DATE DUE

JY 18 '01		
NO 1 '01		
OC 21 '02		
NO 26 '02		
AP 12 03		

Solomon's Sword

SOLOMON'S

— SWORD

Two Families and the Children
the State Took Away

MICHAEL SHAPIRO

T I M E S T B O O K S

R A N D O M   H O U S E

Library of Congress Cataloging-in-Publication Data

Shapiro, Michael.
    Solomon's sword : two families and the children the state
took away / Michael Shapiro.
      p.   cm.
    Includes index.
    ISBN 0-8129-2394-4
    1. Child welfare—United States—Case studies.   2. Family
services—United States—Case studies.   I. Title.
HV741.S4314   1999
362.7'0973—dc21   98-48830

Random House website address: www.atrandom.com/
Printed in the United States of America on acid-free paper
9 8 7 6 5 4 3 2
First Edition
Book design by Susan Hood

For Eliza and Jake

24 And the king said, Bring me a sword. And they brought a sword before the king.

25 And the king said, Divide the living child in two, and give half to the one, and half to the other.

26 Then spake the woman whose the living child *was* unto the king, for her bowels yearned upon her son, and she said, O my lord, give her the living child, and in no wise slay it. But the other said, Let it be neither mine nor thine, *but* divide *it*.

27 Then the king answered and said, Give her the living child, and in no wise slay it: she *is* the mother thereof.

28 And all Ĭs´rā-ĕl heard of the judgment which the king had judged; and they feared the king; for they saw that the wisdom of God *was* in him to do judgment.

—I Kings 3:24–28

Contents

Preface   xiii

THE LAFLAMMES, PART I: "A RISK-FREE CHILD"

1. Cindy   3
2. Gina   11
3. Almost Parents   18
4. Sanctuary   25
5. An Outcomes Judge   32
6. Twisting   43
7. A Merciful Act   49
8. Rescue Fantasy   57
9. Sitting in Judgment   69
10. Removal   76

THE MELTONS, PART I: NINETEEN CHILDREN

1. Maxine's House   85
2. Joseph's Ghost   91
3. "An Undifferentiated Mass"   98
4. A "Dirty House"   103
5. Reunion   109
6. The Child Saver   112
7. "Lost"   119
8. "Laying On of Hands"   127
9. Grandmother   140
10. As She Found Them   148

Contents

11. "I Thought I Was Doing Fine"   157
12. Getting Them Back   164

THE LAFLAMMES, PART II: ANGELICA

1. An Appeal   169
2. Speaking for the Child   183
3. A Room of Her Own   198
4. Infinite Patience   201
5. Court of Last Resort   205
6. Best Interests   211
7. Final Decision   218
8. The Child   224

THE MELTONS, PART II: MISSING MOTHER

1. Expecting   229
2. "No Space for Me"   234
3. The Inevitability of Mother   251
4. The Philosophical Piece   266
5. Surrender   277

Epilogue   283

Acknowledgments   303
Sources   305
Index   313

Preface

This is a book about two families whose children the state took away.

One family is the LaFlammes, a husband and wife whom the state of Connecticut gave an infant to adopt. The state later reversed its decision. The other family is the Meltons, five sisters whose seventeen children the police discovered living in squalor in a two-bedroom apartment on Chicago's West Side.

The state could not leave either family alone or intact. It acted against the parents in order to help their children. The state did not intend to hurt the children, but did so just the same. With the best of intentions the state hurts and fails hundreds of thousands of children, day after day, year after year. It takes children from parents from whom they should not be separated. It returns children to parents with whom they should not live.

The state fails children not merely because its agents are sometimes incompetent or because they are numbed by the volume and nature of their work; rather, there is a debilitating myth that lies at the heart of the state's failure, the myth that the state can save a child, that it can give that child an ideal life in which the past, awful as it might have been, does not exist. The state tries to do this by severing the relationship between a child and the parents who failed him. That well-intentioned but naive mistake sets in motion many of the other mistakes the state makes when it tries to help children.

Half a million children across the country live apart from parents who have abused, neglected, or abandoned them. The number has remained static for a decade, mainly because the child welfare system is filled with children who enter it younger and who stay longer than they have in many years. The longer those children stay in the system, the greater the chance that they will never return home or that no one will adopt them.

The child welfare system lurches from crisis to crisis, the object of contempt and ridicule. It is a world where each failure builds upon the last: The children coming into the system are increasingly troubled by physical and mental illness. Local child welfare agencies can do little to assist these children because virtually all the money they get from Washington must be spent only on housing and feeding them. The children remain in foster care, where their problems often deepen. Those conditions are made worse still because the state often moves children from one foster home to the next. It is not unheard of for children to live in twenty different foster homes in a single year. Within four years of "aging out" of the child welfare system at age eighteen, roughly half of all former foster children have dropped out of school. More than a third have not held a job in a year. A quarter are homeless. Forty percent are in prison or living on public assistance.

The state comes into a home with the stated goal of helping the children. That is only partly true. For as long as parents have failed their children, the state has tried to ensure that those children do not become people like their parents—threats to the public order and drains on the public purse.

I have written this book because I hope to change the way we think about child welfare, its mission, and its practical work. I tell the story of the LaFlammes because their struggle to keep their child reveals the myths that shape our definition of families and of what families are supposed to be. I tell the Meltons' story because in their haplessness, their inability to rise above their sadness, and their crippling limitations, they are the people who succeed only in making the child welfare system look impotent and confused: not the abusive parents, not the killers, but people altogether different and more vexing—parents who love their children and whose children love them but who cannot keep those children fed, clothed, schooled, and safe. These stories both appear to have satisfactory endings. But much needless pain was inflicted upon these children in the well-intentioned desire to save them.

The stories are mirror images of each other. Where the LaFlammes were embraced and pitied by the public, the Meltons were pilloried. Yet just as there existed a bond between the LaFlammes and their child, there was also a bond between the Melton sisters and their many children. Parents do fail their children, sometimes in horrific ways. There are times when the state must intervene in the lives of families. But how can the state do this work without further damaging the children?

I tell these stories in the hope and belief that if we understand why it was that the state felt compelled to take these children, we might begin to understand how to fashion better lives for the children who become the state's. Not perfect. Better.

THE LAFLAMMES,
PART I

―――

"A Risk-Free Child"

Cindy

THE CHILD, known first as Megan Marie and later as Angelica, was born at 1:35 in the afternoon of June 26, 1991, at the Hospital of Saint Raphael in New Haven, Connecticut. She was delivered vaginally and without complications. Her skin was pale and her hair dark. She weighed seven pounds. She cried immediately. She arrived a week before her due date, a fact that at the moment of her birth mattered little to her mother, who was brought to the hospital by ambulance after collapsing on the street. Her mother would later insist that only upon hearing the results of an ultrasound did she understand that the pain she felt on the street was the onset of labor and that she was, in fact, pregnant.

"How far along am I?" asked the mother.

"You're due," she was told.

The mother had received no prenatal care, but there was no evidence that she had abused either drugs or alcohol. The child required no special newborn attention. The hospital record indicated that the mother gave her name as Christina Becolli and her age as twenty-two. Both were lies. She was not accompanied in the ambulance nor through labor, and she received no visitors in her room. She said she lived on the streets and that the child's father was not involved in her life. She said she was a twin, which was the only truthful statement she made. The hospital record noted a "poor social situation." Nine hours after the child was born, the mother disappeared.

The child was alert and vigorous, if somewhat fussy. She had some difficulty feeding. The hospital social worker contacted the Department of Children and Youth Services. The department placed the child under its guardianship and recommended foster care. The department would later insist that it had no way of finding the mother because it had only an assumed name, a false age, and no address. It did not occur to staff within the department to track down the ambulance driver, in the hope that the driver might help them find the mother. On the sixth day of the child's life, the department was awaiting the legal paperwork that would seek a termination of the unknown mother's parental rights and free her daughter for adoption.

The child was twelve weeks old on September 11 when Cynthia LaFlamme took a call at her desk from a caseworker with the Department of Children and Youth Services. Cindy worked as an underwriter for the Aetna Life and Casualty Company. She and her husband, Jerry, lived upstairs from Jerry's aunt and uncle on a street of small and aging homes in New Britain, a working-class town. They had just celebrated their third wedding anniversary.

Cindy was thirty-six years old and childless. Her attempts to have a child during her first marriage had ended with eight miscarriages and the birth of stillborn twins. She and her first husband had spent $16,000 for in vitro fertilization that was not successful. At twenty-eight, after almost dying during her last two miscarriages, Cindy had undergone tubal ligation, ending any chance of her giving birth. Cindy wanted a child. And in the final year of her first marriage she placed her name on the state's registry of prospective adoptive parents.

Before her divorce, Cindy found it painful to explain her childlessness. She enjoyed a respite from the questions about children when she was once again single. But with her marriage to Jerry the questions resumed. Cindy, who could be brusque, replied to questions about pregnancy by saying "I'm not 'cause I can't have a kid."

All through her crumbling first marriage, her divorce, her two years living with Jerry, and their marriage, Cindy kept her application for adoption on file, even though a year on the waiting list was added to her case because, she was told, her divorce raised questions about the stability of a home she could offer a child. Still, nine years after she first applied for a child, the Department of Children and Youth Services called and told her that the time had come for her and her husband to start attending parenting classes.

The state may be powerless to control the sorts of parents people become when they conceive a child. But in the cases of those whom the state can select as parents, it imposes the sort of scrutiny reminiscent of the periodic calls on newspaper editorial pages for a licensing examination for parents. The LaFlammes joined the other prospective parents in classes on parenting skills, classes generally reserved for parents whose children the state had taken away. The LaFlammes were asked about the form of discipline used by their own parents and whether they intended, say, to hit their child. "Spanking," replied Cindy, "didn't work for me." Cindy was asked whether she planned to work (she did), whether she had a history of drug or alcohol abuse (she did not), whether she drank (no), and whether she and Jerry had been rebellious when they were young. "He was," she replied. "I wasn't." She and Jerry were asked what sort of baby they wanted, a baby born to an alcoholic or drug addicted mother, a baby that had been taken from an abusive parent. More than a healthy baby, the LaFlammes told their screener, they wanted a "risk-free baby," a baby whose birth parent had lost any legal claim to the child. The three-hour classes met once a week for two months. The screener, eager to make sure that the LaFlammes were not proceeding with an unwise fantasy of who their child would be, asked, "Do you think everything will be okay when you get this child?"

Cindy replied that she understood that "this would be a child with a past."

The state arranged to visit their home. Cindy had twenty-four hours to get the apartment ready. She washed the walls and ceilings, even though Jerry reminded her that all the caseworker wanted to see was that the house was clean. "I was taking no chances," Cindy said. The LaFlammes' apartment was small and narrow. It had two bedrooms and a living room that looked out over the street. There was a yard in the back. The room Cindy and Jerry intended for their child was next to their own. The caseworker measured the size of the rooms and opened the medicine cabinet to check its contents. She inspected the outlets to make sure that safety plugs had already been installed for a child whom they had yet to be awarded.

As eager as Jerry was to become a father, it was Cindy who assumed the responsibility of talking with and satisfying the agents of the state. Jerry, a truck driver who had been out of work since injuring his back, was a quiet man with thick shoulders, a heavy gut, a drooping black mustache, and sad eyes. Cindy was altogether different. She was quick and incisive. A woman with brown, curly hair, Cindy possessed considerable wisdom and insight about her circumstances and herself. She was determined, above all, to be a parent, but was careful not to let herself dream too fancifully, considering the pain that had for so long attended her dream of a child.

The screening ended in the spring. Then, in August of 1991, Cindy detected what she remembered as the early signs of pregnancy. Medically, she knew, this was impossible. Still, her period was three weeks late, and she was growing nauseous. She began shopping for baby things, pacifiers and "onesies." In early September, not at all sure what was happening to her, Cindy was at her cubicle eating lunch when she took a call from the Department of Children and Youth Services.

"You don't know me," the caseworker said. "Do you have a minute to talk to me?"

Cindy assumed she was calling to schedule yet another home study. When the woman explained that she was the LaFlammes' caseworker, Cindy replied that she already had a caseworker. The woman explained that she was the new caseworker because the nature of the case had changed.

"We have a baby for you," she said. "She's two months old, and that's all I know about her."

Later, Cindy would remember that the caseworker told her, "I know you're not listening to me anymore. Call me back when you get it together."

"So," Cindy later told me, "I'm hysterical at my desk."

Friends walked by and asked what had happened, and when she told them "Jerry and I have a baby," they asked, "When are you getting her?" Cindy first replied that she did not know and then decided to call Jerry and then the caseworker, who told Cindy that she and Jerry had best choose a name. Cindy, remembering the admonition in class that adoptive parents not change a child's name, asked what the baby was called. The caseworker reassured her that the child was known officially only as Baby Girl and to her foster parents as "sweet pea." The child, the caseworker told her, was indeed "risk-free."

The LaFlammes chose the name Samantha Elizabeth but then decided to pick a back-up, in case the child did not look like a Samantha. Cindy thought Samantha suggested a blond child with a button nose. Their name in reserve was Megan Marie.

The child had been living since shortly after her birth with Betty Lou and Louis Cortigiano, licensed foster parents. The state had not found the mother. On July 25, when the child was a month old, John Downey, the presiding judge of the Connecticut Juvenile Court in New Haven, waived the standard twelve-month statutory definition of abandonment—as the law permitted him to do—and terminated the absent mother's rights. Notice of the termination was published in the New Haven *Register*, as was required by law, listing the assumed name the mother gave at the hospital. It advised her that she had twenty days to appeal the judge's ruling. Twenty days passed, and she did not appear. There was no reason for the caseworker to believe she was wrong when she told Cindy LaFlamme that the child was free for adoption.

Jerry drove to Cindy's sister's house in New Jersey and picked up a crib and dresser. Cindy bought Playtex bottles and formula and worried whether she had gotten the right brands. Another caseworker called. Her name was Patricia LeMay, and she asked Cindy and Jerry to come to the department's office in nearby Hamden to complete some forms. She also had a picture of the child to show them. Patricia LeMay told them what she knew of the circumstances of the child's birth, how the mother was a woman with dark hair and appeared to be twenty, perhaps twenty-five, how she gave a false name and said that she came from Florida. The department assumed the mother panicked and fled but could not be sure because she never returned for her child.

Cindy had told Jerry's aunt and uncle and Jerry's mother but was waiting to tell her own mother about the baby. Then she saw the picture of the baby. The baby had dark hair and dark eyes. She looked nothing like a Samantha. She looked, Cindy told Jerry, like a Megan. "Now," she said, "she's real to me." Cindy felt she could call her mother to tell her about her child.

Patricia LeMay came for yet another inspection of the LaFlammes' home. She checked to make sure that they had bottles and formula. Then, a month after Cindy first got the call about the child, Patricia LeMay took them to see her. She had told the LaFlammes to bring a stuffed animal to leave behind so that the child could get accustomed to their smells, to Jerry's cigarettes and Cindy's perfume.

They saw the child for the first time late on a weekday afternoon. She was now almost four months old. Betty Lou Cortigiano wanted her husband to be home for their visit. The Cortigianos had four children of their own. The baby slept in a bassinet in their bedroom. The Cortigianos were pleased that Cindy and Jerry were Catholic.

They asked, "Are you going to bring her up Catholic?" and the LaFlammes replied that they would. They chatted for five minutes, and then Betty Lou said, "Let me go get your baby."

They stayed for two hours. Betty Lou gave the baby right to Cindy. They talked about her sleeping habits and about the foods she liked. The Cortigianos said she liked peaches and bananas. The LaFlammes wanted to know how the child reacted to the Cortigianos' dog. The LaFlammes had a cat and wanted to make sure this would not pose a problem. The Cortigianos showed them the diary they had kept of the child's life with them. It marked the first time she sat in a wading pool, the first time she went to McDonald's, and the first time she threw up on Lou. The smell of cologne made the child vomit. The LaFlammes left the stuffed animal behind. They returned the next day without Patricia LeMay. This time Cindy fed her dinner and gave her a bath. Cindy was happy because when she took the baby in her arms, the baby put Cindy's finger in her mouth.

The LaFlammes were supposed to take the baby home on the Friday of that week, but it was decided they could take her a day early. Cindy could not sleep that night. She woke Jerry and whispered, "She's coming home tomorrow."

Cindy picked out a white dress with hearts for the baby. Patricia LeMay joined them at the Cortigianos. Cindy and Jerry promised the Cortigianos that they would keep in touch. The Cortigianos took pictures of the baby and then, weeping, asked Cindy and Jerry not to linger. They took the baby to their car but could not figure out how to get her into the baby seat. Patricia LeMay helped strap her in. That night Jerry's mother came over, as did Cindy's parents and Jerry's aunt and uncle. They hung a WELCOME HOME sign outside. Cindy and Jerry fed Megan cereal and peaches for dinner and put her to bed at eight o'clock. Cindy lay awake in bed, listening to her breathing on the monitor.

Megan was a good sleeper. She slept through the night and woke at eight o'clock in the morning. Jerry's aunt, who had no children of her own, would come upstairs, pick her up, and dance with her around the apartment. Cindy took three weeks off from work. Patricia LeMay came by to visit and asked whether the LaFlammes had taken Megan to the park. They said they had not because they did not know whether they needed permission from the state to take her on an outing. LeMay assured them they did not.

Cindy's mother threw Cindy a baby shower. Fifty people came. The women gathered around Cindy with gifts. Their husbands came later. Cindy understood that the turnout was especially large because people knew what preceded her finally becoming a mother.

Given the general timetable for adoptions in Connecticut, Megan's adoption was likely to be made final in the early spring, roughly six months after the state placed her with the LaFlammes. The LaFlammes, meanwhile, waited until December to baptize Megan. They asked for permission from the state to do so because even though Megan had been with them for three months, the adoption was not yet finalized. Patricia LeMay granted them permission, and Megan was baptized at the Corpus Christi Roman Catholic Church. In a departure from custom, Cindy and Jerry invited all the members of the family to stand at the altar. The LaFlammes also invited the Cortigianos and Patricia LeMay, who was pregnant and came with her husband. LeMay told Cindy's mother how well she thought things were going with the LaFlammes and their child.

The family gathered for Christmas at the LaFlammes apartment. Patricia LeMay called five days later.

"I want to come out and see you guys," she said.

Cindy, having been told no more but somehow sensing what was to come, hung up the phone, turned to Jerry, and said, "I have a bad feeling. I think Megan's mother wants her back."

Jerry said he did not believe her.

"I just know," said Cindy.

LeMay called again on January 2. This time Cindy insisted that they talk. LeMay hesitated. Cindy challenged her. She said, "Megan's mother is back."

"I don't want to get into it," said LeMay.

"Patty," she bellowed, "just tell me."

Gina

IN THE SPRING of her junior year at Jonathan Law High School in Milford, Connecticut, Gina Pellegrino was, once again, fighting with her parents. Gina thought her parents were too strict. They wanted her home right after work, which meant that Gina could not spend time with her friends. Gina wanted to save her money and buy a car. Her parents, who had divorced when she was seven, remarried when Gina was sixteen. In the years between, Gina's mother moved her children from Connecticut to Texas to Michigan and back to Connecticut. She thought her mother was a vain woman concerned only about her own appearance and not with her only daughter. "She would go and buy the cheapest things for me," Gina told me. "She bought me clothes at thrift shops. She'd leave me alone with my brothers, and they would beat on me." Gina had five brothers whom she could match for rough play until she was nine and decided that she wanted to wear only dresses. "I was pretty much of a school person," she said.

She was of medium height and broad across the shoulders. She had a handsome face, framed by long dark hair. She wore a lot of rings, and on her left hand, between the thumb and forefinger, she had had tattooed the letter *M*, with a small cross beneath it. Gina assumed that after graduating from Jonathan Law she would enlist in the Army and that after her tour she would enter the police academy.

But by the spring of her junior year, life with her parents had become unbearable. Gina went to them and announced, "It would be better if I moved out." Her parents did not protest. She moved in with a friend and found a job as a cashier. "Everything," she later said, "seemed fine after that." She thought nothing of the weight she had begun to gain, assuming she could mask it on warm days with baggy pants and tee shirts. This, and the knowledge of having not once missed her period and having felt nothing that might have been a fetal kick, made the events of June 26 all the more shocking to her.

Gina was outside, walking, when she felt pain so severe that she passed out. When she woke up, an ambulance driver was asking her, "Are you on drugs? Have you been drinking?"

Gina asked, "Can you tell me what is wrong with me?"

After the child was born, and after she left the hospital, Gina returned to the apartment she shared with her friend and to her job as a cashier. She told no one about passing out in the street, of going into unexpected labor, of the birth of a daughter, or of leaving the hospital without her. "It was really hard not to take her in my arms and keep her there," she later said. "It was really hard to let her go. I know I didn't do anything wrong."

It is central in Gina's telling of her story that it be understood she did nothing wrong. People, she said, were unkind to her. Sometimes they were cruel. Although it may have appeared at the time that she did not act wisely, she had not intended to do anything wrong and, really, she had not. She continued believing this and insisting that she had no knowledge of her pregnancy even after a high school guidance counselor reported that Gina had, in fact, spoken with her about being pregnant. The point was not whether Gina lied; rather it was what Gina believed. She believed that she did not know she was pregnant, that she had not intended to abandon her child. She believed that despite a disappearance that did appear intentional, she was and deserved to remain the mother of that child.

"She was so tiny, and she had a full head of hair," Gina said, recalling first seeing the child. "When they handed her to me, she stopped crying. Later a social worker came in. She said, 'Since no one knows you've had a baby . . .' and put this paper in my face, and I knew it was something she wanted to do and I didn't want to do. I screamed, 'Get out of my room, and get this paper out of my face.' I wish I would have known I was pregnant so I could have got some things to-gether, do some shopping, get some essentials for the baby. I broke into tears—what should I do? How can I handle this? I was nineteen years old. They kept putting all these things in my face. A nurse said, if you want to leave, okay . . ."

She intended to come back. But first she had preparations to make. "I told them my real name. I don't know where they got Christina from." She wanted to tell her parents. "I respected my parents."

I asked what they might have said.

"Probably, 'Why didn't you tell us? You're so stupid.' They like to insult me a lot, especially my mom. She's very old-fashioned—'You got yourself into this mess.' I kept being scared. And I couldn't get myself out of the mess."

When she left, Gina said, she told a nurse that she would be back. Gina said she called the next day. A nurse said, "Your daughter's fine." She told the nurse, "I need a little more time, and I'll be there tomor-row." She called the next day.

A nurse, she said, told her, "Your daughter's not here."

"Where is she?" Gina recalled asking.

"DCYS has her," said the nurse, of the Department of Children and Youth Services.

Gina said she asked, "Why is my daughter there?"

"Well," said the nurse, "you abandoned her. You gave a false name. You didn't give an address."

Gina said she called the department. She remembered that the person who answered asked "Who is this?" and Gina, recounting the events at the hospital, said, "This is her mother."

She recalled how the person on the phone said, "You're in a lot of trouble." Gina thought this person might call the police.

Gina told her boyfriend about the baby. "He flipped out. He asked, 'Didn't you know you were pregnant?' "

She returned to Jonathan Law High for her senior year. She was still, she said, "trying to find out what I could." She called the depart-ment. "I didn't tell them my name or what I had done," she said. "It was just for advice."

She learned nothing, not of the termination of her parental rights or of the twenty-day appeal period or of the placement of the child for adoption. She had been gone from her parents' home for almost a year when she called and told them that she wanted to talk with them. Gina told her parents that she wanted them to see her and not merely speak with her on the phone. She told them she wanted them to see "how I've changed."

Gina was afraid of her mother. Her mother had warned her about sex. "Twenty-four, seven—twenty-four hours a day, seven days a week," Gina said. "I thought about that all the time. I thought she was going to kill me. All through my teenage life my mother said, 'Don't have sex.' When my mom disciplines, she yells at the top of her lungs. She's always right. She'd rather hit you first, then ask. Things would always be my fault. She wouldn't ask my brothers 'What happened?' She would leave me to go shopping, and I wanted to be with her. I wanted more from her, and she wouldn't give it to me."

Now, when she told her parents what had happened to her, her father asked, "What do mean you were pregnant? Did you have an abortion?"

"I had a baby, and the state took it away from me," Gina said. "They said I abandoned her, and I didn't."

I asked Gina what her parents said next.

She said they were not angry at her. They felt bad for her. She recalled her mother saying, "We feel so ashamed of ourselves for throwing you out."

———

The next day, November 12, four and a half months after abandoning the child, Gina Pellegrino, with her mother at her side, called the Department of Children and Youth Services. She told Patricia LeMay about the circumstances of the child's birth, leaving no doubt that she was in fact the birth mother. Two days later LeMay came to the Pellegrino home.

Gina did not like Patricia LeMay. She did not like her manner or her attitude and especially did not like hearing that she would not be able to get the child back. LeMay explained to Gina and her mother about the termination of parental rights and what it meant, and how it severed any legal claim she had to the child.

"She was very cocky," Gina said. "She had a smart reaction to everything I said. She was lying in my face to my mother. She said, 'There's nothing you can do because you're not going to be able to get your daughter back.' I knew if I had gotten a lawyer and I just told her the story, I knew that she would find a way to make everything okay."

Gina's mother listened to LeMay explain that the child was lost to her daughter. Then she ordered LeMay out of her house.

Gina and her mother called private attorneys. The first lawyer was a man "with a snotty attitude." The next was a woman who, Gina said, "was pretty nice to me, in the beginning." The attorneys, however, wanted more money than they could pay. Gina called legal assistance in Derby. She hoped she could get a lawyer for free. She spoke with one lawyer who listened to her tell the facts of the case. The lawyer, Gina said, was not interested in her case. Gina waited two weeks and called a lawyer in the New Haven legal assistance office whom the first lawyer mentioned. "She believed me," Gina said. "How could someone lie about having a baby and someone taking her away? I would have gotten everything together. I don't believe in abortion or giving my blood up for adoption to someone else."

In stories where the outcome feels both tragic and wrong, it is tempting to revisit the crucial junctures in the belief that had someone been wiser or better briefed or more sympathetic to a particular argument, then all that followed could have ended right, and not as it actually did. It might also be comforting to discover that at the heart of this perceived wrong lay the hand of a player who was somehow evil or deceitful or intent on causing harm. But in the matter of this child, that was not the case. What made this story so much harder to accept for so many who came to hear about it, and who formed passionately held opinions, was the fact that each player was trying to do what he or she felt was right for the child.

Each believed not only in the correctness of his argument, but in its virtue and in what that argument said about the appropriate relationship between children and their parents and the state.

People believed that the state failed this child, that it acted not in her best interests but, as has happened all too often for so many years, in the interests of the adults who claimed her. In the months that followed the first published reports of the battle for the child—the early rounds were conducted in secret, as is often the case in family court matters—newspaper columnists and editorial writers, lawyers, social workers, the state commissioner of mental health, the state attorney general, and the thirty-five hundred people who signed a petition demanding "justice" for Megan Marie protested what they regarded as the callous way she was treated. Her story was seized upon by campaigners for a constitutional amendment requiring family courts to make the "best interests" of children their paramount concern. The state legislature convened a special committee to review her case.

Because the voices of protest dominated the public debate, and because they were often so angry and bitter, the subtleties were all but lost. Although this was portrayed, in bold strokes, as the struggle between two mothers, it was an infinitely more tangled story. The battle for the child known in court records as Baby Girl B—the initial was taken from the assumed name that Gina Pellegrino gave at the hospital—raised questions that continue to defy resolution: What constitutes a break between parent and child so severe that it is deemed irreparable? When should the determination of a child's future hinge on the question of that child's best interests? These questions, in turn, raised others: What exactly are a child's best interests, and how can they be determined? When does one person stop being a mother and someone else start? Which bond between parent and child is paramount—the biological or the psychological? When do parents and a child become a family?

A teenage woman gave birth to a child whom she left behind, presumably forever. The State of Connecticut took responsibility for the child. The state put the child in a temporary home and then, after careful scrutiny, delivered her into the arms of a new set of parents, thereby giving her the permanency so elusive for most of the children in the state's care. The state's work was done, and seemingly done well. The child was safe and wanted. The matter was resolved satisfactorily, or so it appeared.

This story, like all child welfare stories, was a story of a parent who failed a child. In the early chapters of this story, that failure appeared obvious and clear: The woman abandoned her child and disappeared. But then, as so often happens in child welfare cases, the extent and nature of that failure grew more complex. As it did, the state was forced, sometimes against its desire and instinct, to consider whether the parent it deemed a failure was, indeed, a parent who had shown herself deserving of another chance.

Each side in the battle for this child possessed a compelling argument: Gina Pellegrino, because the child was hers not only by virtue of birth but because of the determination she displayed in trying to reclaim her; the LaFlammes, because they had assumed the role of Megan's parents, caring for her and planning for her future. But because the LaFlammes had not yet formally adopted Megan, the question remained whether Gina had, in fact, failed her child so profoundly that the state was justified in severing her legal claim to Megan. In terminating her rights, Judge Downey had already ruled that she had. In her termination trial, however, Downey was judging Gina in absentia. Now the woman herself stood before him, asking that he reconsider her worth as a parent.

Four months after she left her child behind in the hospital, Gina Pellegrino, with her own mother at her side, called the Department of Children and Youth Services. After months in which she claimed she had called without success, she got through. Patricia LeMay took her call and heard her story and two days later arrived at the home of Gina's parents. LeMay believed, at the very least, that she would be able to gather some hereditary information that she could pass along to Cindy and Jerry LaFlamme.

Almost Parents

Cɪɴᴅʏ LᴀFʟᴀᴍᴍᴇ, having sensed why Patricia LeMay had called her at work and angry that LeMay insisted that they wait to talk in person, demanded to know the true reason for the call. LeMay demurred and then relented. She told Cindy that the child's mother had called her and wanted her back.

"Don't worry," LeMay said. "We've got plans."

Cindy hung up the phone. She sat at her desk. She tried to compose herself. She went to her boss to ask whether she might leave early. Then she began to cry. She got to her car but could barely drive. She became so hysterical that she almost plowed into the back of an orange truck.

She made it home. She ran up the steps and called out to Jerry, "Megan's mother wants her back." She ran to Megan's room. The child was sleeping. Cindy woke her. She hugged Megan and kissed her and made sure not to cry in front of her.

Three days later, on January 5, Patricia LeMay came to the LaFlammes' home. She explained that six weeks earlier she received a call from a woman claiming to be Megan's mother and that she went to see her. LeMay decided to wait until after New Year's to tell the LaFlammes about the call she received two weeks before Thanksgiving—a month after Cindy and Jerry took Megan home—because she did not want to "ruin their holidays."

"Are you sure she's the mother?" Cindy asked.

"The baby looks just like her," said LeMay. She told the LaFlammes about the visit, how this woman asked whether she might help her case by finding a good lawyer. LeMay reported that she told her she did not know.

Now, LeMay told the LaFlammes, the woman had a lawyer and in mid-December the lawyer filed a motion seeking to have her termination of parental rights case reopened. The motion was filed in New Haven with Judge John Downey, who heard the state's original case and who terminated her rights. A hearing was scheduled for the following week.

The LaFlammes realized they needed a lawyer. They checked names in the Yellow Pages and settled on an attorney named William Bloss. Bloss, an even-tempered man who declined to offer predictions, quickly filed a motion with Judge Downey, asking that the LaFlammes as "pre-adoptive parents" be granted a voice in the proceedings. Downey considered Bloss's arguments during the same two days he heard the birth mother's case. He did not issue a ruling on her case for two months. As for the LaFlammes, however, Downey quickly ruled that they were excluded from the case. Megan may have been living with them, but legally she remained the child of the state until her adoption was final. That the state had given Megan to the LaFlammes with the understanding that they would adopt her did not change their legal status as parents-in-waiting. For the moment there was only one question before the court, and that was whether the birth mother could still appeal the termination of her rights. The LaFlammes had no legal standing and, for that matter, no business in court.

Bloss advised the LaFlammes not to come to court until their status was resolved. But Cindy and Jerry insisted. Bloss, at the very least, told the LaFlammes he did not want them meeting the birth mother. Cindy, however, wanted to see what the birth mother looked like. This way, she reasoned, when Megan grew up and asked about her, Cindy could describe the birth mother to her.

Patricia LeMay had described the woman for them. The LaFlammes waited downstairs, and when the session ended, Bloss came to tell them it was time to leave. Cindy insisted on driving. She drove the car to the front of the courthouse. She and Jerry reclined their seats, so they could look without being seen. "I was watching for this long, dark-haired girl to walk out," she said. "And her and her mother walked out, and that's when it really started to click, when I saw a face. That's when I actually connected the baby to her, to a real person. I expected to see this scuzzy, street-worn kid who wasn't anything. But here she was. She was very attractive, nicely dressed. She was not what I had expected, just this creepy type, drug addict type that didn't have any sense of responsibility, that didn't know or didn't care what she was doing. I saw this nice girl who looked like she probably just screwed up. When I saw her, that's when I thought, uh oh. This kid's gonna fight, and so are we. Neither of us said a word. I started the car and left."

Months later, when the news of the case began spreading, the court's initial treatment of the LaFlammes, to say nothing of the child, appeared arbitrary and cruel: Since the state had given Megan to the LaFlammes, hadn't they the right to appear in proceedings that might determine her future? But the state's exclusion of the LaFlammes from a hearing in which they had an interest—emotional, not legal—reflected not so much callousness as ambivalence.

The state did not quite know what to do with people like the LaFlammes. They were not Megan's biological parents. But neither were they foster parents whom the state paid to take her in and who did so knowing that the relationship was temporary. Because Megan's adoption was still months away from being finalized, they were "preadoptive parents." This status carried no legal standing.

The courts, however, recognized that relationships did blossom between children and the people with whom they were placed. The United States Supreme Court had said as much in 1977, when a group of foster parents sued New York State for infringing on the rights they claimed to the children in their care. The foster parents insisted that their devotion to those children and the bonds that had developed between them over time had earned the foster parents a voice in deciding where those children should live, be it in another foster home or back with their biological parents. The Court disagreed. New York, wrote Justice William Brennan, gave the foster parents a voice—specifically, a chance to speak at a hearing before the children were removed from their homes. It was a limited voice; it was not and could not be a voice equal to that of biological parents.

Although limiting his opinion to the narrow question of whether New York's procedures for removing children from foster homes was constitutionally sound, Brennan began building his argument on the question of what, in fact, constituted a family—a group of people whose privacy the law protected from interference by the state. Earlier in this century the Court issued several rulings that protected the sanctity of the family. In one such instance it ruled that the state could not prohibit a private school supported by German immigrant parents from teaching German to their children before the children had mastered English. In another case the Court ruled that Amish parents did not have to send their high school age children to secular schools. There existed, the Court ruled, a "private realm of family life which the state cannot enter." Yet what the Court meant by "family" remained elusive.

Biological ties, Brennan wrote, were not the only measure of a family; the state, after all, created families through marriage. A family, he wrote, evolves "from the emotional attachments that derive from the intimacy of daily association." He could envision a family where, say, a child was placed in a foster home as an infant and remained there for "several years," a period during which the child and her foster parents accomplished the same "socializing function" as a biological family. These parents and child were not, he wrote, "a mere collection of unrelated individuals."

But did the foster parents enjoy the same protection from the state as did the biological parents? They did not. The expectations of that relationship were simply not the same as they were for biological parents. The state made it clear to the foster parents that a child was not being placed with them permanently, that one day the state would take the child back. Biological parents who had voluntarily placed their children in foster care—perhaps because they were sick or overwhelmed by too many problems to be competent parents— had to know that they could get their children back, that the state could not decide that the children were somehow better off with their foster parents without determining that the biological parents were unfit.

Justice Potter Stewart, in a concurring opinion, went a step further. Conceding, as Brennan did, the bonds of affection between foster parents and children, he nonetheless insisted that those foster parents did not enjoy a form of squatters' rights to the children, that the children's having been with them for a long time did not constitute a claim to the children. He then dismissed Brennan's argument about a family evolving when an infant is placed and remains for years with a foster family. That, he wrote, represents not success in the child welfare system, but failure if, as New York law held, the goal of foster care was that it end with the child returning to his "real family" or with his being placed in a permanent adoptive home.

Legal scholars believed that this decision would be used by lower courts as a way to better define the distinction between foster and biological families. Instead, wrote Robert Mnookin of Harvard Law School, it was cited primarily as a rationale for denying foster parents any rights to the children they cared for.

From the layman's perspective it is tempting to ask why the Court did not use this case to settle the question of which ties were paramount—biological or psychological—or at least establish a formula for determining when psychological bonds outweighed the biological. The Court, however, was asked to rule only on the question of New York's foster care removal procedures, and that is all it was supposed to do.

Yet several years later the Court was presented with two cases where adoptive and biological parents competed for the same children. The cases of Baby Jessica and Baby Richard both attracted wide and passionate attention. (Both came after the case of Megan Marie.) In each instance, biological fathers claimed custody of children they had never seen. Both Jessica and Richard were placed in infancy for adoption. Both children were formally adopted. Both fathers, however, argued that they were defrauded by the mothers of their children—in Jessica's case because the mother lied about the identity of the father, in Richard's because the the birth mother told the father that the child had died.

In each case, the extended legal wrangle ended with the state court ordering that the child be handed over to the biological parent, even though no relationship other than the biological one existed between the father and child; they had, in fact, never even met. In Richard's case, the United States Supreme Court declined to intervene. In the case of Jessica, the Court, after a brief review, supported the state court in its ruling.

The lower courts had ruled that the fathers had essentially lost their children because their parental rights were unfairly terminated: They had not been given the chance to act as fathers to their children because they had been deceived or defrauded. But the courts determined that the act of stepping forward to reclaim their children was sufficient.

But if that is indeed so—and the Supreme Court has, in essence, said as much—when do nonbiological sets of parents and children become a family? At the moment of legal adoption? At the time the child is placed in the prospective adoptive parent's arms? When does a different sort of family become, to use Justice Stewart's words, "a real family"?

It is easy to dismiss the Court's siding with biological claims as a cavalier disregard of psychological bonds. If the Court is correct in interpreting the law as an instrument of protection against the power of the state, then its rulings—or nonrulings—are an attempt at leveling the playing field. They ensure that the state will not slip into the role of social engineer, determining the best fate for children in terms of which sets of parents can better provide for them. The Court has also resisted making the best interests of children a paramount consideration in custody decisions prior to determining a parent is unfit. In the hierarchy of Constitutional protections, there is the biological family. It exists until parental rights are terminated. Then the determinant can be, Who will love the child better? Beyond the sheer awfulness of physically taking a child away from the only parents she has ever known, the Constitution must, in the view of the Court, favor protecting biological parents from the power of the state.

In the matter of Baby Girl B, however, Gina Pellegrino was not, strictly speaking, the parent of the child born to her on June 26, 1991. Judge Downey had terminated her rights; her appeal period had passed. The LaFlammes, however, were not yet her legal parents. But they had taken Megan only upon assurance from the state that the relationship would be permanent; they did not want to be foster parents; they were not paid for taking the baby. They had taken her into their home in the belief that she would be their daughter forever.

Later, it was quietly suggested that this case differed from those of Baby Richard and Baby Jessica in the amount of time the LaFlammes had Megan before learning of Gina's return. It was, after all, only four months, not two years as in Jessica's case or five as in Richard's. The argument, however, is absurd: Parents who learn that their four-month-old suffers from a life-threatening illness do not reconcile their grief by saying, Well, at least we didn't have her for years. Parents do not expect to lose their children, not at four months, not ever. At least not anymore.

Sanctuary

IT IS IMPOSSIBLE to write about the history of the family, of its evolution to a sacred form, without considering the frequency and awfulness of what we would now think of as untimely death. For much of recorded history, for instance, parents routinely outlived their children. Children died at birth or within the first year of life. Those children fortunate enough to survive could not be sure that their mothers would live to see them grow into adulthood. These children saw their mothers bear many children, if only to replace the children they lost. The childbearing might come to a sudden end with a mother dying during the birth of her last child.

For all that medicine and science make life less fragile, there remains no quest more elemental and quixotic than trying to find a haven in an unpredictable and threatening world. The family, as we have come to celebrate it, is only the latest in a long history of moorings among the perils.

Until the mid-nineteenth century the nuclear family did not exist as an entity worthy of celebration. Indeed, there was seldom a time before then when most fathers, mothers, and their offspring lived alone. It was not until the coming of the Industrial Revolution that nuclear families found themselves alone, free from the company of the many friends and strangers who lived with them, sometimes by design and sometimes by happenstance. For millennia "family" meant the people who happened to live under a single roof. Life often took place in a single room, where at any time in the course of the day or night, a stranger might walk in, take a seat by the hearth, and if it was late, share a bed if none were free.

Children across medieval Europe were born into a world surrounded by relatives, servants, and the young children of other people—because beginning as early as the age of seven, children were sent away to be reared by strangers as their apprentices. The practice cut across lines of class and sex. It existed for centuries, ensuring that generations of children came of age under the tutelage of people other than their mother and father, who were occupied with raising the children of other people.

This was not a result of parental indifference. Rather, it reflected the demands of a time when mortality, both for children and adults, was extraordinarily high. Societies were filled with widows and orphans, too few able hands and many children to feed. People lived together because they needed one another, to help with the household business—be it farming or trade—to help with the children, who no one assumed could be reared by one mother alone. Children were economic entities, the property of fathers. They were expected to work. The child's formative relationship, however, was with a master who, in turn, was expected to teach not only a trade, but some manners as well. The Catholic church took children, too. Parents routinely gave over their children to the monastery or convent in an act of "oblation," which like so many moments of surrendering children in the Middle Ages was done in the interests of keeping them fed, housed, and alive.

In his seminal work *Centuries of Childhood*, the French social historian Philippe Aries argued that for millennia childhood simply did not exist as a distinct period. Aries, whose work has since come under considerable challenge, built his case largely on the iconography of medieval Europe. Children, he wrote, rarely appeared in depictions of both village and city life, and when they did, it was to perform such adult tasks as, say, serving at a wedding. Aries marked the dawn of the idea of childhood with the increasing appearances of children in art. Where Aries encountered his stiffest criticism, however, was in his assumption that children were not only unseen but unloved. Aries believed that high rates of infant mortality compelled parents to keep their children at an emotional distance, if only to protect themselves from the seemingly interminable succession of deaths.

A second school of historians, however, Peter Laslett chief among them, looked at records—deeds, archives, tax records—and argued that there was considerable evidence to suggest that parents loved their children very much, that they wailed and grieved when their children died.

Friends could provide comfort in the temporal world; the church offered itself for the spiritual. Where the ancient world offered gods and idols, the early Catholic church provided saints, whose shrines became destinations on the lifelong pilgrimage in search of a haven. Catholics believed, however, that the safety that man so desperately sought could be found only in the kingdom and family of heaven.

From roughly the fourth century on, the path to salvation was best achieved in the celibate life of the monastery or convent. But in the twelfth century, the church, eager to shape the lives of the laity as well the clergy, turned to the family, or rather to the Holy Family, as a beacon of safety. This began with the transformation of the Virgin Mary from a distant and powerful figure into a warm and protecting maternal one. This is not to suggest that until then mothers somehow did not matter. Mothers have always existed as a form of sanctuary, whether as the mother goddesses worshipped in the ancient world or as the Virgin Mary. For millennia, however, motherhood—and all it suggested about comfort and safety—had little, and sometimes nothing, to do with child rearing. Motherhood was a shared experience, so much so that even for its most intimate act, breastfeeding, a mother could subcontract the work to a wet nurse.

The cult of Mary, however, made the idealized mother into an accessible, imaginable figure. "The insecurity and real dangers of medieval childhood created powerful, persistent fantasies of protection and rescue by an omnipotent, loving mother," wrote historian John R. Gillis in his study of the history of the mythology of the family, *A World of Their Own Making*. So Jesus was depicted surrounded by his mother, his foster father—Joseph—and his grandmother, Saint Ann. But this was a family only in an idealized form. They were worthy of worship, but not of emulation.

That view changed in the sixteenth century, with the Protestant Reformation. While Protestants also regarded life on earth as a form of exile—and freedom as achieved only in death and in a "gathering in" of that family of strangers—it encouraged believers to model their lives after the Holy Family. Protestants encouraged the faithful to look no further than their own households for an earthly representation of the family of God. But like Catholics, Protestants believed this quest to be worthy but futile.

Protestants at once idealized behavior within a family—a wise father, a dutiful wife—but cared nothing about what good might come from the relationships within the family. Emotional life within a Protestant family was thin, Gillis argued, because affection was reserved for God, so much so that the radical Protestants, the Puritans, discouraged too much affection between family members.

The Reformation marked the beginning of the modern idea of the family as a distinct and private entity. With the Reformation, not only did Protestant churches permit the marriage of their clergy, but the Catholic church began moving toward sanctifying a relationship between men and women. This was accomplished through the effective use of patron saints. Men and women, seeking approval of their union in the eyes of the church, were depicted in the iconography of the time in the company of their respective patron saints, whose company blessed not only their joining together, but the children who stood with them. The presence of the saints, Aries wrote, created "the cult of the family." What had for so long been profane was now rendered holy.

Parents, or rather fathers, who had held the power of life and death over their children, were now charged with their spiritual care. The work formerly accomplished by clergymen was now to be done by fathers as well, who were encouraged by the Protestant churches to read the Bible to their children in the vernacular. Architecture changed as well. The household, with all its many and assorted people living communally, began giving way to smaller spaces where people even had rooms of their own. A father, meanwhile, was responsible for ensuring that his own child would be neither a bother nor an idler. When the growing number of schools began assuming the role of apprenticeship in the seventeenth and eighteenth centuries, the motivating idea was to train children for a productive life and allow parents to keep an eye on their own children so that they would remain uncorrupted by the evils of the adult world around them and in which, as apprentices, they had lived. And if those lessons were enforced by the proctor's rod, the punishment came not out of malice but out of an altogether new idea of the distinctiveness and importance of the child.

At the same time that the child in Europe was being moved closer to the center of the family, the Puritans who had left England for the American Colonies carried with them a different view of the place of the family in society. In the Colonies the family was the essential economic and social unit. Parents were expected to assume responsibility for the care, feeding, and moral upbringing of their children, and when they failed, the state—the public authority in the form of the village elders—would do it for them. The harsh nature, both economically and spiritually, of early Colonial life was such that all people were expected to be productive and to be attached to a family. If their own family, or rather their father, could not do the job, the village was expected to assist financially. And if the parents were dead or idle, the elders, drawing upon the English tradition, were free to place the children with another family as indentured servants, where they remained for years. There was no society, save for England, "so drab and dry of true sympathy as that of Colonial Massachusetts," wrote Robert Kelso in *The History of Public Poor Relief in Massachusetts, 1620 to 1920*. Still, he added, it was a society guided by a clear set of principles: The colony could not afford slackers, nor the morally suspect. The village authority may not have necessarily wanted the children—or the expense of helping with them—but it was not going to tolerate their sloth or dependence. If the parents were destitute, they too were to be "bound out."

The growing acceptance of the idea of children not as threats but as innocents coincided with the emergence of their mothers as people of consequence. Historically, children belonged to their fathers. But with the liberalization of divorce laws, both in England and in the Colonies, mothers began to be granted custody of their children. That, in turn, moved the question of custody from a strictly economic one—the children as revenue-producing chattel—to an emotional one: the well-being of the children. So too did the contractual claim upon a child by a family to whom a child had been indentured recede in the face of a growing belief by the courts of "natural law." A mother could claim heaven on her side, so long as she was viewed as a proper mother who did not shirk her responsibilities to her children. With this "romantic" view of mothers came a "romantic" view of children, writes Mary Ann Mason in *From Father's Property to Children's Rights.* So powerful was this idea of motherhood that the courts, citing what in the nineteenth century came to be called "the tender years doctrine," began insisting that young children were best off close by their mothers.

The elevation of the family to the position it now holds began in earnest with the social upheaval of the Industrial Revolution. With the shift in workplace from home to factory, the strangers who for centuries had been part of the household began moving out. The great movement of people across Europe and across the United States spurred the religious revival, especially among women and young people searching for a sense of order in a rapidly changing world. Yet at the same time that "brotherhoods" and "sisterhoods" were replacing the community of the home or the town, the growing Victorian middle class was taking a new and altogether different look at its own families and, in Gillis's words, finding them "an object of worshipful contemplation."

The family was no longer heavenly or remote. It was exalted, having a status that stood in direct proportion to the need it filled as the antidote to chaos, as the safe harbor in a frightening world. "In a few short decades during the second half of the nineteenth century," Gillis wrote, "the household ceased to be like any other place and became an enchanted world populated by mythic figures."

What is most striking in this history of the evolution of the family is the speed with which it progressed. The "cult of the family" endures essentially intact today as a central and defining component of American society and of the laws that govern it. It is difficult then to imagine that in the civilization from which those laws evolved, parents of all classes routinely abandoned their children.

Children were abandoned, wrote the historian John Boswell, because parents could not afford them, because the children were of the wrong sex, because they did not wish to have the children compete for an inheritance with their other children, or if parents "simply could not be bothered with parenthood." Parents abandoned their children on hillsides in ancient Rome. They sold their children. The church did not condemn abandonment. If it had, it would have been forced, as recently as the late eighteenth century, to include the many parents of Toulouse who abandoned a quarter of all the children born in that French city. "I made no secret of my action," wrote Jean-Jacques Rousseau, who abandoned all five of his children, "because I saw no wrong in it."

Boswell called his book *The Kindness of Strangers*. The title, he wrote, reflected the antithesis of abandonment—the understanding among parents that their discarded children would be found and cared for by people they did not know. The practice of abandonment, shocking not only in its scale but in how recently and openly it was conducted, is now regarded, at the very least, as grounds for the state to sever the relationship between that offending parent and the child. But parents still leave their children. They leave them in Dumpsters, which in the view of some psychologists is tantamount to a wish to perform infanticide: The child is not quite murdered; the parent need not be there to inflict the fatal blow. Parents also abandon their children in places where they know the children will be safe. This is a far more complicated, though troubling, choice in that a parent may be saying that while she does not want the child or cannot care for the child or cannot accept that she has this child, she does not want the child to die. The state, assuming the role once played by the church, is the intermediary. It takes the child and, if the child is fortunate, delivers her into the hands of a line of strangers.

In fourteenth-century Italy, parents who wished to abandon a child could take the child anonymously to a foundling hospital. There, in the wall, was a small door called the *ruota*. The *ruota* revolved, but only enough for a parent to place the child on the outside of the wall, turn the wheel, and deposit the child on the inside. The children whose parents slipped them onto the *ruota* and into the company of other abandoned children almost always died young. The parents presumably could not know this because once the child passed into the almshouse, they never saw her again.

An Outcomes Judge

IN MARCH, two months after Cindy and Jerry LaFlamme saw Gina Pellegrino outside the New Haven courthouse, Judge Downey ruled that although he had already terminated Gina's parental rights, and although notice was published and the appeal period had elapsed, he was nonetheless reconsidering the termination. He granted Gina a new trial to determine whether there were indeed grounds for the state to take her child. The state attorney general's office, appearing for the Department of Children and Youth Services, argued that the state had already proven a case of statutory abandonment against Gina and that she merited no further review of her case. Downey, however, ordered that Gina now be granted weekly, one-hour visits with the child. His decision surprised even the lawyer representing Gina, who based her case not on family law but on an obscure provision in the state's commercial code, one that had never before been applied to a case involving a child.

The lawyer, Angelica Anaya-Allen, came upon a potential loophole in the law, one that might allow the judge, if he saw fit, to rule that even though the child was placed with the LaFlammes, the court maintained ultimate control of her fate. The provision granted the opportunity for judicial review in civil judgments four months after the judgment was rendered. Anaya-Allen then took her argument a step further, to an equally unlikely place: the 1980 federal Adoption Assistance Act. The act was designed, in part, as a legal remedy for foster care drift: It not only strengthened judges' hands in clarifying the conditions for terminating parental rights, but also gave judges the power to review foster care cases so that children in care would not simply slide unnoticed and unattended through the child welfare system. In her brief, Anaya-Allen argued not only that Downey maintained the authority to review the child's case, but that Gina Pellegrino, regardless of her disappearance, still had one final chance to appeal his termination of her rights. It was, Anaya-Allen conceded, a bit of a stretch.

Angelica Anaya-Allen had come east to college at Brown University and law school at Harvard. After traveling around the world, she returned home to Santa Fe, only to discover that legal services had no openings. She and her husband moved first to New Jersey, where she worked as a Legal Aid Society lawyer representing welfare recipients, and then to New Haven. New Haven Legal Services had an opening for an attorney representing parents whose children were in the custody of the Department of Children and Youth Services.

Anaya-Allen's clients were all women and were almost all "a pain in the neck." Her time was spent less on legal issues than on tracking down her clients, reminding them to come to court, and, in the case of one mother, making sure she did not return to court in a black spandex miniskirt. The warning surprised the client, whom Anaya-Allen advised to think of dressing for court as if she were dressing for church. Anaya-Allen's clients had therapists and drug counselors, appointed by the state to assist them in changing the course of their lives. Virtually all her clients were women with drug problems who lost their children to the state by, say, leaving the children home alone, going out to get high, and disappearing for a few days.

Sometimes the mothers were openly hostile, and occasionally they were merely pathetic, like the mother whose child was admitted to the hospital with a spiral fracture of the arm and who could come up with no explanation better than that the child had somehow fallen from her lap. The child was nine months old and a crier, and Anaya-Allen could only guess at what had really happened. "I try extremely hard not to make judgments about what my clients are entitled to, because if you do that you can't adequately represent them," Anaya-Allen said. "You put in a tremendous amount of work on someone's legal defense, and your client disappears; and obviously it's true that a tremendous number of our clients have a tremendous number of problems, so that whatever legal issue they've brought to my doorstep is not the most important thing for them. You get discouraged."

Yet Anaya-Allen also saw, occasionally, just how arbitrary the state could be in judging the parents it deemed unsatisfactory. Early on in New Haven, she represented a twenty-one-year-old woman whose infant child was taken after the child was diagnosed as "failing to thrive." The child was admitted to the hospital suffering from vomiting, diarrhea, and a precipitous weight loss. The mother stood accused of starving her child. Yet Anaya-Allen was struck by how a social worker interpreted the mother's every action: how spending time with her other child, a two-year-old, was seen as failing to spend enough time with the hospitalized infant; how taking her ailing child out of her crib and into the cot where the mother slept in her child's hospital room was duly noted as a violation of hospital rules and as endangering the child. Child welfare caseworkers accepted without question the reports the hospital issued on the child's weakened condition, even though the hospital offered no clear diagnosis of her condition. The hospital, Anaya-Allen discovered, did not like the mother because this mother, feeling she was not being kept apprised of her child's condition, would sneak behind the desk at the nurses' station to read her child's chart. This concern was interpreted as hostility and noted in the growing litany of complaints against her.

Still, in the late fall of 1991, mothers whose dedication to their children was dismissed as endangerment were the exception on Angelica Anaya-Allen's case list. Two mothers were facing termination of their parental rights. The loss of their children, she came to see, did little to motivate her clients to do what the state demanded of them: Too often, they simply gave up.

Then, in November, Anaya-Allen took a call from a colleague in the Derby legal assistance office. The lawyer told her of a case that might interest her. A young woman had a child in the custody of the Department of Children and Youth Services. The woman had been under the impression that the child was in foster care and that she could somehow get her child back. A department caseworker, however, told her she was too late. The woman believed her child had been adopted. She called a private attorney, learned that she could not afford the fee, called legal assistance, and told her story to a screener to determine if she was eligible for free legal services. She had no understanding of her status under the law. She just wanted her child back.

"I liked her," Anaya-Allen said. She and Gina Pellegrino sat in her office, with its exposed brick walls and snapshots of Anaya-Allen's family and of India, from her long-ago trip around the world. Gina told her story of the birth of her child. "She was in some respects a very likable young woman, very attractive, energetic, not really bright but of average intelligence. A very nice young woman who seemed like a kid who had really made a mistake and felt really bad about it. I could see immediately that this was going to be an extremely difficult and time-consuming case."

As they spoke that day, Anaya-Allen knew only what Gina told her. If she was right and the child had been adopted, there might be years of legal appeals and court challenges, to say nothing of questions about the emotional capacity and the parenting ability of a nineteen-year-old who had left her child in the hospital and disappeared. They spoke for an hour. Anaya-Allen warned Gina of what was likely to come, of the toll her case would take not only on her, but on her child and the people whom the state had made the child's parents. "I wanted to make sure she knew what she was doing," she said. She also wanted to make sure that, unlike so many of her other clients, Gina would not quit on her, that she would see this through. "She believed," Anaya-Allen recalled, "that she was this child's mother."

In November, when Patricia LeMay visited Gina Pellegrino and her mother, she advised Gina that her chance to appeal the termination of her rights had passed and that the child was lost to her. LeMay told Gina that adopted children had the right to information about the identity of their birth parents when they became eighteen years old. It was understood, by all parties, that LeMay said this based upon her understanding of the statutes and that that understanding did not encompass an obscure provision in the Connecticut Civil Code.

Still, Gina filed her brief two weeks after the four-month appeal period ended. Angelica Anaya-Allen argued that because the state, in the person of the unknowing LeMay, was insufficiently forthcoming, her client had a reasonable explanation for filing her appeal late: She did not know that time was running out. It did not matter that Gina and her mother, enraged with LeMay and what she told them, ordered her out of their house and, ignoring her advice, starting looking for a lawyer.

"Although mother did not accept Ms. LeMay's information as the final word on the subject," Downey wrote in his decision, "mother's subsequent actions, though prompt, were not infused with the urgency which a correct explanation of the situation would have inspired." LeMay, he ruled, "misled the mother." The late filing aside, the federal Adoption Assistance Act granted him continuing jurisdiction in the matter of this child. The state conceded as much, but argued that the twelve-month review in foster care cases was designed to make sure that there is "progress in making permanent plans for the child." Downey rejected this line of reasoning. He also chastised the state for failing to promptly notify the attorney assigned to represent the interests of the child that her birth mother had reappeared. In July, this attorney, Marion Fay, had agreed with Downey that the birth mother's rights should be terminated. Now, however, she changed her mind. She, too, wanted the birth mother to be granted another hearing.

Angelica Anaya-Allen gave Judge Downey the legal hook upon which he could allow her client a final chance to reclaim the child she abandoned. Downey accepted her argument without qualification or reservation. In the final paragraph of his four-page decision he hinted, quite broadly, at his view of the facts of the case. Anaya-Allen's brief, he wrote, "has shown that genuine issues exist, which, after a full hearing on the merits, could constitute a meritorious defense to the allegations" that the state brought against her.

Megan was now nine months old. She had been with the LaFlammes for five months when a caseworker took her to see Gina Pellegrino for the first time since the day she was born. For the visit Cindy packed toys, a bib, and cookies. "I really felt," Cindy said, "I'm going to lose her."

There are mysteries in this story that lead, inevitably, to speculation. Because the hearings on Gina Pellegrino's case were closed to the public and the press, there is no way of knowing what, precisely, was said in court or how Gina's story was received by Judge Downey. I have heard from those who took the LaFlammes' side, but who were not in court during those hearings, that Downey "liked" Gina, that it was understood that he had compassion for her and was therefore willing to consider her version of things. I have also heard that Downey was known as a "mother's judge," that he favored biological claims over psychological ones. There is no way to know any of this. To this day, Downey has not spoken about the case. That is his right and, strictly speaking, his obligation as a family court judge who is charged with protecting the confidentiality of children, even though the name of this child was soon no longer a secret. Downey declined all written and telephone requests to speak with me about this or any other case. So too did Marion Fay, the attorney for the child, and Patricia LeMay, the caseworker.

But it is the silence of John Downey, whose voice was the one that mattered in determining the fate of this child, that leaves unanswered, and ultimately unanswerable, the question at the heart of this story: If Gina Pellegrino did abandon her child and if she was missing from her child's life for four months and if the child was placed with a family that the state had been assiduous in screening, on what basis could John Downey consider taking that child from the LaFlammes and returning her to Gina Pellegrino?

John Downey was, by all accounts, a respected and admired judge. I have not heard him criticized for being derelict or insensitive or in any way less than scrupulous in his work. Downey was sixty-two at the time of the case. He served as chairman of the state Department of Public Utility Control and ran unsuccessfully for the Democratic nomination for lieutenant governor in 1978 and for the party's nomination for the United States Senate in 1982. He attended Choate and Yale, where he played defensive tackle on the football team and was captain of the wrestling team. A roommate once told *The New York Times* that Downey, a devout Catholic, thought that he might want to be a teacher or a writer, or that he might want to coach. At Choate he was voted "most popular, most versatile and most likely to succeed." The inscription over his Choate yearbook picture read: "Always act in accordance with the dictates of your conscience—and chance the consequences."

A friend told me about meeting John Downey when he came to speak to her class at Harvard Law School. Afterwards, she introduced herself. She had never met him, and this made what happened next especially curious.

When my friend mentioned her name, Downey told her that she had graduated from Yale in 1971. He then told her her father's home address. Seeing that she was taken aback, Downey hurried to explain: There were two kinds of books that his Chinese jailers had allowed him to read. One was the Bible. The other, for reasons not explained, was Yale's annual yearbooks which, during twenty years of solitary confinement in China, he had committed to memory.

———

The Central Intelligence Agency recruited John Downey at Yale. He joined when he graduated. This was 1952, in the midst of the Korean War. Downey's mission was to organize and supply Chinese Nationalist espionage teams operating in Manchuria. On November 29, 1952, Downey's plane was shot down over China. For two years the Chinese released no news of his fate or whereabouts. Then, referring to him as an "arch criminal," the Chinese government sentenced Downey to life imprisonment for spying. Washington insisted that Downey was a civilian and would maintain that fabrication for another twenty-one years.

He lived in a twelve-by-fifteen-foot cell in Brass Bridge Prison in Beijing. He was allowed outside for an hour a day. He read and exercised and chatted with his cell mate. He heard from time to time of events at home, like the assassination of President John Kennedy, news of which was translated for him by prison guards from a small item buried in a Chinese paper. Downey's mother visited three times. A schoolteacher, she had reared Downey and his brother and sister alone after their father, a probate judge, was killed in an accident when John Downey was young. In prison Downey's life stood still. His brother became a Manhattan attorney. A boyhood friend, Thomas Meskill, became Connecticut's governor. Meskill recalled Downey's "dry Irish wit" and believed that if "anyone could go through this ordeal, Jack Downey could, because he's that kind of guy."

In 1973, as relations between Beijing and Washington began to thaw, Downey's name reemerged, as did questions of his fate. China released several other captured Americans, and there were reports that Downey, too, might be freed. In Connecticut, marchers organized rallies, calling for his freedom. Jerry LaFlamme and his father were among the marchers. In January of that year, President Richard Nixon finally conceded, offhandedly, that Downey had indeed been a spy. It is believed that this admission was crucial for the Chinese. Two months later, then-Governor Thomas Meskill, upon learning that Downey's seventy-five-year-old mother had suffered a stroke, called the White House. President Nixon, in turn, contacted Chinese Premier Zhou Enlai and asked whether this news might help speed Downey's release.

John Downey stepped across the covered bridge at Lo Wu into Hong Kong on March 12, 1973. He wore what newspapers described as "Chinese-style" blue pants and a blue shirt. He carried an overcoat and a suitcase. A British helicopter ferried him to a United States Air Force Nightingale evacuation plane, which carried him to Clark Air Force Base in the Philippines. There he met his brother, who joined him for the trip home. His mother, who was slipping in and out of consciousness, was not told that her son was coming until moments before he stepped into her room. He took her hand and sat at her side and talked.

A year after his release, Downey enrolled at Harvard Law School. He was forty-two years old. The following year he married Audrey Lee, who was born in China and whom he met in New Haven, where she worked as a research associate in molecular biophysics and biochemistry. It was noted in their wedding announcement that his wife's village was not far from the place where his plane was shot down. He returned to China in 1983 on a goodwill tour. He expressed bitterness not toward the Chinese, but rather toward former secretary of state John Foster Dulles who, Downey learned on his visit, might well have helped win his release sixteen years earlier were he amenable to an exchange of Chinese and American journalists.

"I knew what I was getting into," he told *The Washington Post* in 1978. "They told me what would happen if I ever got caught. If I blamed anyone, it was myself alone for being so dumb as to volunteer." The years in prison were, he said, "a complete waste."

Downey's political ambitions went no further than his defeats in primary elections during which critics suggested that he was running not on any political experience but rather on the memory of the story of his imprisonment. New Britain, the LaFlammes' town, named a street and a slow-pitch baseball team for him. In time he was appointed to the bench and in 1990 was made the chief administrative judge for the Connecticut Juvenile Court.

It is tempting to seek a connection between Downey's ordeal and the sort of judge he became. But I know of none, other than his having once displayed a particularly powerful sense of idealism. Far more telling was the view of Downey as a judge offered by a colleague of his, Fredrica Brenneman. Brenneman served as a Connecticut family court judge for over twenty years and was so well regarded that, as a senior judge, she was responsible for training the new judges who sat in family court. She was a plain-spoken woman who believed, passionately, in what she called "the process."

The process—the laws and statutes that defined and regulated juvenile justice—was her guide. The laws and statutes showed her how to proceed and also checked any impulses she might have had in trying to achieve a result that was not strictly in accord with the process. Brenneman believed that there were two types of judges—process judges, like her, and "results" judges. Results judges, she explained, drawing upon the writing of Duncan Kennedy of Harvard Law School and the "critical legal issues" school of thought, looked at a case, saw what they believed was the desired result, and then found a way through the statutes to do what they believed should be done. Results judges did not necessarily ignore the dictates of the process, she said, but they would, if it meant smoothing the path to their desired result, interpret the statutes loosely.

This was not, Brenneman explained, a matter of being a stickler for detail. Rather, to be a process judge was to hold a belief in the wisdom and purpose of the statutes: They existed, by virtue of their passage as legislation, for a reason. The process also provided judges with a measure of security one often needed on the family court bench, where judges, trying hard to make the right decision for a child, will often avoid making any decision at all because they are afraid of being wrong.

"I'm not God," Brenneman said. "And when you think you're God and you have to make the right decision, you're paralyzed. And when you're paralyzed, it's always a bad decision." In addition to training judges, she now moved from courthouse to courthouse, often being asked to assist with cases in which a final judgment was too long delayed "because the judge will seek any excuse to get a continuance, to seek a compromise" when what "this kid needs is process." She said, "Frequently I'll come in and feel like I'm some mistral, some wind blowing in saying, 'Guys, never mind about best interests. We're miles away from best interests.' In order to get to best interests, to that bottom line, you have to do a lot of very mechanical kinds of things." By this she meant that the judge first had to determine whether the state had proved its case for parental failure—neglect, abandonment, or abuse—and whether there were grounds for termination. Then the judge had to determine whether the child was adoptable, whether there was a family that wanted him. Only then, based upon what she had learned through the step-by-step of the process, was Brenneman prepared to move on to the question of what was in the child's best interests.

Brenneman admired the speed with which Downey sought a resolution. But she had reservations about his decision to reverse his termination of Gina Pellegrino's parental rights and grant her a new trial.

I asked what she would have done had Gina come before her and explained, as she presumably did to Judge Downey, that she had not intended to abandon her child, that she had tried without success to reach the Department of Children and Youth Services, and that she was confused and afraid and sorry.

Brenneman replied that she would have followed the dictates of the process. And the process would have told her that rights had been terminated and notice published, that the twenty-day appeal period had expired, and that Gina had filed her petition two weeks after the four-month civil judgment appeal period elapsed.

"I believe in the process," Brenneman said. "I believe in the finality of judgments. If the process says the termination is final, it's final because there has to be some finality to 'Who is my mother?' I don't care about blood is thicker than water. The mother had made a decision. And there should have been a time after which it is too late. My heart goes out to Gina, but it's too late. I would have said, tough toast."

Twisting

Dᴜʀɪɴɢ ᴛʜᴇ ʟᴀᴛᴇ winter and spring of 1992, Cindy and Jerry LaFlamme's lives began to resemble, in their uncertainty and power-lessness, the lives of the other people, most of them poorer than the LaFlammes, into whose families the state feels compelled to intrude.

Because the state essentially created the LaFlamme family by giving Megan to Cindy and Jerry, and because Judge Downey ruled that the state still held sway over the future of that family, the LaFlammes could do nothing to advance their own cause. But they were still re-sponsible for the care of the child the state gave them. Judge Downey ruled that Gina Pellegrino was to have weekly, one-hour visits with the child. For the first visit, Cindy handed Megan to a caseworker and watched as she took Megan away. The caseworker drove Megan to Gina's parents' house in Milford, an hour away. Gina saw the child in the caseworker's presence—Downey ruled that the visits were to be supervised. The caseworker then drove Megan back to the LaFlammes.

She was gone for three hours, and when Megan came home all Cindy could see was a wet diaper and the cookie stain on the nice dress she had put her in. "So now I'm mad," Cindy said. She told the caseworker to follow her around the apartment. She took her into Megan's room. She showed her the crib and opened the closet and showed her all the clothes she and Jerry bought for Megan. She took the caseworker to the kitchen. "There was tons of baby food and diapers," Cindy said.

The caseworker talked with the LaFlammes. Usually, it was Cindy who spoke for the couple. But now Jerry, who was most comfortable sitting off to the side while Cindy answered questions, told the caseworker that he would rather see the baby dead than go back to her birth mother.

"All I meant by it was, at least if you had a tombstone you could go and see," Jerry told me.

"You have someplace where you can go and grieve," Cindy explained.

The caseworker, however, took Jerry literally. She filed a report recommending that the child be removed immediately from the LaFlamme home because Jerry was suicidal and potentially homicidal and the child was in danger. The LaFlammes were ordered to see a psychiatrist. Angelica Anaya-Allen, seizing upon the report, also asked Judge Downey to have the child taken from the LaFlammes. Downey, however, dismissed the caseworker's request and ruled that for now the child would stay where she was.

Gina, too, was having a difficult time. When the visits began, she was living with her parents. Then, once again, her parents threw her out. "They said, 'You have to find another place to visit.'" When I asked Gina why her parents asked her to leave, she would not say. Her friends and brother, however, told *The Hartford Courant* that Gina's parents were angry because her boyfriend, Jermaine, was black. Jermaine, who was twenty, would pass in and out of Gina's life in the months to come. Whether he was, in fact, the father of the child Gina has never said. Gina's father, for his part, told the *Courant* that he was not prejudiced but that he did not "like her hanging out with black friends." Gina, meanwhile, moved in with a friend. But her friend's mother did not want the visits taking place at her house. So the visits took place at an office of the Department of Children and Youth Services. Gina, however, did not like the place. It was "filthy," she said, with "dirty diapers in the playroom." She asked to have the visits at her brother's house. "I had a hard time dealing with things," Gina said.

The arrangement for visitation called upon the LaFlammes to bring Megan to the parking lot of a McDonald's. There, Gina and a caseworker were to meet them and take the baby. They were to bring the baby back to the parking lot when the visit ended. Cindy insisted upon taking Megan back and forth, even though this meant having to adjust her work schedule to be in the office by four in the morning.

"Now we're rotating our lives around Gina and these visits," Cindy said. "The visits are twice a week. It's three or four hours back and forth. Everything changed. It started to interfere with my work. Now I can't concentrate. I have lawyers calling me. I have social workers calling me. I got my husband calling me. Everything is a problem, and they can't handle it, and they have to call me. So now even when I'm at work, I'm not working. It started to interfere with our lives at home because now I'm taking time off from work. Jerry couldn't do it because every time he saw Gina, the look on his face was he wanted to blast into her."

Cindy heard from the caseworker that Megan had not done well with Gina's parents. With Gina, however, Megan was more comfortable, if somewhat shy. It would be best, the department decided, if Gina and Cindy did not meet.

"Then one visit I'm outside, sitting in the car," Cindy said. "Gina and the social worker come out, and Gina is holding the baby."

I asked Cindy how she felt, watching Gina hold the baby.

"It didn't bother me because of how the baby acted," she said. "She was kind of twisted away from her. She didn't have her arms around her. So it was kind of like she was the baby-sitter at that point."

Cindy watched from her corner of the parking lot, assuming that the caseworker would take Megan and that Gina would leave. "And they come closer and closer, and I say, Oh my God, she's coming up to the car. Gina brings her all the way up to the car. She walked up to car. She looked at me, and I looked at her. And as soon as Megan saw me, she put her arms out and came flying at me. So we talked for a couple of seconds about the next visit. Then I said, Megan give Gina a kiss and say 'Bye.' And when I turned around, Gina was gone."

Cindy's memories of the early visits with Gina are of Megan never wanting to leave her arms. Sometimes, she said, Megan cried, and sometimes she made an angry face. And when she came back, Cindy said, Megan came right to her. "Threw herself at me." That was the way she always described their reunion. Cindy also remembered how Gina would say, "Go to mommy," and that she would say goodbye to Megan with a kiss on the hand.

Cindy began keeping a diary on March 26, the day Megan first visited Gina. All through the spring she kept the diary on a desk calendar, with room for a few random observations, but little more. Mostly, it is filled with the minutiae of the daily life of a young child—naps, playing in the yard with Jerry, family breakfasts, and middle-of-the-night crying. Cindy noted pediatrician appointments and court appointments and Megan's temperature, when she was running a fever. She marked the progress of the case, but offered little comment on her feelings. The only surprise was the entry of June 18, on which she wrote "Gina graduates." There are occasional barbs directed toward Gina, references to missed appointments and late arrivals and the state of the child when she was returned. Cindy noted family vacations to New Jersey and Megan's first assisted steps. But what is most striking in Cindy's diary is the almost complete absence of any hint of joy in her home: All is bleak. The entries are filled with reports of Megan's disrupted sleep and ear infections and antibiotics. When I asked Cindy whether the diary offered an accurate reflection of the family's life in the four months they waited for Judge Downey to decide whether, indeed, they could remain together, she did not hesitate in saying that it did.

MARCH 26. *I guess the visit went o.k. Gina still does not have bottles . . . Megan had a good time but was not as playful. She kept poking her ear.*

MARCH 30. *I went to work . . . when I bent down to kiss Megan goodbye she pulled my hair and started crying.*

APRIL 3. *Megan's second visit with bio-mother & grandmother at DCYS. I had to sleep with Megan in rocking chair. I played her music tape all the way down to DCYS & we sang together.*

APRIL 4. *All day she followed me around in her walker holding onto my leg. . . .*

APRIL 6. *Why for three days after will she cry at any given time.*

APRIL 9. *Woke up 11:30, 2:30, 5:30 each time I had to hold her or rock her.*

APRIL 18. *Climbed up 1 step by herself.*

MAY 11. *She was happy so long as I was holding her. I slept in the rocking chair all night holding her. Megan ate chocolate ice cream.*

MAY 14. *Megan cried on and off all day.*

Cindy said, "By the time I got home from the visits, I was flipping out because the baby's coming home and she's dirty. One time she came home, and she screamed the whole time coming home because she didn't have anything to drink. She's dirty. She's hungry. Now I pick her up out of the car seat, and she's got pee running down her leg. So now I'm screaming at Jerry to help me get her out of the car, and so now Jerry's aunt and uncle are upset. I'm upset. I'm screaming at Jerry. He's screaming at me, the baby's crying, and everybody's doing everything at once. Jerry's aunt is making a bottle. Jerry is making dinner for the baby, and she's in the sink getting a bath. Within twenty minutes I had her clean, fed, and bottled because everybody helped and everybody's flipping out."

Through all those months, Cindy said, a cloud hung over their home "that never goes away. And now there's distance between us where he's going into the family room because he needs to be by himself and I'm in the living room because I need to be by myself. And it's incredible the things that are going through your mind—that you're going to lose this kid. And if you don't lose her, what are you going to do? This girl [Gina] is going to be in your life forever. What are we going to do? Are we going to let Gina visit her? What role is Gina going to play? So now you're thinking all this stuff."

A psychiatric social worker who later interviewed the LaFlammes and Gina as well as Megan, and who therefore understood the situation in the months of the visits, told me that what was happening in the LaFlamme home that spring was much like what happens in the homes where a child is dying. The parent never stops loving the child, she explained. But out of self-preservation, the parent begins emotionally distancing herself from the child because she is preparing herself for the moment when the child will die. I described this to Cindy.

"It's real difficult to say," she said. "I used to go into her room in the middle of the night and hold her." Cindy insisted, however, that she did not remove herself from the child, that she did not try to protect herself from the sadness of her potential loss. "I don't think I did. I think that's when I developed the ulcer."

In late May the tone of the diary entries began to change. There were still the middle-of-the-night wakings and the dirty clothes at the end of the visits and the bottles that Gina did not, much to Cindy's chagrin, wash. But Cindy also began to note a change in Megan after the visits.

MAY 28. *The visit was from 11:00 to 4:00. They went to a park for the whole visit, Megan had a great time.*

MAY 30. *She woke up with a cold, temp 101. I started giving her Pediacare and Tylenol.*

JUNE 10. *Visit was at Gina's brother. Megan had a great time, she carried a kitten around with her. Gina only changed her diaper once. Megan peed through her clothes.*

JUNE 11. *Everything is perfect. Her ears look fine.*

JUNE 12. *Gina did not show up for her visit.*

JUNE 26. *Megan's 1st birthday. She'll be with Gina . . . I'm very upset about that.*

Cindy put a line through the latter part of the entry. But she did not make the line thick or try to cover over her words.

A Merciful Act

T HE ONLY QUESTION in the case that was now before Judge Downey was whether grounds still existed to terminate Gina Pellegrino's parental rights. If Downey ruled that they did, the next question to consider was whether he believed it best to terminate. Only then, the statutes dictated, was Downey to turn to the question of the child and decide where it was in her best interests to live.

Downey's ruling in March to reopen the case put the state attorney general's office in a difficult position. In July, a month after Gina Pellegrino gave birth, the state argued successfully that the then-unknown mother had abandoned her child. Abandonment, along with neglect, abuse, and the absence of a parent-child relationship, was grounds for termination. The length of time that defines abandonment, like the period of neglect or the specific nature of abuse, varies from state to state. In Connecticut it is twelve months, but a judge can waive any part of that period and decide that a child has been too long abandoned and that it is time to terminate parental rights.

In March the state attorney general's office made two seemingly innocuous but crucial decisions: not to appeal Downey's decision to reopen the case and to amend its case against Gina Pellegrino. The assistant attorney general in charge, Paul Bakulsky, consulted with his associates and concluded that the state could not successfully win a case for abandonment because Gina Pellegrino surfaced before the twelve-month statute of limitations expired. So Bakulsky amended the petition, presumably strengthening the state's complaint against Gina by arguing that not only had she abandoned her child, but that she had no relationship with her. The original abandonment petition against Gina was filed within a week of Megan's birth. It made no sense, Bakulsky said, to continue arguing that the child had been abandoned for less than a week, if the mother was, in fact, missing for four months. "We were under an obligation to bring the court up to date before trial," he said. "Why argue stale evidence?" Besides, he added, "I thought she would have a much more difficult time explaining four months."

This seemingly logical step, however, would prove to be a problem.

Termination of parental rights was, in theory, an act of compassion. In its idealized form it represents the boldest and most decisive act the state can perform in the interests of a child—a legal severing of that child from a parent deemed to have been a failure so that that child can be free to become the child of someone else. The history of termination as a legal action has two parts: before and after the passage of the 1980 Adoption Assistance Act, a law designed to stop foster care drift—children spending years bouncing from foster home to foster home without the state finding them a lasting place to live.

Before 1980, termination was used primarily in cases in which a parent voluntarily surrendered a child for adoption. Mark Hardin, an attorney at the American Bar Association's Center on Children and the Law who has studied termination, recalled speaking to a group of several hundred caseworkers in the late 1970s and asking how many of them worked on termination cases in the past year. The room fell silent until one worker asked whether he meant cases in which a parent gave up a child. No, Hardin explained, he meant when the state acted against a parent. None of the workers could recall such a case. By the mid-1980s, he said, termination cases had surged. This reflected not only a change in federal and state law, but a growing belief in the necessity of finding lasting homes for children.

But noble intentions aside, termination was not necessarily accomplishing its intended goal. In a 1994 study of terminations and adoptions in New York and Michigan, Martin Guggenheim, a professor at

New York University Law School, concluded that the rush to sever parental rights had not succeeded in hurrying children into new homes. Instead, it created a growing number of what Guggenheim called "legal orphans"—children whose parents' rights had been terminated but whom no one wanted to adopt. The children lived in foster care or in one of the state's institutions, but with no legal parent other than the state.

The case law on termination, however, suggests that while judges are ordering many more terminations, they are profoundly uncomfortable with the idea of taking children away from parents, no matter how objectionable the parents. The United States Supreme Court's rulings on termination, for instance, have consistently placed a high burden on the state to prove its cases for termination. It has struck down termination laws that it considered vague and lacking in proof of real and considerable danger to a child if he stayed in his parents' home.

In so doing, the Court weakened, but by no means eliminated, the broad and questionable discretionary power that caseworkers exercised when they went into a home and, after a hasty inspection of the cleanliness of the place or the company the parents kept or the manner in which the parents cared for their children, decided that the children could be better off elsewhere. This is not to suggest that such practices no longer existed. Far from it. Rather the Court succeeded in giving aggrieved parents a legal recourse—that is, if the parents, many of whom were poor and not wise to the workings of the family court and appellate division, understood that the Constitution protected their interests in their children.

"Even when blood relations are strained, parents retain a vital interest in preventing the irretrievable destruction of their family life," Justice Harry Blackmun wrote in 1982, in a decision that overturned New York State's termination of a palpably neglectful couple's rights to their children because the state's standard of "preponderance of the evidence" was insufficient. The Court ruled that termination required the higher standard of "clear and convincing evidence." Blackmun wrote that the power that the state could muster against an individual parent, especially the sort of struggling parents whose children populated the child welfare system, was so overwhelming that it was necessary to put a greater burden of proof on the state if it wanted to take a child. In the contest between the interests of the state in safeguarding children and the interests of a parent in keeping her children, the risk of legally imposed harm to the parent was the greater one and therefore needed the protection of the law.

That was the sentiment of the majority of the Supreme Court in 1982. The dissent, however, written by Justice William Rehnquist (who became chief justice in 1986), was a harbinger. Besides arguing that the majority's opinion was an intrusion of the federal bench into a realm reserved for the state courts, Rehnquist noted that New York had spent four years trying without apparent success to assist the parents in keeping their children. All this help, all the programs and money and guidance had not kept the mother and father from failing as parents in the eyes of the state. It was time, Rehnquist wrote, to allow the state to sever those parental rights, so that the children could move on to new and presumably better lives.

The rationale behind termination as a merciful act was based, in part, on what had evolved into an essential psychological component for making child welfare policy and law—the idea of the "psychological parent." The idea that biological ties between a parent and child were not necessarily paramount for a child was drawn from the work that Anna Freud did after World War II with the psychologist John Bowlby. Freud and Bowlby argued that what mattered most to a child were the people whom she saw and trusted as her parents. Freud and Bowlby based this conclusion on research conducted with children who had been separated from their parents during the war, sent to live for months and sometimes years with other people—foster parents—and who were, at the end of the war, reunited with their biological parents. The reunions, for some children, were catastrophic in that the parents who had sent them away, presumably to save their lives, had ceased, in the view of Freud and Bowlby, to be parents in a psychological sense. The children now looked to their foster parents as their true parents, their "psychological parents," from whom a forced separation would be traumatic. The specter of parents coming to regain children who now rejected them was, in the view of Bowlby and Freud, overshadowed by the prospect of seeing those children taken from the people whom they had come to regard as their mothers and fathers.

Anna Freud later joined the psychologist Albert Solnit and the legal scholar and psychologist Joseph Goldstein in writing three books that have become a reference point in determining questions of placement and intervention. The *Best Interests* books—*Beyond the Best Interests of the Child* (1973), *Before the Best Interests of the Child* (1979), and *In the Best Interests of the Child* (1986)—argued that the disruptions in a child's life be kept to a minimum, which meant that the state should tread carefully when it considered intervention. "Parents should generally be entitled to raise their children as they think best, free of state interference," they wrote, arguing that this belief necessitated "minimum state intervention" in the lives of families. Goldstein, Freud, and Solnit gave a generation of lawyers, judges, legal scholars, and court-appointed psychologists who did not believe that a family was constituted only by biological ties a scholarly argument to defend their position: If the children are with their psychological parents and those parents are not failing their children, leave the family alone.

Years later, however, legal scholars such as Peggy Davis of New York University Law School—a former Bronx family court judge—and others argued that Goldstein, Freud, and Solnit's theories were twisted and distorted by the state: "Continuity of care" became a goal best achieved by terminating parental rights so that a child could be free to live permanently with another set of more acceptable parents. "Under the banner of this principle," Davis wrote, "these institutions have moved doggedly to end 'the limbo of foster care' by terminating biological ties in order that children might be given permanence."

———

Where some advocates argue that termination offered a clear-cut solution that allowed children to begin new and better lives, others believed the concept to be deeply flawed. Termination, they argued, is designed to eliminate one set of parents and replace them with another. And that process often produces competing claims to a child. That contest with its inevitable winner and loser, argue such legal scholars as Marcia Garrison, may not necessarily be in the child's best interests either. Richard Dudley, a New York psychologist and a colleague of Davis's, told me that the idea of such a conflict troubled him: It transforms a relationship—the family—that should ideally be cooperative into something adversarial, as it can be in an especially acrimonious divorce. Why were people talking about "winning" a child or beating the other side by showing that they, and not the opposing party, represented the child's best interests? Dudley, who had spent years testifying as an expert witness on child welfare matters, was not so naive as to believe this was a matter easily resolved by people being civil to one another.

His view of the state's relationship with families was built on an altogether different premise than the prevailing notion of "permanency." He questioned the definition of permanency as a single set of parents, be it biological or psychological. Why, he wondered, was it necessary to limit the child to one parent? There was ample evidence and a rich history of cultures—that of Black America, especially—in which several adults, related and unrelated, took a share in helping to rear a child.

Davis, with whom Dudley taught a class at New York University Law School, went on to argue that the idea of a single "psychological parent" had become so much the accepted orthodoxy of the field that it led people to believe in an idea that was not necessarily supported by fact. She cited the British psychologist Michael Rutter, who evaluated several studies on the strength of attachments between parents and children and found the results not nearly as conclusive as many had assumed. "It is not ignorance as such which is harmful," Rutter wrote, "but rather our 'knowing' so many things are not true."

This argument against a single psychological parent was bolstered by, of all people, John Bowlby. Bowlby insisted that the children of even the most neglectful parents still wanted, and needed, to be with their parents. Because even if their parents fed them poorly and did not keep them clean, the parents still loved them, in their fashion, which meant that the children felt that they were of value to someone.

Time and again, the casebooks tell stories of terminations, which should be conclusive, nonetheless ending with two sets of adults still making claims to a child. The courts, acting on behalf of a child, must decide whose claim prevails. The stories are almost unbearably painful to read: the parent who loses a child because she happens to be white and lives with a black man in a poor section of an Alabama town; the Connecticut mother whose infant dies of SIDS (sudden infant death syndrome) and who loses her other children because the state, dissatisfied with the condition of her home and therefore dubious about her effectiveness as a parent, suspects her of murder and takes the children.

One story in particular haunts me, that of a child named Kristina who was five months old in 1980 when her mother brought the child to the Pawtucket Memorial Hospital in Rhode Island. Kristina had been having trouble retaining food and gaining weight. Her mother, Kate, brought her to doctors and clinics time and again. Now, with her daughter in the hospital, Kate visited frequently and spent the night. But because Kristina was diagnosed as "failing to thrive," the state's Department of Children and Families intervened. And when, after two weeks, her doctors released Kristina, the department took the child and placed her in a foster home. Later she was moved to a second foster home, where she would live for the next five years as her mother and father fought to get her back. Simply put, the department did not think that Kate was providing a good enough home. Visiting caseworkers reported that her two other children were seen with runny noses and without diapers, that there were dirty sheets on the bed, and that the house at times smelled of urine. No one ever saw Kate strike her children. The caseworkers required Kate to attend parenting classes so that she would learn how not to yell at her children. She fulfilled each requirement that the department made of her, missing parenting classes only when she was pregnant. She was allowed to visit Kristina for an hour and a half, every other week. But Kristina, the department ruled, could not go home. A family court judge, on the department's recommendation, weighing all the years Kristina had spent with her foster parents against all of the years that Kate and her husband spent trying to get Kristina back, decided to terminate Kate's parental rights. Kate had not been a bad mother. Rather, the judge ruled, Kristina had spent so much time with her foster parents—and, at the department's recommendation, so little time with Kate and her husband—that Kristina came to see those foster parents as her true parents.

I have read variations of this story in which all the players are trying to do the right thing, and all believe that they have the answer to the question of a child's best interests. Each side has a reasonable claim. But in the interest of achieving permanence, the law uses the bluntest possible instrument—termination of rights—where it is altogether inappropriate and dangerous for the child. For her part, Kate did appeal her termination. And, in time, she regained a child whom the state, attempting to do what it judged wise and fair, had first placed in limbo and then, acting as if this was best for Kristina, tried to just make her mother disappear.

After Cindy LaFlamme heard that Gina's parents had thrown her out, and that Gina was having difficulty finding a place to live, she suggested to her lawyer, William Bloss, that she and Jerry could take in both Gina and Megan. They could all live together; this way the child could stay with them, Gina would have a place to live, and no one would lose. Bloss, knowing the parties, did not think this a wise idea. Jerry LaFlamme, in particular, had little use for Gina, to whom he could barely bring himself to speak. Gina sensed this. "The guy had a snotty attitude," she said. "The woman, she was pretty nice to me in the beginning. Then I understood where they were coming from." Besides, she said, "I live in Milford. I don't know anybody in New Britain. I said 'No way.' It was just so they could be with my daughter."

Rescue Fantasy

Iᴛ ᴡᴀs Mᴀʏ. Megan was eleven months old. She had been with the LaFlammes for eight months. Gina was seeing her twice a week, for two hours at a time. On May 13 Megan had her first four-hour visit with Gina. That afternoon Megan had a bout of diarrhea in the department office. A caseworker gave Jerry a pair of overalls for Megan to wear because she had soiled her clothes. Cindy was upset because when Megan came home she was dirty and her hair was greasy. Cindy stripped off Megan's clothes, bathed her, fed her, and held her in the rocking chair all night. In her diary entry for the following day Cindy wrote: "Megan cried off and on all day and she was very clingy to Jerry and to me all night. Jerry took Megan to the park to feed the ducks and she played on the swings."

Cindy was aware of what was happening to her and her husband and their child, which was one of the reasons she kept her diary. "I really wanted to document what was going on all this time in case we did get to keep her, or in case we lost her. If she ever came back, I could show this to her. Bill Bloss did say that she would probably come back searching for us, wanting to know about that part of her life that was missing. At least this way I could show her what was going on."

This is what was going on. "Things are starting to get very, very stressful," Cindy said.

"Now the visits are starting to get longer. Now the visits are taking place outside, in a park, and the state is making it easy for Gina because now everyone's feeling sorry for her. She doesn't have a home. She doesn't have a job. She has no money.

"I'm trying not to take time off from work. Jerry would bring the baby to Jennifer Hauser [the new social worker]. And Jennifer would take the baby to Gina, and they would go wherever. And then after work, I would pick up the baby.

"On one visit they were late, they were really late, and I'm thinking something's happened, something's wrong. Maybe Gina took off and they can't find her, and Jennifer's out looking for her and no one can come here to tell me. Now even the office is closed, and I'm sitting in the parking lot and I'm waiting for a cop to come and say, What are you doing?

"Finally Jennifer pulls into the gate. She usually motions for me to walk over. Something happened and I don't know what. She said there's a mark on the baby. And I'm very calm about this. And she said, 'It's under her eye.' So we open the car door and I look at the baby, and there's this red mark under her eye.

"She said, 'I have a camera in my car, let me take some pictures.' We turn the baby around to get all kinds of angles of this eye. At home it's gotten ten times worse. It was swelling. It turned black and blue. So I called the pediatrician. There was some guy on call who said, it looks like a bug bite.

"On Monday I called Jennifer and said, 'Her eye is black and blue.' And I kept taking pictures all weekend. This happened on Friday.

"Gina doesn't see her till Wednesday. So on Wednesday Jennifer brings Megan down to Gina, and Gina opens the door and says, 'Oh my God, she has a black eye. What happened?' And Jennifer said, 'This is what happened when she was with you on Friday. Do you want to explain?'

"Gina said, 'I don't know.' And Jennifer kept at her and kept at her. She was now at her mother's again. Finally, Gina admitted that she went out to check the mail and left the baby with her mother, and when she came back, the baby was bruised. So now she's trying to blame it on her mother."

Cindy said, "We never did get the real story." Then she said that she remembered how that spring, when Megan was learning to walk, she would fall down and bruise herself, and that babies bruised themselves all the time for inexplicable reasons and that it did not speak badly about their parents.

———

In early June the question of Megan's interests, independent of the interests of either the LaFlammes or Gina Pellegrino, were at last considered in a formal way. This was done over two days at the Yale Child Study Center in New Haven. The center was assigned the job of assessing both the LaFlammes and Gina in relation to the child and offering an opinion on where her best interests, from a psychological point of view, might lie.

There are two schools of thought on the fate of children whose lives have been, or are to be, disrupted. One argues that children, even young children, are capable of weathering even catastrophic changes, a view perhaps best expressed by James Heiple of the Illinois Supreme Court. After ruling that Baby Richard should be removed from the adoptive home where he had lived since birth and be given immediately to the biological father he had never seen, Heiple insisted that any attendant trauma "will work itself out over time." The opposing view, which was rooted in the work of Joseph Goldstein, Anna Freud, and Albert Solnit in their *Best Interests* trilogy, argued that disruptions, especially to young children, were potentially injurious, that to take a child from the people he saw as his parents risked having that child grow up emotionally stunted, incapable of forming lasting bonds with adults. It was this latter view that informed much of the work and thinking of the Yale Child Study Center, where Solnit, who was now the state's commissioner of mental health—and later, a player in this story—had been director and where his students and protégés were many.

It is tempting to put great stock in the view of experts. But, explained the center's director, Donald Cohen, it was important to understand the limits of what could be determined in watching and talking to children and adults and then predicting what fate awaited that child. Cohen, a child psychologist, was a reasonable man. In a field where ideologues so dominated the debate, this was a welcome quality. When Cohen spoke of the trauma that children were sometimes forced to endure—be it through war, death of a parent, or cruelties inflicted by their parents—he spoke not, as was often the case, of the horrific consequences that came with such losses. Rather, he spoke of children's resilience, of what children were capable of confronting before moving on with their lives. What troubled him were generalities applied to all children, because no two children reacted to a trauma in quite the same way. Cohen framed the question of children and tragedy not in terms of outcomes, but in terms of avoidance. War and death could not be avoided. But disruptions, especially disruptions imposed by the state, could. Why take the chance of making things hard for a child, when it may not be necessary? Why burden a child with that risk?

Cohen was a student of Albert Solnit's, and Solnit's influence was clear in his belief that trauma be kept to a minimum in a child's life. Cohen, however, did not believe, as Solnit had argued, that a child's only place was with the adult she saw as her psychological parent. There were other factors to consider, such as the commitment that parent had to the child. But if a child saw an adult as the dependable and enduring parent in her life, it made no sense to forcibly disrupt that relationship.

Judges, however, often wanted evidence of a bond, not merely an expert's opinion, especially that of an expert hired by a contestant for a child. Judges were free, as Cohen acknowledged, to reject or accept that recommendation. The only measure for assessing the connection between parent and child was the Ainsworth Strange Situation Test. Like all measures that seek to predict the sort of adult a child might become, the test had passionate supporters and detractors among psychologists. The test was developed in the wake of Anna Freud and John Bowlby's work with children who came of age in institutions where they were depressed, angry, and withdrawn. Mary Ainsworth, a psychologist, believed that children needed what she called a "secure base" upon which to build their emotional lives. Simply put, if they knew who their parent was—generally, this meant the mother—then they had a foundation upon which other relationships could be built. Without that bond, that "attachment," children risked growing up emotionally at sea, unconnected and unable to connect. To determine whether a child was securely "attached," Ainsworth devised her "strange situation" test. It began with a parent coming into a laboratory playroom with a child. The child played with the toys in the room. Sometime in the next twenty minutes a stranger came into the room. The parent soon left. Then the stranger left the child alone. The stranger returned, followed shortly afterwards by the parent.

Ainsworth believed that the "securely attached" child cried when the parent left, refused to be comforted by the stranger, and calmed down when the parent returned. Children without that attachment either grew anxious when their parent left and alternately reached for and rejected them when they returned or simply did not appear to care when their parent came and left. Ainsworth compared these latter children to the depressed and angry children whom Bowlby had studied.

———

In late June the LaFlammes brought Megan to New Haven, where psychologists would judge to whom she was attached. The Yale Child Study Center study did not limit its assessment to the strange situation test. But because its work was built on the belief in the psychological parent and the connection a child had with that adult, the test was applied, along with interviews and observation. The Child Study Center was a squat brick building where the hallways were lined with such artistic representations of parents and their children as Picasso's *Maternity*, in which a mother nurses a child and Van Gogh's *First Steps*, in which a peasant, setting his shovel and work aside, takes his child's hand to guide him. Cindy's memory of the first visit to the center is of being observed giving Megan to Gina. Megan was on the floor, playing. Gina came into the room and picked up Megan and whirled her around. Cindy did not believe that Megan wanted to be picked up, that she wanted to play. She did not believe, nor was she likely to believe, that Gina was adept at sensing Megan's moods and rhythms.

The LaFlammes left the room. Megan sat on Gina's lap. Soon, Cindy said, "They called me in. As soon as I sat down I said, 'Hi Gina, how you doing?' and Megan came flying at me. So now Gina leaves and we stay. And Megan's off playing. She knew we were there. Now I'm trying to talk with them, and I'm all upset because how can they see that we've bonded if she's over there playing with toys? So I told them that, and they said, No, that's a good thing. The baby is secure. If they stay with you, they don't feel secure."

Of course, that is how Cindy would want to remember the testing, that it was she, and not Gina, with whom Megan felt secure. Gina's memory of the visits were of many questions about the nature of the child's birth and abandonment, and of her explanation of things as she believed they had happened. The evaluation took place over two days. Shortly before Judge Downey rendered his decision, the center submitted its two-page report.

The report noted that Gina had had some one hundred hours of visiting time with Megan, but that there appeared to be no real connection between them. The report also raised questions about Gina's understanding of what would take place if she regained the child. She was not, the screeners noted, able to articulate any real plans for the child's future. She spoke of perhaps living with her twin brother, even though her brother was not necessarily able to be of help because he suffered from a permanent disability. Gina, they wrote, "seriously minimizes the status of her situation." They noted, too, that Gina's living arrangements were in flux, that she had been in and out of her parents' home, and that she was now living in a room that her lawyer had found for her.

The LaFlammes, they wrote, were "highly sensitive and skilled parents." Megan was "more animated, social and vocal with the LaFlammes." In closing, they wrote, "the LaFlammes are Megan's parents in her eyes."

———

Perhaps that is where the story should have ended. People skilled at assessing children and their relationships with adults had concluded that the child was best kept where she was. But the story could not end there because, strictly speaking, the evaluation had no bearing on whether or not Gina's parental rights should be terminated. Downey read and sealed it. This, as Fredrica Brenneman might have put it, was in accord with "the process." Termination could not be about whether one set of parents was preferable to another. The psychological point of view aside, the law, at this point in the case, was asking only whether the child was still Gina's.

Later, editorial writers and those who wrote letters to the editors complained that the process was flawed. They wrote that the only issue should have been Megan, that to consider her fate in the context of an obscure provision in the state's commercial code underscored the degree to which she was being treated not as a person but as chattel, as the property or potential property of adults. That children had rights under the law—that they could be protected from abuse, that they had a right to counsel, that they could try to use the law to emancipate themselves from their parents—was then a relatively new idea.

It was not until 1895, for instance, that the first conviction of child abuse in the United States was rendered, in the New York case of a child named Mary Ellen, whose barbaric parents were prosecuted under laws that had until then been applied in cases of cruelty to animals. The seminal cases since—such as the 1967 United States Supreme Court decision in the case *in re* Gault, in which a teenager who was sentenced to six years in reform school for making a prank phone call won the right to have a lawyer and confront his accuser— gave children some of the legal protection formerly reserved for adults. This was not greeted with universal approval. The notorious 1992 case of Gregory K., for instance, in which a twelve-year-old boy asked a Florida judge to terminate his parents' rights so that he could be freed for adoption, became a lightning rod for those who believed that children had the right to use the law to protect themselves from their parents. Others insisted that such actions would surely lead to children dragging their parents into court because they did not want to take out the garbage. The judge who granted Gregory the right to bring his "divorce" petition against his parents was reversed on appeal. The appellate court ruled that while the law protected children, children needed adults—the agents of the state—to use the law for them.

The law has never quite known what to do with children. It wants to protect them, if need be from their parents. But it also wants to protect their parents from being told by the state how to rear them. The law does not regard children and parents as equal. This, says Stephen Wizner, a professor at Yale Law School, is as it should be: It is unfair to place upon children the burdens and responsibilities of adults. That is why judges in custody cases make it clear, or at least try to assure older children, that it is the responsibility of a judge to decide where a child lives and that the child need not assume that burden. The law tries to be compassionate, fair, and understanding. And that, ideally, is how it should be in its role as *parens patriae*, or the guardian of all the state's children. But that does not mean that the state can, say, look at a family and decide that the children would be better off elsewhere, with other people who might be able to provide a cleaner house and nicer clothes and better prospects. At least the state cannot do so anymore.

In his autobiography, Malcolm X told the writer Alex Haley what happened to his family after his father's murder. Goldstein, Freud, and Solnit included the story at the end of *In the Best Interests of the Child:*

> When the state Welfare people began coming to our house, we would come from school sometimes and find them talking to our mother, asking a thousand questions. . . . She would talk back sharply to the state Welfare people, telling them that she was a grown woman, able to raise her children, that it wasn't necessary for them to keep coming around so much, meddling in our lives.

Malcolm wrote of his mother's slow decline into madness and of the visitors from the welfare department beginning "to plant the seeds of division in our minds." One by one, the state took her children and sent them to live in different homes. Malcolm's mother suffered a mental breakdown. "I truly believe that if ever a state social agency destroyed a family, it destroyed ours. We wanted and tried to stay together. Our home didn't have to be destroyed." The story is a parable for the way the state's attempt to assist children for whom it wishes only a better fate can end in ruin. Malcolm equated what happened to him and his siblings with "modern day slavery—however kindly intentioned."

In late June of 1992, Gina Pellegrino, having worn out her parents' welcome and having exhausted the alternatives of friends and siblings, went to live in a homeless shelter and there awaited Judge Downey's decision on whether she could have her child back. That the LaFlammes could offer a demonstratively better present, and presumably more secure future, with savings bonds and life insurance and money set aside, could not, and should not, have mattered. All that should have mattered, in the eyes of those who believed that a child's place was with the people she regarded as her parents, was where the child felt she was home. In an often-cited Iowa case in which grandparents fought the husband of their late daughter for custody of their grandson, Anna Freud took issue with an appellate judge's opinion in which he noted the material benefits of the grandparents' home as compared to the spare offerings of the "romantic" father. "Important as external advantages are," she wrote in 1971, about the case of *Painter v. Bannister,* "we have seen too often that they can be wasted unless they are accompanied by the internal emotional constellations which enable children to profit from them." The child, she wrote, saw his grandparents, and not his grieving and absent father, as his "father." And for Anna Freud that is all that mattered.

But the instrument for making a judgment on the fate of a child was the law, or more specifically a judge. And the law made it clear that in the hierarchy of claims to a child the biological tie trumped all others, unless the state decided that the bond was ruptured. Donald Cohen of the Yale Child Study Center, for one, believed that is just what had happened when Gina Pellegrino left the hospital. Cohen, who was not involved in the assessment on the case, then went a step further. In his view, and in the view of others—though not in the view of the courts—Megan became the LaFlammes' child at the moment Betty Lou Cortigiano, with Patricia LeMay as the state's representative at her side, handed her to Cindy LaFlamme.

"My view on this is very severe," he said. "I don't believe that after a child is given for adoption there should be any probation period. That's it. When the baby comes out, the baby comes out. Nobody says we have to wait two hours to see if it's your baby. Similarly when a judge hands the baby to the adoptive mother, he says this is your baby."

But what would he say, I asked, if Gina Pellegrino had come to him and told him how badly she felt about leaving the child in the hospital.

Cohen, an especially gentle man, replied, "You have no baby."

But what if Gina said she had made a mistake, that she thought her mother would get angry at her.

"You had a baby," he said. "I do not deny that you had a baby. You once had a child. But you no longer have a child. Somebody else has the child."

His finality was pleasing. But it was not a view uniformly held by his colleagues. One of them, Barbara Nordhaus, who had conducted the evaluations—but who could not speak directly about them—came to roughly the same conclusion, but from a different and more circuitous path. Nordhaus, like Solnit and Cohen, believed that the courts dealt with children using an adult's sense of time. By this she meant that while a final disposition in a custody matter might take several months of hearings, delays, scheduling conflicts for attorneys and expert witnesses, and closing arguments, that was an acceptable period for an adult. It was, however, interminable for a child. Megan came to the LaFlammes in October. Judge Downey rendered his decision ten months later. Had the Department of Children and Youth Services acted immediately after Gina's call in November, she said, it would have been best to take the child from the LaFlammes, sad as that would have been. "On November 14 [the day Patricia LeMay first visited Gina] it's Gina and the baby. From the baby's point of view it's in the baby's best interest to go to Gina on November 14, all other things being equal. The longer the baby is with the LaFlammes, the less it's in the baby's interest to be moved."

Meanwhile, she said, "the clock is ticking." In January, when Judge Downey decided to reconsider the termination, "two more months have passed and the child has had two significant placements [first with the Cortigianos, then with the LaFlammes] by the age of six months." Just because the child is not "acting out," she added, does not mean the child is not in some way suffering.

Had the agency taken the child from the LaFlammes in November, Nordhaus said, it would have spared Megan, at the very least, the six months of uncertainty and growing tension and sadness in her home. So why, I asked, did the agency stall? Why did Patricia LeMay wait seven weeks to tell the LaFlammes about Gina's return and even allow them to baptize the child?

Nordhaus, who could be blunt and harsh in her assessments, tried to take a compassionate view of LeMay's decision. Consider, she said, that here was a worker with a case for which there was a good ending. It was nothing at all like so many of the other cases that her agency saw and which Nordhaus, who assisted the department in assessing children, knew intimately. This was not a case of a child who had bounced from home to home or an abused child or a child whose innocence had long vanished. This was an infant whom the state could deliver to a couple that had so badly wanted a child. Except that the LaFlammes had made it clear from the outset that they wanted a risk-free child, a child whom they had no fear of losing because Cindy had suffered enough loss. Here Nordhaus was especially angry with the department: It had offered the LaFlammes assurances that were not true; while Gina's rights had been terminated, Megan was not, technically, risk-free. Why, she asked, didn't the attorney general know about that four-month waiting period for appeals?

Perhaps, I said, because no one ever thought that it would be used in a child welfare case until Angelica Anaya-Allen, desperate for a hook upon which to hang her client's tenuous case, tried it.

But for Nordhaus there was more to the matter than failure to know the commercial code. She believed that what was really taking place within the department, even after Gina reappeared, was the desire to make a potentially happy ending real. It was as if that good resolution was there before them, and in a field where the work is often so unsatisfying, here was a case that could be salvaged, if only the birth mother would go away. What was happening, Nordhaus explained, was common. In the trade it was called "rescue fantasy." This was the earnest, innocent, and often woefully wrongheaded idea that if the caseworker could just get the children into the right foster home or if she could only get the mother to complete her rehab or if she could only find the family a clean and decent place to live, this could be a "family" in the way that she thought families could be.

For the department, and a caseworker, eager to perform the small miracle of a rescue, she said, Gina "is unwelcome and you want to make her go away." As for the delay in telling the LaFlammes about Gina until after Thanksgiving and Christmas—which LeMay had explained as "not wanting to ruin their holidays"—Nordhaus said, "the holidays represent some coming to terms with the loss of the fantasy of the idealized family. That is when everyone is together."

Nordhaus did not believe that the department or LeMay acted with deliberate cruelty. But in this contest the department—as child welfare agencies and caseworkers have done for decades and continue doing today—chose sides, or rather the side of the people who embodied the qualities they admired in a parent. The danger in the rescue fantasy, Nordhaus said, is that it becomes a form of aggression against the side not chosen, against the other, less acceptable parent. "We're in charge here, and this baby is now with a nice couple," she said, suggesting the unconscious thinking within the department. "We have resolved this. This is how we want it to be."

But Gina, unlike the other clients whom Angelica Anaya-Allen had represented, who stopped coming to court and relapsed into drug use and who could never seem to gather the strength to do what was necessary to regain their children, unlike the clients of whom Anaya-Allen had grown so weary, Gina, emboldened by her smart and appropriately aggressive attorney, would not go away.

Sitting in Judgment

I DID NOT want the LaFlammes to lose Megan. I liked them. I felt bad when they told me about what had happened to Cindy in all her other attempts to have a child. They were people like me. Gina Pellegrino, for whom I felt pity, was not like me, and I did not believe that she would be a parent like me. I recognize now that this sort of thinking sounds very much like the sort of thinking that Barbara Nordhaus and others applied to caseworkers: that no matter, in Malcolm X's words, how "kindly intentioned," they could not help but apply to their work their own sense of what sort of family was good for a child.

Goldstein, Freud, and Solnit had warned the professionals of the child welfare system against overstepping the bounds of their expertise: Lawyers should limit themselves to arguing points of law, judges to interpreting the law, and psychologists to diagnosis. But this was not possible. People held opinions about children and what was best for children, and when they saw a situation that they did not like and they had the power to do something about, they acted. I recall waiting in line with my children to buy tickets at an amusement park and watching a father turn on his son and, in a rage, start kicking him. The boy, who looked about eight, cried more, I sensed, from humiliation than pain. The father did not much seem to care. He kicked the boy, who had talked back to him, again and again. I wanted very much at that moment to look like, say, Shaquille O'Neal, the mammoth basketball player, and tap the man on the shoulder and say, If you kick him one more time I will kick you. But then the son, weeping and hurt, would have stepped between us and said, Leave my dad alone. I'm sure the child would not have cared in the least had I said, But I was just trying to help.

I had difficulty understanding the decision that Judge Downey had made to reconsider the case against Gina Pellegrino. The logic eluded me. I could not see how, considering the evidence, he could arrive at the decision he reached unless that decision had less to do with logic and more with an intuitive sense of how things should be. Because Judge Downey declined to talk with me, I felt compelled to try to make his case for him, so that I might see how this decision spoke about so many decisions made about families each day by the agents of the state.

In the course of learning about this story, I came upon another case that was striking in some of its similarities. In this case, too, the decision troubled me. The case was heard in Queens County Family Court in New York before Judge Michael Gage. Unlike Judge Downey, Judge Gage allowed me to sit in her courtroom, and in time, and with the understanding that I would keep the names of children confidential, she talked with me about the thinking that brought her to this and other decisions. I tell this story because it suggests how it was that a judge—an equally admired and respected judge—arrived at a judgment, and what that judgment said about when it might be understandable for the state to impose itself upon a family.

The case concerned a three-year-old boy whom I will call Robert. Robert was born almost a year to the day before Megan. Robert's mother was a crack addict. He was born with cocaine in his blood. New York's Child Welfare Administration took Robert at birth and placed him in a foster home. The foster parents had several other foster children. Robert's mother visited him twice, when he was eleven months old. She drifted in and out of drug rehabilitation programs, never getting well. Then she vanished again. The department looked but could not find her. In her report, the caseworker for the private agency that had been assigned the case wrote that the department's goal was for Robert to be adopted by his foster parents. The foster parents had once considered adopting another child but changed their minds when they decided his behavior was too disruptive. But the foster parents appeared willing to adopt Robert.

There was, however, a problem. Judge Gage determined, through her reading of the case file, that the caseworker wanted and tried to make this problem go away. The problem was Robert's grandmother, whom I will call Mrs. J. Mrs. J lived in Baltimore. She knew that her daughter was pregnant but did not know that she had had her child until the Child Welfare Administration sent a letter to her daughter in Baltimore, trying to find her. Mrs. J called the department and found her grandson's caseworker and said that she wanted to see the child.

The caseworker, in the view of Judge Gage, was not pleased. Mrs. J was a pest. She would call and insist on visiting her grandson. She took the bus from Baltimore to New York to visit Robert. Robert's foster parents had no objection to his seeing his grandmother. As Robert grew older, they allowed him to go to Baltimore with her and visit his cousins and uncle and his older brother, whom his grandmother was rearing. Meanwhile Robert was attending Head Start. The side effects of his exposure to cocaine had begun subsiding, and though he was developmentally delayed, he was no longer the infant that the foster mother had to hold day and night to soothe. When Robert was two years old, his grandmother formally asked for custody. The foster care agency moved to terminate Robert's mother's parental rights, to free Robert for adoption by his foster family. That was the issue before Judge Gage.

Gage, who was fifty, had a reputation as a fair and reasonable judge. She was neither an ideologue who believed that biological or psychological ties were paramount nor a lecturer who used her position to tell the people who came before her how to lead their lives. She and her husband, a law professor, had no children. The arguments of the attorneys aside, the case before Gage rested on these issues: the evaluations by two psychologists, the testimony of the foster parents and Mrs. J, and the caseworker's report. The psychologists both performed the "strange situation" test and both concluded that Robert saw his foster parents as his "psychological parents." Gage discounted the testimony of the psychologist hired by the foster care agency because she had not observed Robert with his grandmother, only with the foster parents. She also ignored the summation by the attorney assigned to represent Robert, who in siding with the foster parents spoke of the catastrophe that awaited Robert if he was moved to his grandmother's home. The lawyer was young and inexperienced and, in Gage's view, so oversold her case as to render the argument specious. Gage did, however, pay particular attention to the report of the second, more neutral psychologist, who concluded that either Robert's foster parents or his grandmother could provide him with a suitable home.

Then Gage turned to the caseworker, whose behavior reminded me of what Barbara Nordhaus saw as Patricia LeMay's rescue fantasy for Megan. "The best that can be said for the agency case worker," Gage wrote in her decision, "who was the worker the entire time the child was in care, is that she demonstrated by the evidence to be obtuse and not responsive to efforts to plan for permanency for [Robert]." The caseworker, Gage wrote, tried to stall Mrs. J at every turn. She scheduled visits on weekdays, even though this meant a considerable hardship for Mrs. J. These actions suggested to Gage that the caseworker felt she had found a solution to the problem of Robert and that when an alternative appeared in the person of Mrs. J, she tried to make her disappear.

"Once something is in motion, people are happy to let it continue indefinitely," Gage later said of the thinking that too often guided child welfare workers. A home had been found, and it was a place where the child could stay and therefore avoid the limbo of foster care drift. It was a good solution. But it was not the only solution, and not necessarily the best solution. It was available and convenient, and in Gage's view, that was enough for the caseworker who, in fairness, may have had too few cases with so satisfying a resolution. The presence of Mrs. J, however, meant work for the caseworker. It meant clutter and uncertainty. It was as if the caseworker had said, Look, I have this kid in a good place. Can't we just leave well enough alone? What was left unsaid was Mrs. J's association with her daughter, the drug-addicted and irresponsible mother. And this could not have worked to Mrs. J's advantage. Gage, who was involved with a city-wide committee searching for new answers to the elusive problem of "permanency," was enraged that the caseworker simply took the first solution she came upon. She did not bother to consider whether another solution, in the form of the dogged Mrs. J, might be better. The first placement might well have been the right placement. What upset Gage was that the worker had not even bothered with Mrs. J when it should have been clear that someone so persistent might well be wise to consider.

"This was a perfectly adequate foster placement," Gage wrote. The operative word here, in Gage's view, was "adequate." While Mrs. J was not retreating in her struggle with the child welfare system, the foster mother was tiring of the contest. The foster parents had been interested in having placed with them a child whom they might be able to adopt—"she viewed him as on loan to her," Gage said. The foster father, however, told Gage that he placed great stock in blood ties and wondered whether Mrs. J's home might be where Robert belonged.

The caseworker, and the agency, apparently did not pay much heed to this. "Mrs. J was going to be in the picture for the foreseeable future," Gage said. "And Mrs. F [the foster mother] was growing weary of the struggle."

One day, during the trial, Mrs. J came from Baltimore with her brother, her younger daughter, and the grandson who lived with her. She took the stand and all but begged Judge Gage to give her Robert. It was clear to Gage that Mrs. J harbored fantasies that her troubled daughter, who before her addiction had been a nurses' aide, might one day "get her act together" and come home. Gage accepted that as a sad mother's reasonable dream. She also acknowledged that Mrs. J was prone to smothering Robert a bit and that she was not necessarily facing the difficulties that lay ahead if Robert was moved. One by one Mrs. J's relatives took the stand and talked of their love for Robert and their belief that he belonged with them, his family.

Except that, in the view of the one reliable psychologist in the case, Robert already had a family, the people with whom he had been living since he was born. How could Judge Gage consider moving him? Why could she not make visitation easier for Mrs. J, give her summers and holidays and weekends from time to time, but keep Robert where he was? Moving him appeared, at the very least, to be just the sort of risk that Donald Cohen spoke about. There was no way of knowing what might happen to Robert if he was moved. The psychological evaluations reported some bed-wetting after his first overnight stays away from his foster parents and foster siblings. But even if there was no way of knowing what, precisely, would happen, why take the chance? Judge Gage, however, thought differently.

Gage considered the testimony and evidence and psychological evaluations and ruled that after a period of adjustment Robert would go to live in Baltimore with his grandmother. The foster parents did not appeal.

I had known Judge Gage for over a year, and my initial response was disappointment. How, I asked, could she move this child from his family?

She replied, in her even and measured way, that the key to her decision was the foster parents' ambivalence and fatigue. Mrs. J was relentless in her desire to have her grandson with her. The foster parents may have loved him and wanted to keep him. But they were tired of battling for him. The agency and caseworker could have made things far easier for Robert by considering his grandmother as an option in his life when he was still very young and before his bond with his foster parents had deepened.

"I don't discount that there will be some pain and unhappiness when he leaves the only home he knows," Gage said. But she was moving him nonetheless.

A few weeks later, I spoke with Donald Cohen and told him the story of Robert and of Judge Gage's decision. I assumed that, as a protégé of Albert Solnit, he would have been appalled by her decision.

He was not. He thought Gage had made the wise decision. This opinion was not based on attachment theory or any diagnostic tests for determining the psychological parent. Rather, it was a feeling of the heart. He too heard what Gage heard in the foster mother's weariness.

Cohen asked, "If the child is hit by a truck tomorrow and is permanently disabled, who will give over her life for him?"

Then he answered his own question. "Give the child to his *bubbe*," he said using the Yiddish word for "grandmother," with all that it suggested about warmth and home.

The home into which Judge Gage allowed the state to intrude was not a family, in the sense of people devoted in their actions, and in their hearts, to a child. It was a place where two decent adults cared for a child, but had lost, or never possessed, the desire to fight for him. In a sense they had not quite become a family, at least in the view of Donald Cohen and Judge Gage. Robert may have relied on them. But in Cohen's view, it was his grandmother who had shown that she was the essential adult upon whom he could depend, the adult who in Cohen's view is at the center of a child's family.

Gina was like Mrs. J in one regard: her determination to regain her child. But Cindy and Jerry LaFlamme were not Robert's foster parents, at least in the way Judge Gage perceived them. Just as Judge Gage had based her decision on their ambivalence, so too was the LaFlammes' commitment to the child ample reason for leaving Megan where she was. Never mind that Cindy LaFlamme said that she fell in love the moment she took Megan in her arms. The family that existed between Gina Pellegrino and her child stopped being a family and therefore lost the protection of the law when Gina decided, for whatever reason, to leave her. A new family was formed on the day the LaFlammes took her home. The state was obliged to leave that family alone, unless it believed that the child was in danger. The child was not in danger. If the child was not in danger, how could the state assume that it had the right to impose itself, unless the state, or rather Judge Downey, believed that he could make things as he believed they should be, right and better?

Removal

JUDGE DOWNEY announced his decision on June 30. He ruled that Gina Pellegrino had, indeed, neglected her child and not cared for her. But he rejected the state's argument that these offenses warranted terminating her rights. The child was to be returned to Gina. With that, court was recessed.

A social worker called Cindy fifteen minutes later. Cindy cried and asked how the judge could have made this decision and why she and Jerry were never allowed to be heard in court. She asked the social worker to pick up Megan the following morning at ten. The social worker offered to take Megan that afternoon if the LaFlammes were too upset. Cindy said that Megan would be fine for the night and that she would see the social worker on the front porch the next day.

The following morning Cindy dressed Megan in a white, sleeveless one-piece with a frilly collar. She put on Megan's white shoes and the white socks with the frilly tops. She packed Megan's purple bag. In it Cindy put some toys, a blanket, two pairs of shoes, and a diaper. When the social workers came to the house, they parked in the backyard. The reporters met them on their way into the house. The reporters were from the local newspapers and radio stations and the Associated Press. Channel 3 TV sent a camera crew. Later, Cindy said that Jerry's mother had called the Associated Press to tell them about Judge Downey's decision and that she started getting phone calls from reporters at seven in the morning. The social workers were not pleased. They were not angry with Cindy, whom they hugged and with whom they cried. They were upset with the reporters, especially the camera crew from Channel 3, which later followed them as they drove away from the house.

Megan was sleeping on Cindy's chest when the reporters came into her home. She told them, "I had every reason to believe this would be our daughter forever." The cameraman filmed footage of Megan's room, with the string of colored hearts over her crib and the heart-adorned sheets.

Jerry said, "DCYS gave us a baby and said they'd never, ever take her away. And now she's leaving in fifteen minutes."

Cindy sat at the kitchen table flanked by the social workers, holding Megan and crying. Megan looked sleepy. Jerry gathered a stuffed animal from the couch and put it in Megan's bag. Cindy gave the social workers the bag. Jerry carried Megan outside. They stood next to the car, and together Cindy and Jerry hugged Megan. Then, weeping, they handed her to the social workers who strapped her into a car seat. The photographers crowded around the car and took pictures of Megan, frowning, as she sat slumped in the seat. They turned to the LaFlammes. Cindy stood with one arm around a social worker who was trying to comfort her. Cindy's other arm was around Jerry, whose eyes looked confused and on the verge of tears, as the social workers took Megan away. They were going to take Megan directly to Gina, but decided to go first to their office because they did not want the camera crew to see where Gina was living.

Later that day they drove Megan to Life Haven, the shelter in New Haven where Angelica Anaya-Allen had found a bed for Gina. The shelter was for other homeless mothers and their children.

"It was a nice shelter," Gina said. "They said you can live here as long as you want. Your daughter is beautiful." Gina had been saving money so that she could buy clothing for Megan. "Little pretty dresses for the summertime. I always wanted to have a daughter and dress her up."

One by one, the television crew introduced the players in this drama, all except for Gina, who remained in hiding but who was shown, set against a pale blue background, in a portrait photograph taken as she held Megan. The crew interviewed Angelica Anaya-Allen, who said that Megan was now in a "safe and appropriate environment." The crew went to Brenda Pellegrino's home. She sat at her kitchen table, a heavyset woman in a pale pink shift, wearing a crucifix around her neck. "We want this child," she said. "We have her now. We're gonna keep her now."

The television reporter asked how she learned of the birth of the child. Brenda Pellegrino recalled that Gina told her, "Ma, I didn't know what to do," to which she said she replied, "Gina, you should have called me from the hospital and told me. We could have figured something out together."

Then Brenda Pellegrino asked, "Why did they try so hard to keep my daughter from her baby when they're supposed to be trying to get families back together? Instead they were concerned about getting this child adopted out."

The reporter asked, "What do you say to the LaFlammes?"

"I really feel sorry for the LaFlammes," she replied. "How could they know that after three months someone's coming back for this baby?"

The reporter wanted to know why her daughter was living with the baby in a shelter, instead of with her.

"She wants to live by herself with her daughter," Brenda Pellegrino said. "She really wants to try to take care of the baby by herself. She wants to be a mom."

How will she support herself? the reporter asked.

"She has no job. She has things that will be coming into place when she gets housing. Things like that."

Did Brenda Pellegrino have any doubts of her daughter's devotion to the child, the reporter asked.

"She says she wants this baby with all her heart and soul," she replied. "She wants to be a good mom. She knows she's gonna have to give up things that she wouldn't have normally had to give up if she didn't have her."

The television crew returned to the LaFlammes' home the following day. Cindy told them, "I want my daughter back because she is mine in my heart and soul."

I asked Cindy why she surrendered Megan. In other celebrated cases in which biological parents fought adoptive parents for a child, the adoptive parents kept the child, hoping that a decision might go their way. Cindy said that she believed in following the law and that the judge had ordered that the child be given to Gina and she was obliged to obey.

Later, however, I asked Barbara Nordhaus why she thought the LaFlammes had given up Megan, rather than find a way to keep her or even try to flee with her. Nordhaus had a sense of what life in the LaFlamme home was like in the months leading to Judge Downey's decision and how Megan was in a sense dying before her parents' eyes. By the time Downey ordered them to give up the child, Nordhaus said, the LaFlammes were not so much defeated as resigned to what came to seem inevitable. The surrender was akin to a funeral, and it was time to let Megan go.

Except that Megan was not gone. She was with Gina. And the day after they gave her back, Cindy called a new lawyer, Barbara Ruhe, who asked Cindy whether she had any problem going to the media with her story. Cindy said she did not.

The story of Megan's removal ran across the top of the front page of *The Hartford Courant* and in the papers across the state. The Associated Press story appeared in papers all over the country. Because Judge Downey refused to talk about his decision and because Gina was in hiding, the story became, as Jerry's mother intended, the LaFlammes' story, the moment of their terrible loss and the injustice of a decision that took their child from them. Gina, identified only as a teenager who had abandoned the child, was described as being unemployed and living in a shelter. In the days that followed, the story appeared in such publications as the *Chicago Tribune*, *The Denver Post*, *The Boston Globe*, and *The New York Times* and on CNN's *Sonya Live*. Letters began flooding the editorial boards of the state's newspapers, as well as the office of Richard Blumenthal, the state's attorney general.

Two weeks after the LaFlammes surrendered Megan, Blumenthal, emboldened by the angry letters and a petition signed by thirty-five hundred people, announced that he, personally, was appealing Judge Downey's decision to the state supreme court. He also asked Downey to reconsider his decision. "We will give the judge another opportunity to decide what's best for the child," he said. "Adoptive parents should not have to feel the kind of turmoil that's been in this case."

The story, or rather the public telling of the story of Megan Marie, began on June 30, 1991, with the scene outside the LaFlammes' home, and the imagined scene of the child being handed to her biological mother in a distant homeless shelter. The story began with the moment of Megan's removal, propelling the outrage that dominated the coverage for months to come.

It is hard to tell this story, or to think about this story again and again, and not feel the outrage of the moment the social workers strapped Megan into her car seat and drove her away. The rage is useful in that it calls attention to an event that should never have happened. But when rage dominates the debate, the complexities are lost and with them any chance of understanding how that injustice occurred. Judge Downey did not make his ruling in a vacuum. His decision reflected a long-held—although, in a historical context, brief—idea of what a family is supposed to be and what a child needs a family to be. Megan's removal was the function of a mythologized idea about families that Downey's decision merely reflected.

As a result of that myth a family was threatened and ultimately dismantled. I have yet to hear an explanation of how the months during which Downey deliberated and the LaFlammes waited could have possibly been good for Megan. In the weeks and months after Megan's removal, the two sides in the battle for the child would argue, once again—but this time, in public—the same questions: whether Gina Pellegrino had failed her child to the extent that she deserved to lose her; and whether the LaFlammes constituted a family to which the law extended the same protection it offered Gina Pellegrino when she insisted that the child she abandoned was still her child. The protagonists waited for the state supreme court to decide which family, in the end, would remain a family.

———

In the matter of Megan Marie the state did, in fact, deny a mother her child and a child her mother. The mother was Cindy LaFlamme. Gina Pellegrino did more than leave her newborn child behind in the hospital. She vanished from her life, not for a day or a week or a month. I will grant that Gina acted out of fear, fear of her mother and of the punishment she believed awaited her. Abandonment, like all crimes, comes with explanations. The explanation in Gina's case evokes sympathy. It does not, however, excuse the action. In leaving—albeit in the panic of the moment—Gina said, I do not, at this moment and perhaps ever, want this child. In denying her child for the first four months of that child's life, Gina Pellegrino denied that a relationship between them existed. The state found a new home for that abandoned child. The child's new parents treated her kindly and appropriately; and that is all that they needed to do. Theirs was the relationship that mattered in the child's life. Cindy and Jerry LaFlamme were the child's parents. And the state was wrong to deny them their relationship.

———

Many times each day the agents of the child welfare system arrive at homes across the country and ask to see how the children are doing. Sometimes the agents look around and leave, and sometimes they issue warnings to the parents about making sure the house gets cleaned up and the kids make it to school. Sometimes they ask what help the parents might need and offer social service agency addresses and phone numbers. I can imagine nothing quite so terrifying as the prospect of a knock on the door by a stranger with the power to monitor the way I am rearing my children. But I can only imagine this, or hear what it is like from the people whose circumstances or behavior makes them likely targets for that unwelcome visit. It was highly unlikely to happen to Cindy and Jerry LaFlamme, which is why the imposition of the state upon their family was so unusual. But that did not keep the LaFlammes from experiencing the same powerlessness and anger of poorer people who get the knock on the door. The LaFlammes will go to their graves believing that they did nothing wrong, nothing that merited the cruelty of the state's behavior toward them. Other parents whose children the state takes also believe that they are being punished without having committed an offense. Sometimes they are right.

———

The story of the LaFlammes captures the dynamic of a family that the state feels it cannot leave alone. The more common and more troubling story of the child welfare system, however, takes place when the state imposes itself upon a family where there are serious and legitimate questions about leaving the children where they are or at the very least leaving the parents to do as they please.

The Meltons were such a family. On a winter's night in 1994 the Chicago police stepped into their home and saw a sight so revolting and disturbing that it would guide the state's actions in the weeks and months that followed. In the matter of the Melton family, the State of Illinois acted swiftly and with great purpose. Like the LaFlammes, the Melton family found itself under an attack for which it had no preparation and no experience.

THE MELTONS,
PART I

Nineteen Children

Maxine's House

MAXINE MELTON looked out her living room window, past a flimsy yellow curtain, and watched the police question the crack dealer who worked the corner near the Keystone Avenue Baptist Church. A line had formed in front of the dealer, but people scattered when the police turned onto North Keystone Avenue on Chicago's West Side. The police had picked up a call of shots fired. But the call was an hour old, and the police were left to search the grounds for weapons and bags of crack and, as an afterthought, to investigate a report of drugs being sold out of Maxine's house.

It was just after eleven o'clock on February 1, 1994. The temperature dropped below zero, and light snow was beginning to fall. Inside Maxine's house, the last of the children had fallen asleep. For supper Maxine had opened a large box of spaghetti and two jars of Prego pasta sauce, and when the children finished eating, they watched cartoons and played Super Mario Bros. 3, a video game.

Maxine and the children lived in a two-bedroom apartment on the first floor of a brick house that sat next to an empty lot. The house next door burned down on New Year's Eve. There were once twenty houses on the block. Now there were only five, and their isolation between the vacant lots made the block feel abandoned. Keystone Avenue was a street without distinction in a neighborhood where many of the street names began with the letter *K* (Karlov, Kildare), where crack dealers worked most every corner, and where the landscape was a flat, bleak expanse of "two-flats," stretching out from the faraway lights of the Loop.

Maxine sat on the living room radiator. It was cool. A HAPPY HAL-LOWEEN sign still hung on the broken window. There was nothing to block the cold air from seeping in. When the police came to her door, Maxine, knowing who it was and what they wanted, invited them in. "One of them flashed a light in the window, and I opened the door and let him in, and he asked me was drugs being sold out of here? I told him no," Maxine said. "And he started looking around and looking around, and a couple more officers came in here, and that's when they saw the kids."

There were nineteen children in the apartment. They were crammed, four and five together, on two stained and sheetless mattresses or on the living room floor, near the radiator, huddled under piles of dirty clothes, under a dirty blanket. They slept in their diapers or underwear. One slept on the floor, naked. The children stank of filth. The youngest child was a few months old, and all the rest were under nine, except for a fourteen-year-old who weighed two hundred and eighty pounds and suffered from respiratory problems.

The teenage boy began trying to clean the house, clearing the floor with a snow shovel, hoping that things would not look so bad. Soiled diapers were shoved in the corner. Excrement and toilet paper clogged the single toilet. The bathroom light was out, and the faucet leaked cold water. There was no hot water. There were no towels, soap, or shampoo, and only a single roll of toilet paper. The kitchen sink was piled with dishes caked with spaghetti sauce. The stove was broken and thick with grease. Its door hung open. Cans of lard and some Kool-Aid sat in the pantry. Dripping water stained the bathroom sink black. Cockroaches ran across the floor and in and out of the open boxes of rice and cereal in the pantry. The plaster ceiling was cracked, and the green walls were pocked with holes.

The four police officers who came into Maxine's home were from a special operations unit that dealt primarily with narcotics and with hostage incidents. Two walked in the front door, and two entered through the back. In the living room they watched a child sitting on the floor, sharing a chicken neckbone with a dog. In one of the bedrooms, they found the father of one of Maxine's children, lying on a king-size bed, watching television.

A policeman asked Maxine how many children were in the house. She told them she did not know.

"Take a guess," he said.

"I don't know," said Maxine.

Five of the children were Maxine's. Eleven were the children of her four sisters, Diane, May Fay, Denise, and Cassandra. Diane, who lived there from time to time, left two of her six children at Maxine's. Her other sisters had moved in with their children. So too had Denise Turner, the sister of Maxine's boyfriend, and her three children, one of whom, a four-year-old boy, suffered from cerebral palsy and whose skin was scarred with what the police suspected were cigarette burns. The other mothers were out. Maxine did not know where they had gone, except for her sister Diane, who was, at that moment, in labor at Bethany Hospital.

"They searched the house, but they didn't find no drugs," Maxine said. "Then they started asking me all their names, and the guy told me to get them dressed and everything. They said they were just taking them to the doctor to have them checked, and that's when I knew there was a problem."

Maxine kept asking the officers, "What's the problem?" The police radioed their supervisor, who told them to start assembling, identifying, and removing the children from the house. The children did not have enough clean clothes, so the police dressed them in adult clothing.

The police called for an evidence technician, and their call was picked up by Ken Herzlich, Chicago's version of a modern-day Weegee, the famed New York crime photographer. He worked overnight as a freelance video photographer for the local television stations. Herzlich, whose stock in trade was homicides and fires, listened on his scanner as the police were trying to determine whether they needed ambulances to transport the children or whether they could take them away in squad cars. When he arrived on North Keystone Avenue, Herzlich noticed that the officers were taking turns coming out of the house for fresh air. Later, he went around to the back of the house and poked his nose through a broken kitchen window. The stench was overwhelming—rotting food, dirty diapers, must, dog stink. The police, who knew Herzlich well, asked him to stand across the street when they brought the children out. He aimed his camera at the doorway and, panning from side to side, caught the image of the children being carried down the front steps and out into the falling snow. He thought it odd that the children being taken from such a home were wearing new Nike gym shoes.

By then Cassandra and May Fay Melton and Denise Turner had arrived home. Together with Maxine and the two men staying in the house—Johnny Melton, their brother, and Gregory Turner, the father of Maxine's fourth child—they were taken to the local precinct house and charged with misdemeanor child neglect.

The children appeared to have been fed, and only the child with cerebral palsy displayed signs of physical abuse. The police then brought the children to the Department of Children and Family Service's twenty-four-hour emergency shelter, housed in a modern granite fortress on West Montrose Avenue. The center was the entry point for most of the twelve hundred children absorbed from Cook County into the state's child welfare system every month. Scores of other children were already at the shelter, sleeping.

The children arrived "dirty and confused," said Father John Smyth, director of Maryville City of Youth, an agency of Catholic Charities that ran the shelter for the state. The shelter's staff escorted them into the bright and airy foyer, past the playroom called Scooterville, and the poster that read ANYONE CAN MAKE A MISTAKE. THAT'S WHY PENCILS HAVE ERASERS. The children held the staff members' hands. The staff washed the children, who then ate as much pizza, fruit, and ice cream as they wanted. The staff played Simon Says and Pin the Tail on the Donkey with the younger children while the oldest gave each of their names and then blamed himself for not having kept the place neater.

"He said, 'I was supposed to take care of my brothers and sisters,' " Father Smyth said. "He thought he failed. We said, 'You still are taking care of them. Now tell us who they are.' "

The staff wanted to keep siblings together, so they began moving beds and cribs around the small, softly lit, pastel bedrooms. The staff gave the children clean clothes. They assigned the boys blue beds and the girls, pink. Some of the children stood with their new clothes in their hands, staring at them.

"They asked, 'Can we keep them on the bed?' " Father Smyth said. "We said, 'You can do whatever you want with them. This is yours.' "They asked, 'This is mine?' "We said, 'This is yours forever.' "

The children did not ask about their mothers that night. They were most concerned with being separated from their siblings.

Their mothers, meanwhile, sat in the station house lockup, all except Diane and Denise Melton. No one could find Denise. A cousin finally brought her by in the morning. By then all the mothers but Maxine were released. Maxine was on probation for possession of drugs with intent to sell and would remain in prison for almost a year for violating the terms of her probation when the police charged her with misdemeanor child neglect. But that night, as they waited on a holding cell bench, handcuffed, the sisters began to doze. Before they drifted off to sleep, one of them asked, "Do you think we'll get our kids back?"

Ken Herzlich sold his footage to six local television stations, which featured the story on their morning broadcasts. Herzlich called CNN, which ran the story, too. The *Chicago Sun-Times* and *Tribune* ran front-page stories the following day. So did the networks. ABC News wanted his film not only for *World News Tonight* but for *20/20*. *The New York Times*, *The Washington Post*, and *USA Today* played the story prominently. Two days after the police happened upon the Melton children, President Bill Clinton, at a prayer breakfast, held up a clipping from the *Post* and lamented that this particularly shameful case of parental neglect was happening "not in Calcutta but in Chicago."

On the day after the police took the children, Chicago's mayor, Richard M. Daley, asked, rhetorically, how so dismal a life for the nineteen children could have proceeded without anyone apparently noticing or acting. "You wonder first about their parents. How about their neighbors? How about their family members? Where are they?"

Close by, it soon became clear, but remote. In the days that followed, as social workers searched for homes for the children, they discovered that the Melton sisters and their mother, Josephine, had many relatives living in and near Chicago. These included Josephine's sisters, brothers, and cousins, many of whom, Josephine later said, had nice homes and decent jobs and little use for her and her children. "That's the way it looked to me," she said. "I told my kids always stay with each other and be there for each other. That's all we had ever since we've been here, just each other."

Joseph's Ghost

THE MELTON CHILDREN stayed in the emergency shelter for three days. Then, because the shelter had to accommodate all the new children brought in each day, they had to move on. Father Smyth sensed they would have liked to stay. With no place else to put the children, the department moved them to temporary foster homes. This meant splitting up siblings, but with the promise that once something more permanent could be found, they might be reunited. Meanwhile, attorneys in the Cook County Public Guardian's office assigned to represent the children began assembling a cross-referenced tally sheet, linking each child with a mother and one of what was estimated to be eighteen different fathers. Prosecutors searched public assistance records and discovered that the women living in Maxine's $300-a-month apartment were together receiving some $5,500 a month in public assistance and food stamps. "It's up their noses. It's in their arms. That's where the money is," Kathryn Gallanis, the lead prosecutor, said. The Meltons denied this charge and insisted that the money was spent to feed and clothe nineteen children and seven adults.

The Meltons' timing could not have been worse. Almost everyone I talked with in Chicago about their case admitted, ruefully, that had the police walked in and seen, say, five or even eight children living in much the same conditions, they would, in all likelihood, have admonished Maxine Melton to clean up her home and gone away.

Nineteen, I heard again and again, represented some sort of critical mass, especially in Chicago. In no city was the growing sense of revulsion and rage with the plight of failed children more apparent than in Chicago, where there appeared to be an inescapable connection between abusive and neglectful mothers and such brutish statements of urban life as that of the existence of an eleven-year-old hit man and of teenagers throwing a toddler out of a window because his brother would not steal for them. Forty-seven thousand children across Illinois were living in foster homes, group homes, and orphanages. That number had mushroomed by thirty thousand since 1987. The state expected to take another ten thousand children from their homes in 1995. Each caseworker for the Department of Children and Family Services supervised as many as sixty families, twice the department's recommended load.

In Chicago the anger at the parents and at the department that was supposed to safeguard their children had been building since 1993, when a woman named Amanda Wallace, who had been in and out of mental institutions, nonetheless managed to regain custody of her three-year-old son. The state had taken Joseph from her three times and placed him in foster care. Two months after a judge ordered them reunited, she took him home from a visit with a relative, stuffed a sock in her son's mouth, secured the sock with tape, wrapped an extension cord around his neck, stood him on a chair, and, as he waved goodbye, hanged him.

Amanda Wallace represented the horror confronting agencies like the Department of Children and Family Services, but the Melton sisters embodied the grind of the department's everyday business. "This was not an isolated case of behavior that could be explained as an aberration, even by someone who works in child welfare," said Jess McDonald, the department's director. He became director several months after the police took the Melton children. "What are we going to do? Will they be safe if we leave them in this condition? Is there any harm that might come to them? And what is it? And how soon? And that is a tricky business. The child protection folks will tell you you've got thousands of families like this out there. Just get ready."

The Melton sisters were not Amanda Wallace, and that only made the department's task of what to do with them and their children all the more difficult. The department, like so many child welfare agencies across the country, was in a bind from which it could not seem to extricate itself: It did not necessarily want the children it took, but once it took them, it was very reluctant to give them back. The department's caseworkers, supervisors, and director recognized that the state seldom, if ever, provided a better, and lasting, alternative to all but the most abusive homes. They also understood that if they did not take the children from troubled parents, they risked another Joseph Wallace tragedy.

The circumstances that led the court to reunite Joseph Wallace with his mother and the memory of Joseph's awful death cast a cloud over the Melton case that never quite went away. Because the story of the Melton children was told in the context of the Wallace case, there was the inevitable blurring of events that were similar only in the most superficial way. This often happens when child welfare stories are told. A parent kills a child, or beats a child senseless, or abandons a child for weeks on end. A child dies at the hands of a foster parent or a boyfriend of a parent, and the understandable outrage that follows propels both the telling of the story and the public reaction—the desire to punish the offending parent and the agency that should have protected the child. The fact, however, is that the death of a child at the hands of a parent is an aberration. It is not a true reflection of the nature of the crisis in the child welfare system. Parents have killed children for millennia, and parents, evil and psychotic parents, always will, and sometimes there is very little the state can do to stop them. That it could have done so in the Wallace case transformed the subsequent child welfare crises into events that surely could be prevented, if only caseworkers were vigilant and judges were brave, informed, and decisive. Yet by the time the police discovered the Melton children, Joseph Wallace had become the martyr in whose name other children might be saved.

The Melton sisters wanted their children back, and there was no assurance that they could, on their own, be anything but failures as parents. The state was faced with two unpleasant options: It could keep the children, or it could help their parents. If the state helped the mothers, it risked being accused of wasting public money on the undeserving and dependent poor. If it kept the children, it risked dooming them to a life of drifting from foster home to foster home because the first set of foster parents could no longer keep them, or because the children were beyond control, or because there were reports of abuse and neglect in that foster home, too. If the state kept the children with their mothers but gave them less and less money and assistance, it ran another risk, the responsibility fifteen and sixteen years hence for yet another generation of children born to teenage girls who embarked upon motherhood as their mothers had. There was no solution, no program, strategy, or plan of service that anyone connected with child welfare in Chicago or elsewhere could point to with any real conviction as the answer for the quandary posed by the Meltons.

———

The Melton sisters, meanwhile, believed themselves to be not only isolated but wronged. They listened to the accusations of their neglect and, in shouted responses following court appearances, insisted that the fault for what was found on North Keystone Avenue lay not with them. They blamed the police. The police, they said, not only trashed their home but hauled in the garbage they claimed to have found and even planted spaghetti-encrusted dishes in the kitchen. They claimed that they were good mothers who were being punished only because they were poor and could not afford to live without one another's help and public assistance checks. A group calling itself the National People's Uhuru Movement stood outside the courthouse of the Cook County Juvenile Court demanding reparations from the government for the "illegal arrest and detainment of the Meltons." A few days after the police took the children, a representative from *The Bertice Berry Show* arrived on Keystone Avenue in a stretch limousine and offered vague assurances that the Meltons would indeed receive a new couch if they agreed to appear on the show.

Josephine Melton and her daughters Diane and Denise did appear, several days later, on an hour-long segment, styled after *Oprah*, titled "Inside the House of Shame." All through the taping, Denise rolled her eyes at questions she did not appreciate, including the seemingly simple query from the host: "You brought food. What did you do with it?"

"Put the food in the house. What else am I going to do with it?" she snapped as her mother scolded her "C'mon with a better attitude than that."

The studio audience was divided. Many, black and white, applauded what were characterized as Josephine Melton's efforts at keeping her daughters and grandchildren from the streets. But others, most of them white, took the microphone and, trying to frame their questions gently, asked why, for instance, the Meltons had not cleaned the accumulated filth. "Our refrigerator wasn't filthy till they made it filthy," Denise replied. Even the host, who had wept as Josephine spoke about her daughters, appeared to doubt her. When another woman rose and gently told Diane, "Your child was just born cocaine-addicted. That's severe child abuse as far as I'm concerned," Diane first asked what the woman had said and then replied, hazily, "I have no answer."

The sisters, meanwhile, still lived in Maxine's apartment while Maxine sat in the Cook County Jail. "I didn't want to talk to nobody or watch the news," she said. "I needed to be by myself, just thinking about what the people were saying, which I didn't really care, and thinking about my kids."

Of the five Melton sisters, Maxine appeared to possess the most promise. Her older sister, Diane, who was thirty-one, was at one point a one-hundred-dollar-a-day cocaine and heroin user who once told a social worker that she had been clean only once—for two days, in 1989. The state had already taken three other children from her; a fourth lived with the child's father. On the night the police removed two of her children from Maxine's house, Diane gave birth to her seventh child, a daughter born with cocaine in her blood.

The middle sister, May Fay, who was twenty-five and, by her own description, "wild wild," began running the streets in earnest when she was fifteen and newly pregnant.

Denise, who was twenty-four, was a drug user like May Fay and Diane. She could be sullen and angry, especially when her older sisters left their children with her and went out.

Cassandra, the youngest at twenty-one, was judged by social workers and psychologists to be the least capable of the sisters. She had four children. One of the fathers was seventeen and would later be arrested for locking a rival drug dealer in a closet and torturing him with a pit bull. Another father was sixty-one and lived in a retirement home.

Where Cassandra, Denise, and May Fay were, like their mother, overweight, Maxine was of medium build and height. She wore her hair piled atop her head and, when she was happy, carried herself with an ease and flair that at times was coquettish. She had a wonderful smile. And though she liked to joke and laugh, a cousin who knew her well believed this had nothing to do with joy. "That's why I say she uses the laugh to cover it up," the cousin said of Maxine's unspoken sadness. "Until she learns how to let go of all the joking, she'll be crying inside."

Maxine was twenty-six years old when the police took her children. She said that she worked once, briefly, years before, as a file clerk for the Department of Human Services. Like her sisters, her sole means of support was public assistance. This was also the case for much of her upbringing. She left school at seventeen, in her junior year of high school, when she discovered, after a period of denial that ended only with the onset of labor, that she was pregnant with her first child. She had lived all her life on the West Side, together or close by her mother and sisters. Maxine could be funny and engaging, but she was also prone to despondency so profound that it left her all but incapable of standing up. She had liked school, especially math, and had harbored vague dreams of one day starting a business of her own. "I'm trying to remember what kind of company," she said. "I wanted to do so much, man. There was so much I wanted to do."

Maxine rented her apartment on North Keystone Avenue assuming it would be large enough for herself, her boyfriend, and her five sons. Then, in the summer of 1993, Cassandra, Denise, and May Fay and their children moved in. They were sharing May Fay's $550-a-month apartment until she fell behind on her rent. The landlady told May Fay her sisters could not stay, and May Fay calculated she could not afford the rent without their public assistance checks, too.

On North Keystone Avenue they shared a house where the distinction between weekend and weekday, let alone between day and night, ceased to exist. People came, people stayed. People slept where they happened to fall asleep. When they were hungry, they ate what they found or went down to the corner and brought back an Italian beef sandwich. The house was almost always deafeningly loud with what Denise Melton, who could never bear it, called "little kid noise." "Running around, screaming and hollering when they're playing," she said. "It made me mad. My sisters didn't mind the noise. They tell me to shut up and leave the kids alone, so I shut up and leave the kids alone. I told them to be quiet and stop all the noise."

The children who were old enough to go to school missed weeks of class at a time. Diane Melton's fourteen-year-old son could not read or write. Denise Melton had inadvertently admitted to how seldom the children attended class on *The Bertice Berry Show* when she was told that one of the children said he never went to school. "He just made six, and he can barely talk, so I know he didn't say it," she replied. People in the audience began to laugh.

Maxine and her sisters, however, refused to accept the view that someone might come into their house and look at the state of their children and their surroundings and conclude that the children could not stay there. When I asked Maxine if she had hesitated before opening the door, if she wondered what the police might say and do when they came inside and saw the children, she said she had not. She did not see why she should have.

"They were taking our kids for no reason," she said.

And what had she thought as she watched her children being carried away?

"Why?" she replied. "Why me?"

"An Undifferentiated Mass"

THE MELTONS were among the poor and threatening people whom the rest of society has struggled to control and, in its kinder moments, to understand. They were to Chicago what beggars and vagrants were to the more fortunate classes of sixteenth-century Paris or London or Hamburg who saw them, in the words of the French philosopher Michel Foucault, writing in the mid-1960s, as an "undifferentiated mass" and "a class of society that lives in disorder, in negligence, and almost in illegality." The idle poor of the sixteenth century were chained in pairs and sent to work in Paris sewers. They were placed in warehouses—the Hôpital Général in Paris, the Zuchthaus in Germany—where they were set to work. What Foucault called "the birth of the asylum" was the rest of society's effort to protect itself from a "dangerous" madness "which rose from the lower depths of society."

The children of the poor were also feared, reviled, and incarcerated. A sixteenth-century city chamberlain of Exeter warned that the growing swarms of young beggars and thieves and homeless who "as the Caterpillars, Frogs, Grasshoppes and Lice of Eygpt, shalbe [sic] the plagues of this your common welth." Sixteenth-century London began placing orphans, vagrants, and the children whose parents "were thought unable to keep" them in "hospitals" that had once been attached to monasteries. Citizen committees ran the hospitals. They raised money and bought feather beds, blankets, uniforms, and cuts of meat the likes of which the children presumably had never seen. Matrons fed and clothed the children. Schoolmasters taught them writing and grammar. The children learned to sing from the music teacher. The clever children were prepared for the university. The others learned a craft, which they could apply as apprentices for masters who were carefully chosen. Each Sunday the beadle of London's Christ Hospital would round up the children who slept in the streets around St. Paul's Cathedral and bring them to the House of Occupation at Bridewell.

England's relationship with its poor children—its belief that they needed to be protected from the evils of their parents' world, its insistence that the path to salvation lay in work and study, and its attempt to make helping the poor a public responsibility (fund-raising has always been a problem)—mirrors all that would happen two hundred years later, when America began finding itself just as overwhelmed with children in its city streets. The Elizabethan Poor Laws, which were codified in 1601, placed the burden of the poor on local parishes. The Privy Council offered its authority to help in collecting public monies that went to the deserving poor and to house poor children who could not be indentured. If the local authorities failed to attend to the poor, justices of the peace fined them. Printed guides reminded workers to treat the poor with compassion, to consider their work as God's work and the poor as their flock, and to dun the wealthy for cash. Scholars have praised Tudor England's efforts at kindness toward the poor: the money given to poor and large families, and the desire to make the "hospitals" into places where children might come of age in relative comfort and with some sense of spirituality. But they lamented that the good works were undercut by a chronic shortage of money and a failure by the Privy Council to lend its muscle to the effort.

Inherent in the English treatment of the poor was an ambivalence about their worth. While the Franciscan idea of the holiness of the poor had diminished since the fourteenth century, there remained a sense of obligation to the poor—especially to the poor who were not perceived as idle, but who were regarded as simply down on their luck. The Poor Laws of 1601 made charity mandatory; prison awaited those who failed to pay. Still, sixteenth-century England did, at times, punish the poor with branding, boring a hole through the ear, and enslavement. The harsher view of the poor reflected the radical Protestantism of the Puritans, who believed not only in assistance, but in the sin of idleness. They carried that perception of the poor to the Americas.

In the Colonies, survival demanded that each person be part of a family and that each family contribute to the community. Those who were not part of a family, or whose families were a drain on all the others, were indentured to families that were willing to house and feed them in exchange for their labor. The Colonial and post-Revolutionary village may have looked upon its poor with disdain. But it did so with the understanding that their poverty may well have been the result of a personal failing that in no way reflected badly upon the community. The poor were the local poor. They were familiar. They were people with names to whom help was extended, with money if the family was deserving and with indentured servitude if it was not.

Such generosity, or sense of responsibility, however, did not extend to strangers. Communities were expected to take care of their own. They owed no obligation to outsiders, who were routinely sent back to the villages where they came from, there to be dealt with as idlers.

This relationship between the poor and the people around them began to change in the early 1800s. The America that existed before the Jacksonian era was primarily rural. But in the first twenty years of the nineteenth century, Americans began leaving the countryside for the cities, where they joined many other people who suddenly found themselves surrounded by—and counted as—strangers to whom no assistance or allegiance was owed. In the place of village arrangements for the poor came the impersonal and institutional option: the almshouse and the orphanage.

The asylum boomed. In 1790 there were 200 orphanages in the United States and 1,000 almshouses. Thirty years later, in 1820, the number of orphanages had ballooned to 1,500, and the number of almshouses to 3,000. Thirty years, or roughly a generation, later, in 1850, there were 7,700 orphanages across the country and 17,000 almshouses.

At the same time as the surge in migration from the country to the city, immigrants, primarily from Ireland and Germany, began coming to America in numbers that appalled and terrified the people who had arrived before them. The angry rhetoric used to depict the coming of the Irish to Boston—"pouring like muddy water"—sounds, not surprisingly, much the same as the modern-day characterization on Capitol Hill of "welfare mothers" as "alligators" and "wolves."

If the adults were beyond redemption, there was at least the hope of saving the children from becoming people like their parents. In the early part of the century so-called houses of refuge rose up in cities like New York, Philadelphia, Boston, and St. Louis. There, in the company of poor adults, children learned to eat in silence, to rise and sit and march according to the sound of bells, and above all to learn the skills that would save them from lives of idleness. The more enlightened reformers of the nineteenth century argued that it was wrong to warehouse children alongside criminal, insane, and idle adults. They urged, and succeeded in convincing, local governments to build orphanages where children could safely be housed and at the same time prepared for a suitable life.

This emphasis on acquiring and using a skill also had a commercial component, one dating to Tudor England. The children's workhouses in the industrial city of Norwich emphasized spinning, for instance, so that the city might use children as young as three years old—they were believed to have nimble fingers—to provide a cheap source of labor. This, in turn, made possible centuries of child labor, a practice that in the United States stopped only at the turn of the twentieth century. Still, the chief work of the orphanage was to separate children from the corruptions of the adult world, the world of their parents, so that a nation feeling itself beleaguered by its sudden growth and by the stampede to the cities, writes David Rothman in *The Discovery of the Asylum*, could somehow re-create the social order of the rural world left behind.

What the village accomplished with its sometimes stifling social compact, with the belief that acceptance by the village meant playing by the village rules, the city could approximate through the institution. That enduring need to restore the safety and order of a more manageable world by imposing order on adults who appeared oblivious to the rules remains at the core of the child welfare system's mission. The nature of the institution has changed repeatedly in the intervening 180 years, from orphanage, to foster home, to orphanage, to foster home, to children at home with their struggling parents. What has not changed, what has instead become the accepted wisdom of the relationship between society, the poor, and their children is the need for the institution. It is hardly surprising that the early houses of refuge were grand and imposing structures, with towers and turrets and ornate facades. It was as if only buildings so massive and complex could fill the void of rules and understandings that defined a simpler and presumably better world.

A "Dirty House"

K ATHRYN GALLANIS, the assistant state's attorney, brought to her prosecution of the Meltons a zeal that was neither surprising nor, strictly speaking, necessary: She had a very public case that she was unlikely to lose. The state had already taken the children from the sisters and from Denise Turner. In April of 1994—nearly three months after the police first knocked on Maxine's door—a criminal court judge found the Melton sisters guilty of misdemeanor child neglect. Their jail terms were suspended, and they were placed on probation and ordered to attend job training and parenting classes. Their successful prosecution in juvenile court, which would allow the court to make their children wards of the state, was not seriously in doubt. Maxine, who was already in prison, had pleaded guilty to neglecting her children in the hope that this might help her regain them sooner.

After Gallanis made clear her sense of outrage—"You saw a never-ending cesspool"—she explained that the state's goal, nonetheless, was to reunify the mothers with their children. That, at least, was the stated intention, if only because then the state could qualify for federal funds earmarked for family preservation projects. Unless it was prepared to place a child for adoption, the state was obligated to help mothers regain their children by teaching the mothers how to find and keep a job and how good parents behaved. This tutelage often included drug rehabilitation. Mothers threatened with the loss of their children were offered "family preservation," widely used eight- or ten-week in-house tutorials on everything from planning a menu, to discipline without beating, to simple home repairs. These lessons were all designed to keep children out of the child welfare system. For Gallanis, however, there remained a moral qualification required for reunification. The Melton sisters, she said, would have to "show they are worthy of their children."

Meanwhile, the public defender and court-appointed attorneys assigned to defend Maxine's sisters had little to build their case on other than accusing the state of unjustly taking children from poor mothers who were doing the best they could.

"The state says it's more than a 'dirty house' case, but that's all it is," Gerald Block, the public defender who first represented May Fay (he became ill and later died), said one afternoon before a session of the trial. Block approached the case with the sort of weary fatalism of someone who had seen all this, and worse, many times before. "They were well-nourished," he went on. "There were no telltale signs of abuse—burn marks, fractures, loop marks from belts, imprints on the face. These were just six mothers who unfortunately were living in an apartment whose size should have been for one family. On the West Side of Chicago there are probably thousands of houses like this. You don't take the kids because the family is poor."

Gallanis insisted, however, that in the matter of the Meltons, poverty was not the issue. The juvenile court judge, Lynne Kawamoto, felt much the same way. She had already said publicly that she did not believe "this is just a dirty house case" but rather one that "shows there was a lack of care." It was a view echoed by Chicago's most widely quoted voice on child welfare, Patrick Murphy, the Cook County Public Guardian, whose office represented the rights of the Melton children. Murphy liked to say that after years of seeing the cruelties that parents inflicted upon their children, he had concluded that the best thing society could do for the children of abusive and neglectful parents was to take them away. He decried attempts at family preservation as futile, advocating instead a return to orphanages for the children of families that could not—and should not—be saved.

"The child welfare crowd that bills themselves as advocates for children and push family preservation call this a 'dirty house' case," Murphy said one morning, sitting in his office, the sleeves on his dark green work shirt rolled up for work. He leaned back in his chair, looked into the middle distance, and spoke with an intensity so controlled it approached fury. An editorial writer for the *Chicago Tribune* told me that he could count on receiving a hand-delivered letter from Patrick Murphy most every day, primarily denunciations of the Department of Children and Family Services, which Murphy dismissed as "an equal opportunity incompetent agency." "What makes this so different is that you had these people come together to pool their money and buy drugs," Murphy went on. "These women were narcissistic, selfish human beings. Ninety-nine percent of the people who are on welfare do a hell of a job raising their kids under the most Spartan situation possible. The message is that these people can't raise their children properly, which is a lie."

Murphy had moved past the Meltons and, inevitably, on to a broader and more revealing point I heard often among people who have spent years in and near child welfare: whatever compassion they might have once felt for the mothers who've lost their children to the system had all but evaporated. "In trying to get her on her feet, the family preservation programs are missing the point," Murphy said. "We can't get her on her feet. It's like pissing in the ocean."

I expected this from Murphy and should not have been surprised hearing much the same thing from Gordon Johnson, who had been the director of the Department of Children and Family Services for seven years and who was now president of Hull House Association, which the great child advocate Jane Addams founded in 1889 as a safe place for the children of the poor and the streets. His response to the Melton case "was that these parents should have been locked up immediately. They mock the state." He wondered aloud why it was necessary to pass a test to get a driver's license but that there was no equivalent examination for becoming a parent. His voice grew loud and animated, and in the vernacular of the street, he ridiculed the Meltons: "I'm gonna have children. I'm gonna get my check."

The Melton sisters were oblivious to the angry mood around them, especially when they talked about the future and the help they would need when their children came back. Now, in Chicago and elsewhere, people who might have once thought it prudent to feign compassion about the women's circumstances could summarily dismiss these mothers as pariahs who surely had had so many children in order to pad their monthly check from the state. The Meltons did not help themselves, not on *The Bertice Berry Show* and not in court.

Because Maxine had already pleaded guilty, she was spared the public trial that her sisters and Denise Turner would endure. The trial began in September of 1994 and was open to reporters, which was rare in child welfare cases. By October, nine months after the police took the children, the Meltons still warranted coverage in the *Sun-Times* and *Tribune*, and even by ABC News. Maxine, by this point, had been moved from the Cook County Jail to a women's prison in Dixon, Illinois. Diane, now pregnant with her eighth child, was in the Cook County Jail. May Fay and Denise both lived in residential drug treatment centers. Cassandra had just come from visiting her children. She brought their pictures to court to show her sisters.

The portraits of the children were taken at Sears and placed in a sleeve with circles cut out for the faces. They wore red sweaters and blue pants and skirts and posed with their hands on their laps. The sisters passed the portraits back and forth. They leaned over each others' shoulders, admiring Cassandra's children. Even Diane, who wore jailhouse fatigues and who mostly sat with her jaw set glaring at no one in particular, now looked at the pictures and offered a smile. The sisters talked with their lawyers and most of all with one another. Cassandra wore a Green Bay Packers sweat suit and Denise a Sylvester the Cat sweatshirt. May Fay, dressed in Doc Marten boots, white polo shirt and jeans, and big gold hoop earrings, leaned back in her seat, crossed her arms over her chest and assumed a pose of bemused indifference. Denise stared at Kathryn Gallanis and began bobbing her head slowly, as if she were bored in class. Denise Turner dozed.

Judge Kawamoto watched them. She glanced at the sisters as they looked at Cassandra's pictures. She turned away and then looked back, lowered her head onto her hands and studied them. The sisters, briefly reunited, did not notice her, and soon the judge turned away.

The prosecutors had arrayed before Kawamoto large bulletin boards covered with color photographs of the house on the night the police came. Alongside the photographs was a floor plan of the apartment and a chart with the defendants' names and the names of each of their children. The state, wrapping up its case, produced representatives of various social service programs that the Meltons could have availed themselves of, had they so chosen.

With that, the state rested, and the defense called Cassandra Henderson Melton, a cousin of the Melton sisters and one of the few relatives who the sisters believed liked them. Cassandra Henderson Melton was a tall, broad woman with a round face and a voice that almost always seemed a shout. Having conceded that the house was a shambles, Gerald Block wanted Cassandra to show that her cousins fed their children, if only because she helped with the shopping.

She testified that every month she drove to Maxine's and with the sisters' pooled food stamps and public assistance checks, she took Maxine from market to market, looking for specials. Cassandra saved her receipts because stores sometimes printed special offers on the back. She recalled the shopping trip a few weeks before the police removed the children, when she drove Maxine to the Jewel, where she had a rain check on bacon and to Dominic's for steaks, corned beef, milk, and the buy-one-get-one-free special on cereal. At the Kokomo Market on Harrison, she bought rabbits and slab bacon. Block submitted as evidence a receipt for $347 and asked Cassandra to describe the family's final Sunday dinner together.

Maxine cooked the big dinners, she said, and that Sunday the family ate a picnic ham, collard greens, four cakes, ten sweet potato pies, and macaroni and cheese. They drank Kool-Aid.

Gallanis, on cross-examination, asked where so many people ate.

"The dining room, darlin'," Cassandra replied, adding that they ate from plastic plates.

"Are you sure you saw everyone eat?" Gallanis asked and Cassandra said that she had.

"Did you see them take money and buy heroin, too?"

Cassandra replied she had not. She made a marvelous witness. She was engaging and blunt, a reliable advocate for her cousins. But she also represented a problem for the Meltons, who suffered, inevitably, by comparison. Here was the relative who lived in the same neighborhood and who had become a mother as a teenager, but who worked as a nurse's aide at a suburban nursing home. She was still married to the father of her three children. The mantel in her living room was lined with plaques and awards won at Marconi Middle School for debating and Academic Olympics by her oldest child, Crystal. Cassandra and her husband put away $45 every two weeks so that Crystal might have the money to attend Spelman College.

Reunion

THE TRIAL OF the Melton sisters and Denise Turner stretched over two months, which was not unusual in juvenile court, where the swelling volume of children in the state's care meant judges were often hearing twenty-five cases a day. In the meantime, the Melton sisters were being observed. But the observers did not believe this concerned them. That, at least, was how it appeared at the family's first reunion. The private foster care agency contracted by the state to handle the case arranged the reunion. There was not enough room in the agency's offices, so Cassandra, Denise, May Fay, and their mother, Josephine, gathered with eighteen of the children on a weekday afternoon in a church basement. Maxine was in jail, Diane chose not to come, but a few fathers of the children came. Ten agency workers looked on.

It had taken the agency several days to track down all the children after they were moved from the emergency shelter to their first foster homes. When the workers began calling to locate the children, they found that the children were not where they were supposed to be or that the foster parents did not want them anymore. "They'd put them in an emergency foster home, and the foster parent would say 'I don't want this kid. I can't handle him,' " one worker said. Some of the foster parents wanted the children taken back because the children needed to be brought in for testing and the foster parents said they did not "do transportation."

The Melton children were scrutinized by their social workers, by physicians and psychologists, and by the foster parents who reported what they observed. The social worker spoke about the children's affect. Some of the children were withdrawn to the point of silence, she said. One six-year-old boy sat in her office with his eyes down and refused all offers of milk and cookies and would not begin playing until he was ignored. One of the girls refused to let anyone fix her hair. The social worker sensed this girl did not believe she was worthy of looking pretty. A five-year-old could not eat with utensils. "One of the things you saw was how thirstily they responded to positive attention, and that's a bad sign," she said. "A kid that will go to anybody has never established that parent-child bond."

The children, she said, told of their grandmother giving them beer at breakfast. They said that drugs were sold out of the apartment. The social workers pieced together what they believed to be a map of a home in which territory was established by mattress, with children knowing which corner of the room and the floor was theirs. One child did say, however, that for his birthday the walls were painted blue. Talking to this social worker, an earnest and compassionate woman, I could not help but feel a certain sense of "ah ha!" on her part, as if she had found the bits and pieces of evidence that showed just how badly these children were living. Yet I had heard much the same thing from a neighbor who lived across from the Meltons and who himself was a recovering drug addict. "If you hear somebody hollering at their kids all the time," he said, "never showing any emotion except anger, it's kind of hard to think these kids are getting all the love they need. You know what I'm saying?"

The reunion, the social worker said, struck her as a remarkably unself-conscious re-creation of the family's shared life. After the initial cooing over the newest child—Diane's daughter born the night the police took her cousins—and the pizza and juice, she said, "it became what their home was." The mothers talked and the children played, and when the children got loud, their mothers yelled at them. One mother reached to undo her belt to administer a beating. The social workers noted this. So, too, did they note the way the mothers teased the children when they fell down.

I asked why she believed the sisters behaved this way even in front of people who could help them regain their children. "They don't have the knowledge that they did anything that was a problem," she said. "They don't have the ability to get inside of somebody else's head and think what it's like to be made fun of. If the kid does something stupid, like spills juice all over his shirt, it reflects on them."

The social workers took Polaroid snapshots so that the children could have a souvenir book of the reunion. A woman came to read stories, and it appeared to the workers that the children reacted to the story as if no one had ever read them one before. When the storyteller was done, she started a project for the children. She gave them paper that they were to roll up and make into trees. The mothers wanted to make the trees, too. They asked the storyteller to help them with their trees. "Her kids could have been waving the tree in her face saying, 'Look mom, see what I made,' and she'd say, 'I'm making my own tree.' "

The Child Saver

THE PIETY THAT still guides the saviors of children was especially pronounced in the mid-nineteenth century. The work was then undertaken by religious people who believed that they were competing not only against the evils of the city, but against Protestants, if they were Catholic, and against Catholics, if they were Protestant, for the souls of the children they believed they could save.

First they built asylums in the belief that institutional life provided children with the order they so desperately lacked. The orphanage, with its rows of beds and endless bells, prevailed as the great repository and training ground of poor children until the middle of the nineteenth century, when thinking about what children needed was transformed, in good measure, by a young minister named Charles Loring Brace.

Brace endures as the embodiment of all that is decent—and all that is naive and potentially destructive—in attending to the welfare of children. He came to New York City from Connecticut in 1851, a missionary in search of a calling. He was twenty-five years old. He had long, dark hair, a thick beard, and piercing eyes. A graduate of Yale and of the Union Theological Seminary, Brace began working with the poor of the squalid Five Points district of Lower Manhattan. The place repelled him. Twenty years later, in his seminal work, *The*

Dangerous Classes of New York and Twenty Years Among them, Brace wrote of the "Sisyphus-like work" that "soon discouraged all engaged in it." He described a world of drunks, thieves, and prostitutes living in "double rows of houses, flaunting with dirty banners, and the yards heaped up with bones and refuse. . . ."

Brace had little use for the adults he met. They were, he believed, beyond help or redemption. He despaired for, and fretted about, their children. "These boys and girls, it should be remembered, will soon form the great lower class of our city," he wrote. "They will help form the great multitude of robbers, thieves, vagrants, and prostitutes who are now such a burden upon the law-respecting community." He concluded that it was imperative to break the cycle of what he called "hereditary pauperism."

The asylum, Brace believed, could not accomplish the task. It did not elevate lives, he wrote; it stunted them. "They breed a species of character which is monastic—indolent, unused to struggle; subordinate indeed, but with little independence and manly vigor." They were also expensive and, despite the boom in the asylum trade, insufficient for the thousands of children he reported roaming the streets of New York. So two years after arriving in New York, Brace founded the Children's Aid Society. He believed that the work of attending to poor children was best done through a single agency that could offer many different forms of help, from schools to training academies to such well-intentioned gatherings as "Boys' Meetings" at which the children might be exhorted to better themselves. The society opened "lodging houses" for the newsboys whom Brace found living on the city streets. Some were orphans; others had parents who could not afford to keep them. Brace, however, was not content merely with providing the children with a clean and safe place to live. The greater mission, he wrote in the society's first circular, was "to be the means of draining the city of these children."

The Dangerous Classes is a remarkable document: Almost 120 years after its publication, it endures as the template for the argument that justifies the necessity of saving children from their parents. Brace believed that there was no hope for children unless he could keep "this disease of pauperism" from becoming "mingled in the blood." There was nothing in the relationship between those parents and children worth saving. Indeed, Patrick Murphy's characterization of the Melton sisters echoes Brace's description, a century earlier, of a family living in an almshouse:

> A mother, in decent circumstances, with an infant, was driven into it by stress of poverty. Her child grew up a pauper, and both became accustomed to a life of dependence. The child— a girl—went forth when she was old enough to work, and soon returned with an illegitimate babe. She then remained with her child. This child—also a girl—grew up in like manner, and, occasionally, went forth to labor, but returned finally, with *her* illegitimate child, and at length became a common pauper and prostitute. . . ."

Just as Murphy claimed an understanding of why poor women smoked crack, Brace had claimed the same understanding of why they drank. "Every woman drank hard," he wrote, "I suppose to forget her misery." That, however, was the extent of Brace's compassion for poor women; he recognized that they had reason for their misery—the men who beat them, the "dark, damp, and chill" of cellar homes that reeked of filth and of the animals that slept alongside their beds, the lives of "no work, no friends, rent to pay and nothing to do." But he would not tolerate the way they treated their children, sending them out to scrounge for coal, to beg, to peddle fruit by night in brothels.

The parents may not have been worthy. Their children, however, were not only capable of being saved, but deserving of the effort. Unlike their parents, they still possessed spark and promise. For Brace the children were, above all, innocents—"Saddest of all sights was the thin child's face, so often seen behind prison-bars. . . ." The children in Brace's writing were endearing, if misguided urchins, equally capable of picking a pocket as marveling at the feel of a bed of their own—"it's 'most as good as a steam-gratin'."

"It seemed to me if I could only get the refinement, education, and Christian enthusiasm of the better classes fairly to work here among these children, these terrible evils might be corrected at least for the next generation," he wrote. So he went to the homes of the wealthy and told them stories about the children and their world. He convinced "some of the most gifted women of New York" to assist him in his work. But this exposure of the poor to a presumably better world went only so far, in that the children remained at home or on the streets or, at the very least, in the city. So he proposed sending the children to the country. He envisioned new lives for city children growing up on farms where they might learn the value of work in the care of "good Christian" adults. The plan, called "placing out," came to be known as "the orphan trains."

It is hard to see how Brace could have come upon an answer any less crystalline. If the parents and the city were the sources of all that was bad for the children, and if the mission was to save the children from the evils inflicted by their parents and the city, it was therefore logical, by Brace's reasoning, that the children had to be separated from their parents if the children were to be saved.

Brace's plan was equally simple—"simple," he wrote, "and most effective." His agents first gathered children, be they orphans or children of the streets, into the society's offices and lodging houses. There they were washed, fed, and given clean clothes. The society sent circulars to newspapers in country towns, seeking homes for children. The children were not to be bound over as servants. Rather, Brace wrote, they were to become members of the family. A foster parent could contribute to the cost of transporting a child; but the society expected no payments. It asked only that the adults feed, house, and "train up" the children.

Brace paid little heed to the requests for "a perfect child": "To those who desired the children of 'blue eyes, fair hair, and blond complexion,' we were sure to send the darkeyed and brunette." Appearances, he wrote, did not matter at all once adult and child met; he offered long testimonials and letters recounting fast and loving bonds between unlikely pairs of children and adults. The society, meanwhile, could not keep pace with the demand for children. "Hundreds of applications poured in at once from the farmers and mechanics all through the Union," Brace wrote. So Brace decided to speed up the machinery of placement by loading groups of children onto trains and, with an agent at their side, dispatching them to the villages and farm towns of Pennsylvania, Missouri, Ohio, and Illinois.

The children arrived after three or four days of travel to find the townspeople waiting for them. The society's agents had already posted handbills, announcing the coming of children in need of homes. By the time the children came to town, couples who wanted a child or who needed an extra hand had gathered in the town hall. "The sight of the little company of the children of misfortune always touched the hearts of a population naturally generous," he wrote. "In every American community, especially in a Western one, there are many spare places at the table of life."

Brace's account of these meetings, of course, is filled with scenes of tearful embraces and smiling children. Some of the children, however, remember the moment of their selection differently. In their documentary *The Orphan Trains*, the filmmakers Janet Graham and Edward Gray tracked down the aging men and women who had been sent west in the last years of the orphan trains. They recounted for Graham and Gray the memory of standing in semicircles as strange men and women looked them over, checking their muscles and inspecting their teeth. Siblings were split up. Children not chosen were gathered by the society agent who boarded them onto another train and headed for another town, searching for homes.

Placing out was not new; the difference was the scale. The society was shipping scores of children west every two weeks. Brace believed that his "ingenious scheme" could empty the city of five thousand children a year; he estimated the cost to the taxpayer as a tenth the annual fee of keeping a child in an orphanage. All that stood in his way, he believed, were the forces of ignorance—chief among them Catholic priests who did not wish to see children brought up by Protestants and, even more perplexingly to Brace, the parents themselves. He could not fathom how people in dire circumstances would resist his offer of new lives for their children. "We are perfectly ready to do the same for the outside hard-working poor," he wrote. "But their attachment to the city, their ignorance or bigotry, and their affection for their children, will always prevent them from making use of such a benefaction to any large degree. The poor, living in their own homes, seldom wish to send out their children in this way."

The Children's Aid Society sent 100,000 city children west between 1854 and 1929, when the orphan trains fell out of child welfare fashion. The plan's legacy is not as Brace predicted. Early on, there were complaints from the midwestern states that the society was dumping troubled and troublesome children who were running away from their foster homes and ending up in jail. The society, which had relied on letters from grateful children and adults as evidence of its plan's success, began sending agents to check periodically on the condition of the children. The complaints continued; the society conducted its own investigations and in 1874, twenty years after the placements started, reported that none of the 5,000 children sent to Illinois or the 4,000 children in Michigan had ever been imprisoned. Later, however, the Minnesota State Board of Corrections and Charities, however, tracked down 340 children placed between 1880 and 1883 and found that within three years 100 of those children had left the areas where the society had placed them; 30 had disappeared. In 1922, a study of all the children sent away by the society in five different years was similarly mixed: about half the children had what were deemed successful placements, in that they stayed in the homes where they were placed and did not end up in prison or as runaways. Girls fared better than boys; younger children had a better chance of success than older children.

When she talked decades later with the elderly men and women who rode on the orphan trains, Janet Graham heard stories that underscored the same, mixed legacy. The men and women talked about the people they came to see and love as their parents. They also talked about longing to see their birth parents and, when they were old enough, going back to New York to try to find them. Indeed, many of the children sent west did not wait to go home; they ran away and worked their way back to their parents. Graham came across a letter from one child that read "I would give a hundred worlds like this if I could see my mother."

That tug, that pull toward a past that was sometimes no clearer than fog, came through in many of the letters Graham read. The children, she said, wrote to their birth parents if they could or to the agents that had escorted them to their new homes. They told of the skills they had learned on the farm. But, she added, if they were free to write what they liked, they would ask about people from home. Time and again, Graham said, they would ask "Do you think of me? Do you miss me?"

In one of the society's annual reports, an agent reported that some foster parents resisted paying for the children's transportation, presumably because if they did not want to keep the child, they would have then lost nothing in the transaction. That sentiment, the agent noted, often changed, and the concerns of the initially reluctant foster parent became not of returning the child but of the fear that someone might come to take the child back. The agent told them, "Don't you understand? They're nobody's child."

That, Graham said, was the society's perception of its own spirit of generosity. It had given these children new homes and lives. "They saw themselves as real saviors," she said. "We're providing opportunities for these children, clean slates for these children."

"Lost"

THE ONLY SURPRISE in the trial of the Melton sisters was how Judge Kawamoto would frame her opinion. When she rendered her decision in late October, she chose outrage, which could not help but go down well. I did not doubt the sincerity of the sentiment. Even Denise Melton, who had been such a hard case, began to cry when Kawamoto read her decision.

"Children are life's most precious gifts," she began, leaving no doubt about where she was heading as she repeated what the police had discovered nine months before. "Instead of care, they found squalor. Instead of devotion, they found filth." Poverty, she wrote, was not to blame. Nor was "Government" or the Department of Children and Family Services. She blamed the mothers. Their neglect was so pervasive and so profound, she wrote, that it had become a form of abuse, of which she then found them guilty, as well as of neglect.

In late December of 1994, two months after the verdict, Maxine was released from prison. She went first to her godmother in downstate Illinois, with whom the state had placed her five sons. Then she returned to Chicago, where she set about trying to earn them back. She started slowly. She moved in with her cousin, Cassandra Henderson Melton, who granted her two weeks to relax and then, recognizing Maxine's inertia, began hectoring. She reminded Maxine that to regain custody of her children she needed, at the very least, to show her caseworker and Judge Kawamoto that she had found a job and a home of her own. Maxine listened and argued and sulked and slept late and assured her doubting cousin that her caseworker had something lined up.

Maxine tried to visit her sons every other weekend. She got a ride downtown to Union Station and took the Amtrak train south to Kankakee. When she got to the station, she called her godmother, Claudine Christian, and announced that she had arrived. Because she often came unannounced, she waited until Claudine could find someone to drive the hour to the station to pick her up and bring Maxine to her house. Maxine liked to come on Friday afternoons, when the boys were getting home from school. She stayed for the weekend, and when she left on Sunday, she told her sons that, yes, she would be back for them but that she had things to do in Chicago and they could not go with her.

"They ready for us to be back together," Maxine said. "If I could take them back now, I'd take them back. I think they should be with me because I'm their mother and I can raise them better than anyone else can. I need a house, money, some type of income. Before August I should have my boys back. I have to show that I can be a good mother to my boys, that I can put them in a better environment."

She said this almost in a singsong, as if she had rehearsed what her caseworker and the judge would want to hear. We were sitting in Cassandra Henderson Melton's living room, and Cassandra, who had testified on the sisters' behalf, asked her, "But how can you do that with an Aid once-a-month check? Let's say you make six dollars an hour. That's six times forty hours. Two hundred some dollars a week. It's still hard."

"It is," said Maxine.

But how would she show that she was a good enough mother to regain her sons? She turned to Cassandra, smiled, and asked, "You're a good mother. What should I say?"

Cassandra started to talk but stopped herself. Maxine sat silently for a while. Then she said, "I can't say yet."

Cassandra asked her, "What does it take to be a good mother?"

"Raising your kids the right way," said Maxine.

"What is the right way?" Cassandra asked.

"Good education. Decent place to live. Some type of income so that you can take care of your kids. I don't feel like I didn't do no good job. I just got caught up in a messed-up situation."

I asked Maxine about the first time she got pregnant. Maxine said she did not want to be pregnant. Her mother told her she was pregnant, but Maxine did not want to believe her. "I think I was about three months or more," Maxine said. "She said, 'Girl, you pregnant.' " Maxine denied it. "She said, 'You pregnant like a dog.' "

Maxine said that Cassandra took her to a clinic to confirm the pregnancy, and when the results were positive, Maxine remembers thinking, " 'It ain't happening to me.' Everybody asked who the father was." The father, she said, "was alright with it." He visited the baby for two years. By then Maxine was pregnant with another son by another man, so her first son's father stopped coming by. Each time Maxine discovered she was pregnant, it was her mother who told her; and each time Maxine insisted she was wrong.

I asked Maxine whether she thought about aborting her first pregnancy, considering how little she wanted to be pregnant. She said she had not, nor did she consider aborting any of the other four. By the time she was pregnant for the fifth time, she said, "I had the rest of them so I had Gregory, too."

I heard much the same sentiment from almost every mother I met in Chicago who became a mother as a teenager: None said they wanted the baby, but then none of them said they did not. Rather, they told of how they awoke and much to their surprise found themselves pregnant and continued being pregnant until their child was born. No one used the word "decided" or any word that hinted at volition or desire. Richard Calica, the director of the Juvenile Protective Association in Chicago, said that while the work his agency did with mothers was built upon the principle of parental "responsibility," he had spent years at the Sisyphean task of trying to teach responsibility to women for whom even the most profound event in their lives took place as a passive acceptance of an often unwanted fate.

"They are engaging in a process that has nothing to do with adult sex," he said. Rather, for so many young women, though not necessarily for the fathers of their children, it is "cuddling in the night that leads to sex." It is the same sort of longing that keeps these women sleeping in the same bed with children who are five and six years old, Calica explained: "they"—and here he meant the mothers, not the children—"are afraid of the dark." "The wish," he said, "was that this baby was 'going to take care of me.'"

Cassandra listened as Maxine spoke in cloudy terms about her desire to regain her children. She asked Maxine precisely how she planned to do this. Maxine checked the time and said she had to go to meet her caseworker.

———

Cassandra Henderson Melton had often been to Maxine's house on North Keystone Avenue. She tried to be of help, if only because she felt a debt to her cousins for helping watch her children when she was in school. Cassandra was careful to avoid criticizing her cousins, even though when she was young and overwhelmed by the burden of her children, she found herself unable to bear the dreary and interminable days her cousins lived. She wanted to defend her cousins, but at the same time she drew a clear distinction between her life and theirs.

How was it, I asked her, that she had not become the sort of mother her cousins became? Why was her life so filled with purpose, both for herself and for her children, while only a few blocks away, her cousins and their children lived lives in which the future barely extended past that night's dinner?

If Maxine's vision of the future remained, at best, vague, Cassandra was well along in tending to the details of the new lives she wanted to help her cousins fashion. She wanted the sisters to be ready when their children came back to them.

"I would like to see them all in a low-income house," Cassandra explained. "I would like to see May Fay, Maxine, Cassandra, Denise at home with their children, spending time with them, showing them how to love somebody, showing them how to appreciate what they have." She offered no explanation for omitting Diane, to whom she still felt grateful for helping her look after her firstborn, Crystal. More and more, Diane had come to be seen as a lost soul, a junkie who showed little interest in the children she bore, all of whom she managed to lose. But now, thinking of the others, Cassandra went on. "And I would like to be the one to buy their silverware, their first comforters, their sheet set. I would just like to give them the things the state said they didn't have."

Cassandra believed her cousins could be competent mothers. "I've seen all of them do what a mother is supposed to do, as far as cooking, taking them to school." And if they could not, say, wash clothes as well as she could, it was only because she had her own washing machine and they did not. The sisters came to Cassandra's house to wash their children's clothes.

Still, it was all well and good for the sisters to perform the rudimentary tasks. What did Cassandra believe they needed to know in order to offer a purposeful life to their children?

"Take them children to church," she said. For Cassandra, a religious woman, the house on North Keystone Avenue, like the lives her cousins had lived with their children, was lacking not only in order, but in faith. It was as if her cousins had no sense of their place in the world, of who they were and what might be expected of them. Cassandra harbored no such doubts. "Who am I?" she asked, rhetorically. "I'm thirty-two years old. I know I'm a mother. But what is my reason for being on this earth? I see them being lost."

Despite her impatience with Maxine's inability to work at regaining her sons, and despite all her remarkable certainty in how to shape the good life, Cassandra nonetheless understood the depth not only of the chaos of her cousins' lives, but of the depression that defined the lives they had lived long before they arrived on North Keystone Avenue. She spoke of Maxine as a young mother, but all the while she was thinking about herself. "There are things she felt she could have done and didn't do," Cassandra said. "Then she has to watch her girlfriends go out, and she's stuck home with kids.

"It's depressing to sit at home and wait for the check once a month. You walk the kids to school. You come back home. You prepare the other kids for a nap. It's the same routine. And you clean your house. By eleven o'clock you're done cleaning, so you watch the stories on TV or you read. You try to do something to keep you from getting bored. But there's not much to do. There sure isn't. You call your girlfriends. Maybe they come over. You cook. You feed them. They go home. I had girlfriends who started going out and getting high because they were depressed. Maybe they had boyfriends. He started getting high, and she started getting high. She ended up being alone, just her and the kids. Some of them started running the streets. It's very easy if the mind isn't that strong. I've been through it, you hear me?"

Did her children know she felt this low?

"I would tell them, 'Momma does not feel good, and I feel a change is gonna come.' But you wonder when that change gonna come. I said, 'Just stay by [me and] hug me and kiss me.' They would laugh because they didn't understand where I was coming from. What made the change come? Seeing them and knowing what they had to deal with when they walked outside my door. If you look beyond what's out there, if you use your imagination, you can see a whole better world."

———

Cassandra Henderson Melton became a mother at seventeen. She was not married. On the way home from the clinic where her pregnancy was confirmed, Cassandra's mother made clear her disappointment. "She told me, 'Now you're pregnant. Now you gonna see what I tried to tell you all these years, what motherhood is and just how hard it is.' " Then Cassandra's mother told her daughter she was staying in school and remaining at home. "She told me, 'You don't know if Jake is gonna stay with you. You don't know what it cost for a baby-sitter. You don't know whether they gonna sleep all night or have the colic.' She got up at nighttime, changed diapers, got up in the morning, fed her, got her to the baby-sitter's. She was right there. She was mad, but she was right there. My daddy was the one bought the cases of milk. He was mad, but he came to baby-sit."

Cassandra spoke of the order and clarity that her mother imposed upon her life after Crystal was born. She spoke of God and of the hope her faith engendered. And then, without feigning modesty, she talked about herself. "I was always more determined," she said. "I had to go out and do something for myself. I wanted something for me, and Aid didn't have it and they wasn't gonna give it out."

But why, I asked, did this work for you and not for your cousins? It was early afternoon, and Crystal, a tall, thin girl, came up the front steps and into the house. She took off her coat and said hello. When I asked about her school trophies, she talked about them matter-of-factly, without embarrassment and without boasting. She acknowledged that it was not always easy being the smart one in school. "Like when I was in sixth, seventh, and eighth grades winning all those trophies, people couldn't stand me," she said. "They said they thought I was too much. And my mother said if I listened to them, those trophies wouldn't be up there in the first place." She said she wanted to be a lawyer or a social worker. Her mother had wanted to be a lawyer, too.

I asked Crystal whether her mother was strict with her.

"Sometimes she tell us we can't go outside and she don't want us to be around a bunch of boys because now a bunch of my friends are coming up pregnant and that could have been me." Her friends, she said, "are excited that they're pregnant. Some of them, yeah, they go out and show. Girls, they like to show, like when you're young and you're having a child and your friends see you pregnant."

What would your mother do if you came home pregnant?

"Murder," she said.

"I'll be sick for at least a year, but she wouldn't have an abortion," Cassandra said. "There wouldn't be 'No, I'm leaving, I'm grown.' There wouldn't be none of that."

———— ⸱

Maxine returned. And from the back room, where she had been sleeping, May Fay emerged. Several months had passed since I had seen her in court. She no longer carried herself with the indifferent swagger she displayed in front of Judge Kawamoto. She wore a tee shirt and gray sweatpants, and her hair was wrapped in a small bun that she wore on top of her head. She padded across the dimly lit room and stood for a while by the window. Where Maxine denied and, left without a choice, accepted her pregnancies, May Fay said that if her mother told her she was too young to have a child, she would have obeyed her. "I was a kid then," she said. "I didn't know nothing about babies at fifteen. My mother wasn't saying that I was old enough to make these decisions or nothing. I guess she was letting me see how it was to be out here raising kids when I was fifteen years old."

By the time I met May Fay, she had been released from her residential drug treatment center and, like Maxine, she had moved in with her cousin Cassandra. Cassandra was pleased with May Fay, who had enrolled in a high school equivalency course at a local community college. May Fay had had months of group therapy and enforced abstinence from drugs. She was beginning to admit that she had not done right by her children.

"I always loved my kids, but I didn't show love to my kids because of me being out there getting high and everything," May Fay said. "So I'm just basically wanting to take things one at a time, one day at a time, and gradually slide right on in and show my kids the love that I really have for them and be able to sit down and talk to them and do things talking with them, but you know really sit down and have a hard, long talk with my two oldest. My two youngest ones, they wouldn't quite understand right now. But my two oldest ones, they're very smart. They'll understand. Just sit down and talk about everything that happened and what their momma was going through and that she never really meant to hurt them."

How did you hurt them? I asked.

"Before I started getting high there was nothing my kids asked me for or my kids needed that I couldn't give them. And then it got to the stage where they could ask for things and I would say, 'Just leave me alone.' I finally pushed them away, and I would sit down and think about it and think I shouldn't have said that to my kids."

May Fay's four children lived in a foster home. She saw them once a week. She said they were "ready to come back home."

Were they doing better now, living apart from her?

"I can say Crystal and Joshewa and Darshay are," she said. "Leon, he still the same. He's doing the wrong things. I guess he's doing these things because he's not with us. He's ready to come home to his mama. He was with his father, and then his father let him down. I guess it's just a big disappointment to him. He figured, don't nobody really care. I said, 'Your momma's trying to get herself together. She's trying to do the things that people are asking her to do so she will be able to get you all back home and we can be a family again.' "

"Laying On of Hands"

THE DEPARTMENT of Children and Family Services had known almost nothing of the Melton children. There had been prior, vague reports of one or more of the sisters failing to provide "adequate supervision," none of which the department investigated. But beginning in August of 1983, just as May Fay and Denise had settled in with Maxine, the department began receiving complaints on its child abuse hotline about life at the house on North Keystone Avenue. The calls came from one of the grandmothers of Denise Turner's children. The hotline, however, received some 400,000 calls a year, of which the department investigated about 70,000. About a third of those cases warranted intervention.

The calls about the house on Keystone eventually prompted a visit by one caseworker who could not get inside. The case was passed to another worker, who had been with the department since 1986. The caseworker visited the house twice. She was not allowed in. The caseworker did not call the police, which was the standard recourse when access was denied. Instead, she went away. The last complaint on the hotline came on January 28, 1994. Three days later the police came, by chance, to the house.

Governor Jim Edgar's first response after the Keystone story broke was to call for the dismissal of the caseworker. That was to be expected. It was hardly a secret within the department and among its critics—it had no public advocates—that caseworkers were fair game in Chicago, especially since Joseph Wallace's death at his psychotic mother's hands. The Republican president of the Illinois senate, James "Pate" Philip, told a suburban paper's editorial board that "minority" workers at the department "don't have the same work ethics that we have" and "don't tend to turn on or squeal on their fellow minorities." He singled out the caseworker in the Keystone case: "Of course she was a minority. Her boss was a minority."

Jess McDonald, the department's director, called the accusation "horse hockey," black legislators called Philip a racist, and the criticism of caseworkers continued. Even the special counsel whom the governor appointed to oversee the department, Anne Burke, made a point of telling me of the shoddiness among caseworkers and their supervisors that she found at the department.

"It was far worse than we thought," said Burke, an attorney and the wife of Ed Burke, an especially powerful Chicago alderman. "Very, very ineffective people. There was no accountability whatsoever. And part of that was a lack of supervision. People would be listening to a phone ringing and just let it ring because no one has the responsibility to answer it. There was no notification to another employee if there was a changed court date. It's not their case. Why should they tell another employee?" Burke said she had heard that there were caseworkers, like those who went to the Melton home, who never got inside the homes they were supposed to investigate. "And truly, I believe a lot of them didn't bother."

This perception of incompetence and laziness was not about to change, even with the recommendations that Burke had made about equipping caseworkers with beepers and cellular phones so they could get in touch with the police and voice mail so they could actually get messages from their clients, many of whom had to rely on pay phones to maintain contact.

Child welfare agencies exist in a bureaucratic vacuum; they are unseen until something awful happens, like the death of a child. Then they become the target for all the public and political frustration at the inability of the state to care for children. The criticism of incompetence is, in good measure, well founded. What goes on in child welfare agencies is appalling. I have never heard people talk in flattering ways of a child welfare agency. And this is the view both of critics and directors.

The agencies are viewed with suspicion, in good measure, because they operate behind a cloak of confidentiality. This is done in the name of "protecting" the children. But this is merely a cloak to avoid public scrutiny. It does not serve the agencies well. When a child welfare story breaks, the press descends upon the agency, which generally announces that no information can be released in the name of protecting the confidentiality of the child, who at that point may well be in the office of the medical examiner. The press assumes that what is going on behind the agency's closed doors is not only incompetence but wrongdoing. The inevitable leaks follow, and leaks seldom place bureaucracies in a good light in that they come from people who are angry or who have scores to settle. Scandals in child welfare are almost always followed by days, and sometimes weeks, of endless stories in the local newspapers and on TV—and, if they are especially bad, by the networks and news weeklies, as happened with the Meltons—and by denunciations of the very people who were supposed to "protect" the children from their parents. This assault on the agency, in turn, only makes those within the agency hunker down and reveal little about the case, for fear of making themselves look worse. And that, in turn, only adds to the frustration of the journalists and the public who are by this time absolutely convinced that a child died because somehow the agency allowed that child to "slip through the cracks." Because child welfare agencies command attention only at tragic moments, the perception of failure endures from crisis to crisis.

Yet it is naive to assume that the shameful treatment of children by their parents and the state might be resolved merely by demanding that child welfare agencies improve their performance. This does not mean that the agencies bear no guilt for the plight of abused and neglected children. It would be wonderful if punishing the caseworker, or the supervisor or the director of the agency, might somehow make up for what went wrong for a child. It does not. Someone else comes along, be it a new director or a court-appointed monitor, takes on the same job, and holds his breath, hoping a catastrophe does not happen on his watch. It will. And when it does, the denunciations and inves-

tigations will begin again. So too will calls for reform; or for disman-
tling the bureaucracy; or for a lawsuit demanding that the system be
placed under court supervision; or for more money; or for opening
the agency to greater scrutiny. None of these changes, however, will
ever go far enough. None alter the relationship between the state and
poor families whose behavior violates the general societal view—a
view that, in the case of the Meltons, cut across lines of class and
color—of how families should behave.

Reform takes place all the time at child welfare agencies across the
country. Its impact, however, is sometimes difficult to detect. In Illinois, for instance, Jess McDonald ran an agency that had hired a thousand new caseworkers in the prior twelve months. And even then,
McDonald said, "we can't keep up with the caseload." The department had based its funding request from the state on a projection of
39,000 children in out-of-home placements. But by the end of 1994
the department had in its care 44,000 children. There was no sign of
a letup, especially in the panic that followed the high-profile cases
like those of Joseph Wallace and the Melton children, when the number of children the state took surged.

Caseworkers were supposed to handle between twenty-five and
thirty cases. But many were now handling twice that number. The department could not train or place the new hires quickly enough.
From the six months between the time the jobs were advertised and
the applicants were hired, trained, and placed, the department was
projected to take another 7,200 children whose cases were being
handled by workers working ten hours a week of mandatory over-
time. After five months of this grind, McDonald said, the department
decided it had to cut back on the hours because caseworkers were either burning out or making bad decisions.

Nor was the department necessarily hiring good people. The new
hires, who started at about $24,000 a year—"not bad pay as pay goes
in this field," McDonald said—needed only a bachelor's degree,
which was supplemented by thirteen weeks of training, some in the
classroom, some working alongside a supervisor. Not that those supervisors were always capable of teaching. McDonald acknowledged
that his supervisor corps, which had been decimated several years before by layoffs, was "weak." He now required all supervisors to hold a
master's in social work. That he had supervisors who had risen only

on the basis of seniority and with only a bachelor's degree, he said, was a situation "that no self-respecting agency would settle for." He did not think the caseworker training adequate. Once the caseworkers were out in the field, they were left to learn from the experiences they encountered. Burnout, in Chicago and in agencies across the country, was high. But McDonald was under court order to hire more people, some of whom, he admitted, had no business working in his department. "Are we just going to hire everybody and anybody?" he said. In truth, he was. McDonald admitted that his agency was hiring people who had been dismissed from private agencies. "We do have people, I'm sure, who were 'counseled out,' which doesn't show up as a discharge."

As it happened, the day before the police discovered the Melton children, the department found itself, once again, the object of a public shaming. Since 1991, the department had been operating under the supervision of a court-appointed monitor; this was part of a settlement of a class-action suit brought by the American Civil Liberties Union, which claimed that the department was in such horrendous shape that it was harming the families it was supposed to be helping. The department pledged to fulfill ninety-three separate reforms. The monitor, a retired Cook County judge, reported that almost half those promises remained broken. The department, he wrote, still did not have enough foster beds. It had no systematic way of treating children for their health, nor parents for their drug addictions. Its case files were incomplete, and the department was still too slow to either send children home or terminate their parents' rights. The monitor did credit the department with publishing a handbook for parents accused of abuse and neglect and with soliciting the opinions of panels of outside advisers—even though it had not yet acted on any of their recommendations. He also noted that the department had succeeded in opening a residential floor with seventy-three beds at its Chicago offices so that children were no longer spending the night sleeping in offices.

The suit was one of eight that had been brought against the department since 1984. The department was accused, by turns, of conducting "unreasonable nude searches" of abused children, of not having enough Spanish-speaking caseworkers, of not having enough foster care beds, and, inevitably, of not acting quickly enough to find permanent homes for children. The suits, all of which the department lost, put an even greater financial strain on them: In 1991 alone, the department had paid over $2 million in fees to the New York law firm of Skadden, Arps, Slate, Meagher and Flom—a cost that critics insisted was far greater than the less expensive services of the state's attorneys general. The department replied that with so many overlapping suits, it was easier having a single firm handling its defense.

The department was established in 1964 as an umbrella agency and lobbyist for all the private foster care agencies that had been operated autonomously for decades. It still contracted out much of its work, but remained the agency ultimately responsible for wards of the state. "People have the expectation that we are like a huge human waste management corporation," Jess McDonald said. "That communities, when they get sick and tired of families, say 'I'll call the state. Get them out of here.' "

The department McDonald inherited was still suffering from budget cutting and layoffs in 1993. Money problems were not unique to Illinois. Until 1980, the financial burden of child welfare fell primarily to the states. In 1974, however, with the passage of federally mandated abuse and neglect reporting, the numbers of child welfare cases rose and with them the pressure on the states to pay the cost for those investigations and caseworkers. That same year, federal funding for child protection services was capped at $2.5 billion. Twenty years later it was still only $4 billion. Setting aside the possibility of funding keeping pace with demand, if the money from Washington had been indexed for inflation between 1977 and 1992 it would have ballooned to $36 billion. The burdens on increasingly strapped child welfare departments only grew in 1980, with the Carter Administration's passage of the Adoption Assistance Act. The new law sought to end the decades-long problem of "foster-care drift" by pushing states to either assist failing families or free children for adoption. The slight rise in spending that accompanied the bill's passage was quickly reversed by the Reagan Administration, which not only cut federal funds by 25 percent, but provided the funds to the states in the form of block grants.

By the time the police took the Melton children, the federal government was still paying the bulk of child welfare services. But at a time when more and more child welfare departments were trying to devise ways of doing their work with greater flexibility, Washington's money came with strict limitations. Part of the legacy of the 1980 Adoption Assistance Act was a belief that government should not too aggressively impose itself upon families. The federal government split its money into separate allotments for foster care and for all other child welfare services. Seventy-five percent of that money, however, went to foster care, on what is known in the trade as "hots and cots," for feeding and housing and little more. Washington, in fact, required the states to return money they did not spend on foster care. This decision, in turn, served only to perpetuate the belief among many critics that the child welfare system was little more than a business that made its money by placing children in foster homes.

By 1994 departments like Jess McDonald's were caught in the bureaucratic nightmare of too little money, too many demands, too many clients, and virtually no room for flexibility. This is not to suggest that money is the solution for failing families and failing child welfare agencies—only that the virtual absence of money, at least money that can be spent for things other than room and board and mandatory abuse and neglect investigations, makes any possibility of reform that much more difficult.

In Illinois, however, even attempts at reform had gone poorly. In 1988 the department seized upon what was then the popular idea of family preservation and launched its own version, a $20 million plan called Family First. Modeled after the nation's first and widely copied family preservation project—HomeBuilders, which was opened in 1979 in Tacoma, Washington—Family First was billed as a plan that would reduce the single greatest cost in child welfare, to the state and to children: indeterminate time in foster care. The Illinois plan placed caseworkers into the homes of families deemed by the state in danger of having children removed. For up to three months, longer than in many other such programs, caseworkers were to assist the families in remaining intact. This meant everything from mending broken windows to preparing a weekly menu to teaching parents to discipline children without striking them. The legislature insisted that the program be monitored by the Chapin Hall Center for Children at the University of Chicago, one of the nation's leading schools of social work. The center followed sixteen hundred families over three years.

Its report was damning. Not only had Families First failed to differentiate between struggling families and those that were truly on the verge of losing their children, but it had not been able to reduce the chances of failing families losing their children. In short, the report concluded, the state had spent $20 million to save $2 million in foster care fees.

The report was seized upon by critics of family preservation—Patrick Murphy, the Cook County Public Guardian, chief among them—as proof that some families simply were beyond preserving and that the state did a grave disservice to vulnerable children by assuming that a short course on parenting skills could make their parents competent. In the years to come, the criticism of family preservation grew, even as funding increased in various states and from the Clinton Administration—which in 1993 budgeted $930 million over five years for such programs. The problem with family preservation was the promise that it made: here, at last, was the way to save money *and* families, in a relatively brief encounter.

The problem with family preservation was that those who championed it did so in the belief that because it worked for some families, it would surely work for all families. The Edna McConnell Clark Foundation, one of the large charitable organizations that tried to fill the shortfall in funding that came with the Reagan Administration's drastic cuts to social programs, was a great booster of HomeBuilders, so much so that it spent $30 million supporting and marketing that model and that model alone to child welfare agencies across the country. It was as if the secret to assisting failing families had been discovered in Tacoma and no deviation from orthodoxy was permissible. What this meant, wrote one critic, Paul Adams, of Portland State University, was that other estimable but somewhat different approaches were ignored by states eager for a share in the Clark Foundation's money. And because HomeBuilders was not, and never could be, the answer for all families, it became easy prey for critics, who seized upon its inevitable failures as proof that the approach was hopelessly wrong.

The idea that families like the Meltons could be patched together and made to work on their own in a matter of weeks, or even months, was as simplistic as the argument for a hasty termination of parental rights. Family preservation worked when parents, though mired in hard times—poverty, drugs, no work, illness, often all at the same time—were nonetheless sufficiently capable and motivated to become competent parents, with help and perhaps a push. No short course was going to help the Meltons. They would need more, and more would be costly. Family preservation was supposed to be about doing this on the cheap.

In late January of 1994, shortly before the Keystone case broke, McDonald got a reprieve of sorts. The ACLU, whose suit had forced the department's reorganization and caseworker hirings, entered into a new agreement with the department. It essentially conceded that the department was doing the best it could to comply with the terms of the suit's consent decree. But in the three and a half years since the decree was signed, the number of children entering the system had doubled and the number of cases being closed was being far eclipsed by the number being opened. McDonald conceded as much, saying that there were now some fifteen hundred cases that the department had kept open for no apparent reason. This meant that the children remained wards of the state, and the parents subject to state-mandated behavior. The former supervising judge in Cook County Juvenile Court, William Maddux, said that there were hundreds of cases still open in which no one even had any idea where the children were living.

Even the department's critics talked admiringly of Jess McDonald's ability to understand the dimension and degree of the department's incompetence and of his capacity to instill in his employees a sense that child welfare was a noble cause. Yet six months after assuming his position—he had been director of the state's department of mental health—the passion I had heard so much about seem muted by weariness. He spoke like a man who believed that people did not understand that the things for which his department was being blamed were not necessarily in his control.

"Everyone treats us as if we were a manufacturing business," he said, "that it's predictable, that we have some mysterious powers that allow us to motivate people who have been basically unmotivated about much of anything most of their lives. They dropped out of school. They were educated on the streets. They dropped out of everything, and now because of the laying on of hands of social workers, something's going to turn around. If it happens in ten percent of the cases, that's marvelous."

We sat in the Chicago office, where he spent the two days of the week when he was not in Springfield, the capital. He took off his tweed blazer and sat in his shirtsleeves, finishing breakfast. I had expected someone with a more polished veneer. But he rambled a bit, as he worked to distill what his department was supposed to accomplish. "In the Appropriations Committee they asked, 'Why are your damn caseloads going up so rapidly and what are you doing to control them?' I said, 'We have laws; we have these expectations; the courts are saying take everyone into custody. There's only one logical conclusion: It goes up. That means it costs you more.' "

He was frustrated, as well, by people looking at his department as the sole agency responsible for children. "Where have all the advocates been? Where have all the schools of social work been? They haven't been helping this agency. This agency has been on its own. But if everyone says it's impossible to work with these families, let's just change the law and write them off. But no one wants to give up on families. Literally, financially, we can't afford it. And I think we'll have generations that will curse us if we give up on families. If we do, we're saying, 'If you're poor, turn your kids over to us and save [the state] the time and trouble.' "

I asked McDonald what his department was trying to do. On what basis was he deciding what was best for a parent or child?

First, he said, it was essential that every child be safe. "Safe now and safe from any future harm," he said. It was a tired phrase, convenient and vague. Safe from whom? The parents? The state? McDonald, to his credit, conceded that the goal of safety did not get you very far. "That's when it starts to get muddy. A family comes into the child welfare system. They're involved with drugs. They're impoverished. And we say, 'How about some counseling today? Maybe some parent education programs?' Why in the world do we think these things are going to work?"

McDonald had been in the field for twenty years. He had been a caseworker in downstate Illinois. Child welfare, he believed, had evolved into a reactive agency: It responded, as did the police, when people acted badly. But unlike criminal behavior, the rules on unacceptable parenting were vague. McDonald believed he was not asking that much by insisting that parents accomplish the obvious things, like feeding their children, getting them to school every day, and making sure they were inoculated and that they lived in a house that did not pose a danger to their health, either because the house was a shambles or because the parents were too high or too often absent to notice.

He wanted to help the parents. He did not want their children. But he also did not want his agency liable for an injury or death because one of his caseworkers thought it all right to leave a child at home. The burden, he argued, was misplaced. It was not on his department. It was on the parents. "They are the ones to change. We don't," he said. "And that's what the basic relationship is all about, not just authority. We've got the courts, the state; we've got everyone else reminding them of what they've done and what they have to do. Our job is to help them figure out how to do it. It is their job to make the change. You apply a whole bunch of things to people and hope that something hits."

McDonald's difficulty in articulating a vision for his agency was just the sort of imprecision that plagued one Chicago caseworker I came to know. His name was Sidney Goldberg. He had been a caseworker for fourteen years and was forty-nine years old. I visited him late one cold and rainy morning. He invited me into his living room and showed me to a chair that did not quite face his, so we had to strain a bit to look at each other. Two cats silently patrolled the room. He offered tea and did not turn on a light, which left the room gray. He was an Orthodox Jew; his shelves were lined with books— religious texts and books on such psychological matters as cognitive therapy. For years, I had heard, Goldberg had been trying to place his increasingly unsatisfying work in a philosophical framework. The task remained incomplete.

There was so much to talk about, he said. And with that he began. He spoke in a great hurry, as if he were rushing to a place he could see, hazily, out there. He was that rare person who in his carriage and being and speech embodied the frustrations and questions that vexed him. Again and again, he apologized for rambling. He wanted to know whether he was making sense.

"Number one, there's a lack of thought," he said. "Number two, people sometimes see situations as if they were straight child welfare issues. They are more complicated than that. In many of the families we deal with, there are levels of hopelessness. What kinds of lives are they leading? How can they be expected to have more competent lives including in the area of parenting? Lately I've been feeling like a parasite, getting a salary and not accomplishing much. I used to feel that this was the most important job in the world. Now I think the opposite. There's nothing more intrusive in peoples' lives than child welfare. I believe that now, more than before, there's a lot more intrusion. People are quicker to remove children. I could sit here and talk about kids who are removed, and it's outrageous. And once they're removed, there's nothing for them."

He tried. He talked about attempts at assisting parents with their children, about parenting classes and the counseling of depressed parents and children. He wondered what the thinking was behind making any decision for any family. What was he supposed to be accomplishing?

Goldberg had come up with something on his own, the idea that people who were in some way successful had one area that so interested them that it gave their lives a sense of purpose. I heard from others in the department that over the years Goldberg had worked with parents in trying to find something, anything, that mattered to their children. If he discovered, say, that a child liked the clarinet, he found a clarinet and bought music books and found out about concerts: He helped the child build a life around the clarinet. "Most parents who do not have a tenth of a brain make available to their children what I call interest development," he said. "I'm not talking about some after-school activity that's good for the kiddies."

But he understood, too, that the worst thing that could happen to his idea was for the department to implement it by dispatching every caseworker to ask the fifty or sixty children on his or her caseload what they liked to do and then provide some assistance in their doing it. This approach would miss his point. He was struggling to articulate a philosophy about creating a life. This was not, he believed, a quality that could be programmed and placed in a series of directives and stapled into a handbook and then used—and this was his biggest irritation—the same way for each child in each family that came into the system. How it would work for more than the occasional child who happened to display such an interest to an astute and resourceful caseworker was not yet clear. He did have great hopes for his new director, Jess McDonald.

We talked for an hour. When I said I had to leave, Goldberg said he was disappointed because there was so much more to talk about, so much more he had not yet resolved. "There should be a way for people to be helpful," he said. He stood at the top landing and talked to me as I walked down the stairs. When I got to the door, he was still there, looking down, his presentation incomplete.

———

Later, I asked Jess McDonald whether he had talked with caseworkers about the philosophical dimension of their work—about what they thought they were supposed to be doing.

"They may ask that," he said. "But at some level they don't want us to define that. You want a certain amount of rules. But you want to know: 'To what extent can I exercise my own judgment about what needs to be done?' At every point you have to make a decision. And how do you make that discrete judgment? 'What do I look for?' People will make a lot of mistakes in that. That's the subtle stuff."

Grandmother

JOSEPHINE MELTON had been a nuisance to the private agency responsible for her daughters' children. She wanted custody of her grandchildren and got upset because, she told one social worker, other grandmothers got their grandchildren and she wanted hers, too. The social worker told Josephine that she was "part of the problem."

The social worker had watched Josephine when she came to visit Diane's children. Josephine would comment on how a child looked and then watch the child play. When the child spilled toys on the floor, the social worker heard Josephine say, "All you do is throw toys on the floor." The social worker did not believe that Josephine knew how to relate to her grandchildren. Josephine did not understand how someone could think this way. She had never been in trouble with a child welfare agency with her own children. She believed she had been a good mother. "And there wasn't a night when my kids wasn't with me or their father," she said. "I didn't let my kids spend the night in other people's houses like other kids."

Josephine was fifty-two. She was a heavyset women who, like her daughters, favored sweat suits, often with cartoon logos. She wore her graying hair cut close. In addition to her five daughters and twenty-two grandchildren, she also had two sons. Josephine was staying on the West Side at the home of a woman whose daughter she was watching while the woman was in prison. Josephine brought the child with her to Cassandra Henderson Melton's house. Cassandra, May Fay, and Maxine took turns holding the child, who was several months old. She was plump and dressed in pink and frills, and in two hours I did not hear a cry or sound from her. Maxine, May Fay, and their cousin Cassandra walked the baby around the dining room and cooed at her, as they would be asked to do the following week when Josephine went into the hospital for gallbladder surgery. "Y'all better not spoil her when I go in the hospital," she told them every few minutes. "When I come back, I have to deal with it."

Now that the state had judged her daughters guilty of abusing and neglecting her grandchildren, Josephine wanted to believe her daughters had learned important lessons from losing their children. "I hope they realize from what happened," she said. "Get them a job or whatever they got to do to get their kids and raise them and explain to them that what happened was a mistake and they love them and try to make it up to them."

Josephine had often been to the house on North Keystone Avenue. She watched her grandchildren when her daughters went out. Although she was aware of the condition of the home, she did not fault herself for the lives her daughters provided her grandchildren. She said she tried to tell her daughters the house was too crowded. But this did not work. She did not blame herself for the sorts of mothers her daughters became. "I did the best I could when they were coming up. But after that they got it wrong," she said. "I still told them when I thought they was wrong, but they just didn't listen—a whole lot of stuff I can't remember now. I didn't have no problem with my kids when they was little—being hardheaded, chasing boys, missing school. My girls never gave me no real serious trouble more than having babies. Started having all those kids and no way of taking care of them."

Josephine's daughters had only kind things to say about her. They said she was a "great" mom. They said she "loved kids" and denied them nothing. When they were little, they said, their mother cooked big dinners and invited relatives. They were aware that some relatives did not come to the house. The sisters said they had nice birthdays. "I got baby dolls, skates," Denise once said. "I got stuff I never thought I'd get."

Josephine said, "They say I was too strict."

May Fay, who sat holding the baby and listening to her mother, said, "She was strict in a way, and in a way she wasn't. She was strict in a way that, if she said for us to do something, she meant what she said. As far as her putting us on punishment, we had to stick to our punishment. She shouldn't have been more strict. It was cool the way she was."

I asked Josephine how she learned how to be a parent.

"My grandmother taught me," she said. "My grandmother raised me. She tried to tell us all about things. Going to church. How to be nice. How to treat people. Don't treat people bad because they do you bad things. She did the best she could with us. She kept us clothed and she fed us. She had eleven kids of her own, and she had three of us, four of us. Me and my two sisters and my brother. I ain't got no problem with the time she gave us. She did the best she could for all of us. But it still wasn't like being at home with your own momma. It ain't. I missed my mother."

The social worker who had gotten to know Josephine said that on the day they met, Josephine told her the story of how her mother had left her behind when she moved from the Mississippi Delta to Chicago. And that, the worker said, "is the story of her life and the meaning of her life."

Now, when I raised the subject of her mother, Josephine smiled and shook her head and said that she did not want to talk about her mother. Her refusal lacked the ring of finality. Soon, though reluctantly at first, she began to talk about her growing up. "When my mother came to Chicago, my sister Joanne was about a month old. She left her. I was maybe a year old, better than a year."

I asked when she next saw her mother.

"I don't know," Josephine said. "She came back to visit sometimes." And what of her father?

"I knew him when I was real small," Josephine said. "I remember him when I was real little. That's all I remember."

She looked across at the child in her care, who sat silently on May Fay's lap. "She wants some milk in her bottle," Josephine said. Then she went on. "I started out with a lot of disadvantages if you ask me. My mom and I didn't get along, and I can go on and on, and I'm not gonna do that. I tried to do different with my kids than the way I came up. Maybe I gave a little too much because I didn't want them to come up like I come up. I had to work in the fields and stuff. I got blamed for stuff I didn't do."

Josephine grew up in the Delta town of Lexington, Mississippi, a place made famous by Hazel Brannon Smith, one of the few white newspaper editors who challenged white extremists; by a blues guitarist named Lonnie Pitchford; and as the birthplace of the Church of God in Christ, the largest African-American Pentecostal denomination. The headquarters had since moved, along with over half the population of the town. Now there was little left behind. What had once been a town dominated by farming—mostly sharecropping—had by the late 1980s slipped into a sorry torpor. Where once there were over six thousand farms, there were now just over four hundred. Holmes County, of which Lexington was the county seat, was the poorest county in the country, with a per capita income of $3,400 a year. Lexington's streets were lined with empty stores and boarded-up windows, and the unpaved roads on the outskirts of town were lined with shacks overgrown with weeds. The county was overwhelmingly black and poor; roughly three-quarters of the dwindling population lived in poverty. The county clerk, Jamie Moore, told me, "Welfare is our biggest industry in Holmes County."

Josephine came to Chicago when she was eighteen and pregnant with Diane. "I looked my mother up," she said. She found her mother living with one of her sisters and stayed with them for a while. "Then I found my own place. I stayed up here until I had the baby. My mother wanted me to go back. She wanted me to come up here to go to the hospital. I didn't come here to stay. She never told me to go. I was ready to go myself. I didn't really want to stay."

She bore two sons in Mississippi and then returned to Chicago. When her children were young, Josephine had worked at a leather company, making belts and wallets, and on an assembly line, wrapping straws. She supplemented her incomes with public assistance. "I worked when I wanted to," she said. "And then I went on public aid. That was the only way I could take care of my kids."

The Melton sisters shared the same father, a manual laborer named Arthur Anderson, who died several years ago. The sisters were fond of their father, especially Diane, who once told a psychologist that she was his favorite. Their father lived with them, on and off, until Maxine was eight years old. Then their mother took up with someone new.

"They didn't like the fact that I broke up with their dad," Josephine said. "They started going different ways than before me and their father broke up. I told them I had to live my life, too. I wasn't doing anything to hurt them. But they didn't like it at all. They would always do things they wasn't supposed to do. Like they were going to school, but they started ditching school. Staying out longer than they would."

I asked whether she thought she was losing control of her daughters.

"They wouldn't listen to me," Josephine said. Then she turned to Maxine and asked, "Maxine, how old was you when me and your daddy split up?"

"About eight or nine," Maxine said. The memory of her parents' split saddened Maxine. She asked, "How would you feel if your father just up and leaves?"

"Your father didn't decide to leave," said her mother.

"Well, to leave your mom to take care of eight kids?" said Maxine.

"That wasn't your daddy's fault," Josephine said. "Your daddy wouldn't have went nowhere."

"I know that," said Maxine. "I'm just saying it was a hurtful situation."

I asked Josephine who helped her with her children.

"Their father and another friend that I had," she said. "That's all the people that helped me. My people did nothing for me. All of my people is up here, and none of them did nothing for me." Josephine had a brother in Milwaukee and two sisters who lived near Chicago. "I ain't seen them. I ain't heard from them. Nothing."

Why not?

Josephine said, "I've been asking myself that for fifty-two years. Ain't nothing too good I can say about them."

Now Cassandra Henderson Melton, who was the one relative whom Josephine could rely upon, felt the need to offer her view of things. "The animosity," she said, "is still in the heart."

"I don't know what it is," Josephine said.

I asked Josephine whether she felt rejected by the people she assumed would be closest to her.

"That's the way it looked to me," she said.

With their father gone and their mother with someone new, the Melton sisters, said May Fay, began "running around. Outside all the time. Not in the house all the time. We used to stay outside till the morning time."

"They was doing drugs," Josephine said. "Maxine didn't fool with no drugs. I used to tell them all the time what drugs do and everything, and it wasn't no good. And I guess that her and Cassandra was the only ones who listened."

I asked how she knew.

"How did I know? I used to do drugs. I ain't gonna lie to you. And I used to tell them that they didn't want to get off into that. Maxine listened."

Cassandra laughed and said, "Maxine was addicted to her boyfriends. There's all kinds of addictions."

May Fay said, "She used to stay outside. The only reason she cut it out and slacked down was because she got involved with Greg. [Gregory Turner was the father of Maxine's fourth son, but an even earlier boyfriend.] I figured if Greg hadn't come into her life, she'd be the same wild thing hanging outside like we used to be."

"I changed myself," said Maxine.

"I'd be like that, too," said May Fay. "If I'm told not to go outside by my boyfriend, I'm gonna go outside. But I'm gonna be back in when he gets here. That's how Maxine used to be because every time we was having fun, she was turned around looking for G." Maxine's devotion to her boyfriend at the expense of her sisters saddened May Fay. "We just couldn't really have no fun together. We was all together. We was cool together. It was straight."

"They was getting into no trouble outside drugs," Josephine said. "That's the only problem I had with my kids."

Neither boyfriends nor pregnancy could slow down May Fay who, pregnant at fifteen, was unsure whether she wanted to keep her first child. Her mother offered no guidance, other than to tell her that if she wanted to keep the child, she could keep the child, and if she wanted to abort the pregnancy, she would assist her in finding a doctor. "So I called the baby's father," May Fay said, "and talked about it, and he said he wanted the baby." So she had it.

Later, after all the Melton sisters became mothers of several children, May Fay and her sisters had their mother watch the children so they could go out. "Every time everybody go somewhere," May Fay said, "it's 'Mom come keep the kids.' "

I asked May Fay whether she wondered whether her mother was reluctant to tell her what to do when she first became pregnant because Josephine was afraid that May Fay might get angry at her and run away. Josephine's daughters knew the story of her growing up and knew of the strain between their mother and their seldom-seen grandmother, who had remained in Chicago. They understood that their mother needed them. She needed them close by, and she needed them to need her, if only to watch the growing number of grandchildren. And if the sisters ignored their mother when she told them that they needed to find places of their own, or that they had too many men, and too many friends staying with them, they nonetheless made sure to call and, as May Fay said, "to tell her I love her." The Melton sisters had experimented with lives lived apart from their mother. They left her home and went to live with boyfriends or with the parents of the fathers of their children, or with friends or with each other. Each time they left, they stayed away for a year or two and then moved back to their mother. Even when they moved away, their mother came to see them. And they would call her, too.

"I think she needed us around by her not growing up with her momma," May Fay said. "Her kids was the next best thing. So she tried to keep all of us around. I had a friend, and there was nothing he wouldn't do for me. He tried to get me to move away from my family, always telling me they need things from me. I didn't listen to him. And when he wanted to move on the South Side, my momma said, 'No, you can't move to the South Side. He just want to get you away so he beat you.' I always listened to my momma when I should have been trying to make those decisions myself. If I moved to the South Side, I probably wouldn't have been in this situation. The house [on Keystone] wouldn't have been so crowded then, and if the police would have come up, then there wouldn't have been so many kids."

May Fay explained that had she moved to the South Side, she might have been a better parent because, she reasoned, the South Side, dangerous as it was, was not nearly as forbidding as the desolate West Side. "I probably would have been down a lot of times," May Fay said. "But I would have stuck with it." Instead, she stayed on the West Side, and when her mother warned her that there were too many people living in the house on North Keystone Avenue, she ignored her. "She said all the time, 'This is too much. You need to get your own place.' But me being the stubborn person that I was, I wouldn't listen."

Cassandra listened to her cousin's lament and, trying to steer May Fay toward her own path of redemption, said, "When she was twenty, whatever she would have wanted out of life, she could have gotten it. It's just the same as me when I was twenty-two. That was my goal in the world. I had to achieve something for my kids to see. My oldest girl can see: If mom and dad can do it, then I know I can do it."

May Fay and her sisters did not blame their mother for what had happened to them—for the loss of their children, or for not stopping them from having their children, or for not insisting that they not drop out of school, or for the fact that their lives in no way resembled that of their cousin Cassandra. Josephine Melton had no reason to fear losing the affection of her daughter had she insisted, when May Fay was fifteen, that her child was too young to become a mother.

"I wouldn't have left her," May Fay said, "regardless of what she said."

I asked Josephine whether she ever thought of telling her daughters that the time had come for them to live apart from her. She laughed and said, "I ain't said it yet. I thought about it." Then, thinking of her brother and sisters who had no time for her, she added, "We just didn't grow up like no sister and brother should, loving and caring and helping each other and being together. That's how they supposed to grow up."

When her daughters began having their babies, Josephine taught them what she knew. "Feeding and clothing and talking to a baby. She told me everything," Maxine said. "How to hold a baby when you feed him. When to give them a bath and stuff like that. The right temperature for shampooing and all that. I'd ask, 'Why is he crying?' And she'd say, 'He want a bottle' or 'Change him.' "

I once asked May Fay whether her older children ever told her what they wanted to be.

"My oldest girl says she wants to be a lawyer so she can take care of me when I get older and can't take care of myself," she said. "Leon doesn't really say what he wants to be. He just wants to be able to take care of me when I get older."

As She Found Them

In OCTOBER OF 1994, a few days after Cassandra Henderson Melton testified on her cousins' behalf, the Art Institute of Chicago hosted a series of talks on the status of poor children. Anne Burke, Governor Edgar's special counsel, spoke about the responsibilities of government and communities in caring for children. Judge William Maddux, who had grown up in Boys Town and who was now the supervisor of the Cook County Juvenile Court, spoke about the nation's first juvenile court—an institution whose critics wanted to abolish it for, among other offenses, the leniency they insisted it extended to murderers who were not yet fourteen years old. There was also a play about Jane Addams.

Almost sixty years after her death, Addams had achieved a status approaching sainthood in Chicago, primarily for her forty years of work among the poor at Hull-House. More than anyone who came before her and more than many who followed, Addams understood the poor and their children, who they were and, most importantly, what poor individuals and poor families needed. Addams recognized, in a way that Charles Loring Brace did not, that there was no helping the poor without a relationship with them. For Addams this relationship was similar to, but involved greater compassion than, the one that existed in towns and villages across the country in pre-Jacksonian America. Brace may have believed the orphan trains were more humane than the orphanage. But because Brace regarded the

148

poor not as people but as categories—worthless parents; salvageable children—his approach assumed, as most zealous endeavors do, that what worked for some surely had to work for all.

Addams and the settlement house movement's encounter with the poor began with nothing more complicated than listening to them— if only to hear what they might say about the particular circumstances of their lives.

The play, commissioned for the Art Institute talks and so a celebration of her legacy, nonetheless succeeded in portraying Addams without resorting to hagiography. This was important; it would have been hard to imagine Hull-House working had its neighbors been forced to endure a relationship with a deity. Addams, by her own admission, could be difficult. She suffered bouts of melancholia. She doubted herself. She was often ill when she was young and was sensitive about it; her back was so badly misshapen that as a child she worried that the mere sight of her would embarrass her father if they were seen together. She was a sad child, she wrote in the first volume of her autobiography, *Twenty Years at Hull-House*, whose "happy busy mother" wondered why she was not "a very happy girl," given the advantages of a prosperous home. "The mother," Addams wrote, "did not dream of the sting her words left. . . ."

Addams studied medicine in Philadelphia but was forced to withdraw when her spinal ailment worsened. She spent six months on her back in a bed in her sister's home, delighted to be reading Carlyle and not, she wrote, Gray's *Anatomy*. The life of the mind, however, felt altogether too rarified. Battling what she called "nervous exhaustion" and seeking a place where she might do something with herself and not merely contemplate what she might do, she left for two years in Europe. There, on a bus ride through London's blighted East End, she had her epiphany. Years later she would recall that of all the many haunting sights of the place, the enduring image was of the hands— "empty, pathetic, nerveless and workworn . . . clutching forward for food which was already unfit to eat." She traveled on, visiting Rome, the Riviera, all the while devising a plan.

"I gradually became convinced that it would be a good thing to rent a house in a part of the city where many primitive and actual needs are found," she wrote. She took as her model Toynbee Hall, the East End residence where a group of Oxford men, inspired by the writings of Ruskin and William Morris, worked and lived among the poor. She shared the plan with her friend and traveling companion Ellen Starr. She returned to the East End and Toynbee Hall. In January of 1889 both women, now back in Chicago, set about looking for the place of Addams's dream. They settled on a large, vacant house in the slums on South Halsted Street. They kept the name of the house's original owner, Charles Hull, and nine months later moved in.

Addams spent the rest of her life living in that Victorian house on the corner of Halsted and Polk Streets. She lived among people she liked, and people for whom she had little patience—she could be particularly astringent on the habits of Italian immigrants—but for whom she was and remained a neighbor. Addams recognized that she was not merely another person on the block who, with her degree and background and growing staff, might know a bit about making do. She had a mission, and the mission was to elevate lives that, in the most elemental way, she accepted as she found.

—→ Her idea was simply to make herself and her house available. People came and if they needed, they stayed or they ate. She did not dictate a method for assistance. Rather she reacted to what she saw. Hull-House and the growing settlement house movement attracted a staff of women much like Addams herself, middle-class, educated, and searching for a role. "They must be content to live quietly side by side with their neighbors, until they grow into a sense of relationship and mutual interests," she wrote. She did not want her people coming to Hull-House with a philosophy to impose. "The one thing to be dreaded in the Settlement is that it lose its flexibility, its power of quick adaptation, its readiness to change its methods as its environment may demand."

Addams filled her autobiography, as Brace had done in his, with story after story of the people she met. Yet the stories served entirely different purposes. Where Brace used his to justify the urgency of his mission—this is the child in need; this is the failed parent; the recourse for the child is clear—Addams offered her anecdotes as evidence of the variety and complexity of the lives of the poor and of the many different sorts of help they needed. She wrote of women "bearing the burden of dissolute and incompetent husbands" who left them with the children and little else but whom the women would nonetheless forgive, sober up, dress, and feed when they returned. She did not judge the women harshly, only to write that "some of them presented an impressive manifestation of that miracle of affection which outlives abuse, neglect and crime. . . ."

She was accepting, too, of the abandoned or widowed women with children too young to be left alone when their mothers were forced to go to work. She recalled one such mother whom she met late at night on her knees scrubbing the marble tiling at the board of education. When the woman rose, Addams saw that the front of her dress was soaked. "She left home at five o'clock every night and [had] no opportunity for six hours to nurse her baby. Her mother's milk mingled with the very water with which she scrubbed the floor until she should return at midnight, heated and exhausted, to feed her screaming child with what remained within her breasts."

She saw the children, too. They began appearing at the Hull-House door during the settlement's first summer, she wrote, searching for a cool place on a hot day. She met children who had been crippled in falls, or burned when they were left alone. She recalled one who suffered from curvature of the spine because his mother, fearful of what might happen if he was left unfettered, tied him each morning to a table leg, there to be fed at lunch by his older brother, on break from the factory. "We kept them there and fed them at noon," she wrote. In return they would offer the pennies their mothers had given them in the morning for lunch, before their mothers went to work. She recalled how warm the pennies felt after being gripped in a child's hand all morning. The children sometimes stayed for naps. The casually supervised naps gave way to beds in a nearby apartment, which eventually gave way to a day nursery that Hull-House operated for sixteen years until a large charity opened a home on South Halsted Street for immigrant women and their children.

Compared to Brace's writing, Addams's is unsentimental. That was a gift. By portraying her characters as more than people caught in confounding circumstances, she allowed little room for judgment. The mission at Hull-House was utilitarian. "We early found ourselves spending many hours in efforts to secure support for deserted women, insurance for bewildered widows, damages for injured operators, furniture from the clutches of the installment store." Hull-

House, she wrote, was a go-between for its neighbors and the "hospitals, the county agencies, and State asylums [that] are often but vague rumors to the people who need them most." She envisioned the settlement as something akin to "the big brother whose mere presence on the playground protects the little one from the bullies."

The settlement house movement expanded its advocacy role after the depression of 1893, when those who had been content to take their cues from their neighbors became social reformers as well: The need was too great to ignore the forces that made people poor or the problems so many newly poor people shared. For her part Addams was not, strictly speaking, a visionary, wrote one of her biographers, Daniel Levine, in *Jane Addams and the Liberal Tradition*. She borrowed from the ideas of the times, whether those of E. Stanley Hall on the development of children or those of John Dewey on a progressive view of education fitted for the child and the place. When she saw that working mothers in her neighborhood needed a place to leave their children, she created not only a kindergarten at Hull-House but, in time, a role for herself in the growing kindergarten movement. Hull-House became an amalgam of programs and clubs, each suited for a group or need.

Inevitably, she made enemies. She angered local politicians when she would not support them or when she suggested that the simple act of paving a street was an excerise in corruption. Still, in the years before World War I, Addams was often chosen in public opinion surveys as the most admired woman in the country and, at times, as the most admired American.

———

For all that Addams was celebrated, for all the many other settlement houses across the country that followed Hull-House, for all of Addams's acolytes who later played roles in shaping New Deal policy for the poor (Harry Hopkins and Frances Perkins both worked in settlement houses) and despite Addams's lasting reputation for selflessness, her movement failed to transform the state's relationship with the poor. The principles that guided her movement endure. But they are generally seen only in the occasional, isolated social service program that seeks to recapture the intimacy between worker and client that Hull-House achieved on South Halsted Street. These efforts take place on the periphery of the child welfare system, where the vastness and distance of the bureaucracy brings to mind the numbing, bell-driven mechanism of the nineteenth-century orphanage.

Addams's approach was based on the belief that there was no way of determining the resolution of a poor person's plight until the details of that plight were understood by those offering to help. The uncertainty inherent in that approach and in Addams's insistence that her workers carry out their work without a philosophy to impose proved discomforting, especially to the men who wrote Hull-House's checks. By the 1920s, a generation after Addams first opened Hull-House, the settlements were falling out of fashion. Although more and more public money was being spent on poor families and children, the private money that had helped support the settlements came from community chests. Those chests, argues Walter Trattner in *From Poor Law to Welfare State,* were controlled by bankers, politicians, and businessmen who preferred safer enterprises than the increasingly suspicious settlements. Hull-House itself had already been branded a hotbed of anarchism for Addams's criticism of the incommunicado detention of President William McKinley's assassin. Her embrace of immigrants who made up so many of Chicago's poor and her refusal after World War I to join in curbing immigration made her and her movement the object of growing suspicion, especially with the rise of Bolshevism. These, at least, were the ostensible reasons for cutting funds for assistance that, in the minds of most everyone but Addams and her disciples, was always less about compassion than about keeping undesirables at bay.

Addams did share a Nobel Prize in 1931. When Edmund Wilson came to visit a year later in the midst of The Great Depression, he found Addams absent—she was then seventy-two and had been advised by her doctors to work only four hours a day. Wilson's story was a bouquet to Addams. Yet as he walked through the great Victorian house, he found it difficult to escape both Addams's unseen presence, and the obsolescence of the institution she had created. Hull-House, he wrote, was "planted with a proud irrelevance in the midst of those long dark streets."

Rather than accepting, as Addams had, the inevitable and frustrating clutter of the lives of the poor, the state gravitated in the early twentieth century, as it has historically, toward simplicity and rigidity. This came even as it embraced new thinking on what was best for children. The turn of the century brought what the social historian Viviana Zelizer has called the "sacralization" of children: As child labor came increasingly under attack and as more states made the practice illegal, children were no longer viewed merely as income-producing entities. Instead they became sentimental innocents, a view bolstered by such early child psychologists as E. Stanley Hall, who argued that children were not miniature adults, as was long believed, but a category unto themselves, who came of age in distinct and identifiable stages.

This embrace of children coincided with the elevation of their mothers, whose value as parents rose at the expense of their long-powerful husbands. With the growing acceptance of Victorian England's "cult of motherhood" came the desire to see children kept at home, to be reared by their mothers. In 1909, the first White House Conference on Dependent Children—the culmination of a movement on behalf of children and their mothers that had been growing since the turn of the century—concluded with a call reaffirming the belief that a child's place was at home. If that was not possible, the child should be placed in a close approximation, a suitable foster home.

It was understood that some mothers needed more money than they had if they wanted to keep their children at home, if only so that they would not have to leave them alone to go to work. This was considered wise, so long as the mothers were considered "worthy." The idea of worthiness has troubled many historians who have argued that the condition of worthiness meant excluding women who were, say, morally suspect because after their husbands abandoned them, they took up with someone new. Drinking was a sign of unworthiness; so too was failing to send children to school because as children stopped going off to work, it was accepted as imperative that they go to school. There was, however, a growing sentiment against people losing their children merely because they were poor. State after state passed laws offering mothers' pensions. The money, however, came with strings attached: In order to ensure that public monies were indeed going only to the truly deserving, local governments screened and in many cases continued to supervise the recipients. Absent a monitor, the poor could not be trusted with the money they were given to help them rear their children.

Financial relief was criticized by some as simply a way to keep women at home and by others, especially the large charitable organizations, as establishing a dangerous precedent in turning assistance into an entitlement. There was some justification for this argument: Mother's pensions did evolve into Aid to Dependent Children, which in 1935 became Aid for Families with Dependent Children, an entitlement that endured until 1996, when President Bill Clinton signed into law massive welfare reform.

The state did attempt to collect money from missing fathers; but that was as difficult to accomplish then as it is today. Although a woman may have been widowed or abandoned, if she did not qualify for a pension, she had to work. And that might well have meant leaving the children unattended. That, in turn, brought the family to the attention of the private child protection agencies who, beginning in the late nineteenth century, started dispatching agents to poor neighborhoods in search of children in need. Those agents were later replaced by the agents of the state.

Then, as now, the state proceeded at cross-purposes. Its stated desire may have been to keep children at home, and it may have been willing to help poor women keep their children. But only up to a point. Children in poor and morally suspect homes were not believed to be best off with their mothers. Quite the opposite. They were best off far away from their mothers, just as Brace had argued half a century earlier. Yet for all of Brace's hope of replacing institutions as the repository of children with what later became known as foster homes, orphanages remained the place where the state put poor and abandoned children. As late as 1923, the Census Bureau reported that almost two-thirds of all dependent and neglected children lived in orphanages. There were simply not enough foster care beds, nor was the state willing to spend enough money to pay foster parents, despite warnings that people would not necessarily take the children for free.

Increasingly, however, the orphanages were public institutions, as local governments beginning with Indiana in 1891 began establishing county child welfare boards. The number of children in public institutions doubled from 10 to roughly 20 percent just in the four years from 1900 and 1904.

———

At the same time, the work of attending to the poor had also changed, shifting from the intimacy of the settlement to the more "professional" approach of what was being called "social work." By the 1920s the term had entered the lexicon of a field filled with people who no longer wished to be regarded as charity workers, or "friends," or as well-educated do-gooders who spent two or three years living among the poor. They wanted themselves and their field to become professionalized. They found a scientific basis for their work in the data on the poor that had been compiled for years at the settlements and which provided the basis for writing and thinking at the new schools of social research. The dawn of the age of the social worker coincided as well with the growing interest in the writings of Sigmund Freud. This, in turn, led to the creation of an even more elevated subset of social work—the psychiatric social worker.

Social workers had a bible of sorts, Mary Richmond's five-hundred-page *Social Diagnosis*. Richmond, who believed that the causes of poverty had less to do with individuals than with the places where they lived, wrote a guidebook for identifying the problems that social workers could expect to encounter in their work. Richmond died before she could complete a companion book, detailing the solutions for these many problems. She called her approach "casework"; it endures today as the most frequently used approach in meeting and attempting to help people in need, be they families, children, or the elderly.

"I Thought I Was Doing Fine"

ONE BY ONE Judge Kawamoto remanded the Melton children to the custody of the state. She ordered only one termination of parental rights. That was for Diane, who altogether had seven children. Four were taken in 1989 after one of them tested positive for cocaine at birth. The police took two more from Maxine's house. The state took the daughter born the night the police took the other children. Diane had been in rehab at Cook County Jail but was thrown out after a day. In February, a year after the police took the children from North Keystone Avenue, Diane gave birth to her eighth child, a daughter. She too was born with cocaine in her blood. The state took the baby away at the hospital, where Diane had checked in under an assumed name.

For the other sisters, however, Judge Kawamoto kept open the possibility of reunification—even for Cassandra Melton, who was twenty-one and in jail for violating the terms of her criminal court probation by missing mandatory parenting classes. Yet many people who worked in child welfare doubted the Melton sisters would ever get their children back. Among them was Bernardine Dorhn, a notorious student radical in the 1960s who became director of the Children and Family Justice Center at Northwestern University Law School. Dorhn said that because there had been so much attention given to the case, the state would have to be absolutely sure that the children were returning to homes where there was no possibility of backsliding. While that seemed a reasonable goal, realizing it was unlikely, said Jess McDonald.

The problem with child welfare, he explained, was that it was easy to know when something *was* very wrong—say, a beaten or cocaine-addicted child—and impossible to predict when things *might* go wrong. But that was just what his department was being asked to do: make failed mothers into mothers who would not turn around and again do the things that hurt their children. Keeping the Melton children away from their mothers was the safe course, except that it assumed that the children would remain in their present foster homes for the duration of their childhoods. That was unlikely.

"Very few kids are going home," said Robert Mindell, who worked in Governor Edgar's office on child welfare issues. "The main problem is that the back door is closed. People are afraid to send children home." The messier things got, the longer children stayed away. The children "bonded" with their foster parents, or so caseworkers told judges as justification for awarding them permanent custody. Mothers found the jobs and homes required of them and completed rehab and parenting classes and then, say, missed an appointment downtown with their caseworker, who then told the judge that the client had been insufficiently cooperative and was not ready to regain her children. "Once you're gone for a year or two, a new set of conditions gets thrown into play," said Bernardine Dorhn, whose work included defending mothers who had lost their children to the state. "Life is different for the mothers and their children. If the children have bounced around to four placements and if the mom lost her apartment or had another baby, everyone comes back to the reunion in different shape. The cost paid by the family and children is so high that it's unlikely they'll ever heal. It's a fairly hollow victory."

Mothers became discouraged and gave up, or started smoking crack again and disappeared for weeks at a time. While the caseworker might have wanted to recommend terminating her parental rights, she knew that the foster parents did not much want the children either. The caseworkers wanted to resolve cases—to return the kids or keep the kids, one way or the other. So too did their supervisors, and the juvenile court judges and the legislators who enacted laws and regulations intended to create a glide path toward clear and final resolutions on the fate of children for whom the state was responsible. But no legal remedy or departmental directive had accomplished the task.

In the early winter of 1995, a year after the police took their children, Maxine, May Fay, and Denise were proceeding in the belief they were doing what was expected of them and assumed that this would mean they would get their children back. Denise was especially determined.

One day, shortly after Judge Kawamoto issued her decision, I met Denise in the office of her lawyer, whom she consulted in whispers about questions she was unsure how to answer. Sometimes Denise simply looked at me, rolled her eyes, and stared. She would soon be released from the residential drug treatment center where she lived. She had come to like her life there. She had many chores, she said, such as cooking, washing, and cleaning floors. "I already know what's my job function," she said. "And I just get up and do it." Denise felt motivated. She did not need people to tell her what to do. She believed she was gaining the skills that would help her find her first job. She once tried to find a job at a Wendy's, she explained; but the friend who was supposed to help her get the job did not call when she said she would call, and the job did not work out. "Right now, I'll take any job that's offered me," Denise said, "cooking, cleaning, doing laundry. I'll have a job where I can support my children a little better. Ain't gonna be waiting on welfare once a month."

Two of her children were living with cousins in a Chicago suburb. The third was with his paternal grandmother in a house with a pool in the back. Denise did not feel bad knowing her cousins' house had a big backyard and a bedroom for her children to share. "Right now, they think that's their home," she said. "They ask when am I coming home. I say, 'Yeah, I'm coming home soon.' That's where I want them to be till I get my life together; and when I get my life back together, they're going to come home and probably be in a better house than they is now."

Denise thought she had been a good mother, although, she said, perhaps she should not have gone out at night and come back the next morning and then gone out again the next night. She took her children to the park. She read to them. When her oldest daughter developed a rash on her scalp, she bought the medicated shampoo—she remembered the bottle; it was black and gold—and washed her daughter's hair even though the shampoo smelled bad. Her daughter, she said, used to follow her everywhere "like a shadow."

Now she saw her children every week and talked with them on the phone every other night. "They tell me how they be doing in school," she said. "We sing and we spell. Say ABCs and count over the phone. We always say we love each other." When Denise visited, the children showed her their new possessions, "all their books, their homework, and stuff. Their new coats." This did not sadden her, she said, because the children had had nice things like new winter coats before they were taken. On Keystone, they would wake her early in the morning. Her son would pull her head away from the pillow, and her daughter would kiss her on the forehead. "I thought I was doing fine," she said.

Nonetheless, she had learned that when her son came back from his grandmother's and ran around the house and tore things up, the appropriate response was to talk with him, "tell him he can't do this and he can't do that."

It was still difficult, however, for Denise to envision the future. She knew only that she wanted her children back and believed that she had only to complete "a couple of things" and then they would return. "I be ready," she said.

And what, I asked, would that new life be like?

"They living back home," she said. Then she paused. She thought for a while, and when she started again, she was still searching for an answer. "Love them more. Do nice things with them. That's about all I can think of."

———

Her mother, sisters, and cousin Cassandra were proud of Denise. One afternoon, at Cassandra Henderson Melton's house, Cassandra and May Fay, Maxine, and Josephine Melton sat at the dining room table, talking about Denise.

"When she get out, she gonna get a job at a restaurant," Josephine said.

"When I see my probation officer on the sixteenth, she should have mine lined up," said May Fay.

"I went down there yesterday," said Maxine. "It's a computer school. But see, these jobs ain't in Chicago. These jobs are out in the suburbs."

"I don't know nothing about no suburbs," said May Fay.

"Me, too," said Maxine.

"It ain't hard for me to learn as long as they teach how to get back and forth and don't just send me out there and leave me out there," May Fay said. She laughed nervously.

Cassandra turned to Maxine and asked, "Is it what you want?"

"I ain't got no type of income," Maxine replied. "But I refuse to get on public aid no more for nobody."

"There ain't nothing wrong with your working," said Josephine. "But there ain't nothing wrong with them helping you out too. You ain't gonna get a job right away to get your kids and take care of your kids by yourself."

"That's why I say, now that she's out and around doing nothing, get into a school," said Cassandra. "Why they hesitating? They know it's hard."

May Fay said, "I'm not hesitating."

"She's going to school," said Cassandra.

"I'm not hesitating," Maxine said.

May Fay said, "I go to school from Monday to Thursday from one fifteen to three o'clock. I ain't been the whole week. I don't know why. I just haven't. I just didn't get up to go."

"You can't be being lazy and get your kids back," her mother scolded her. "You always got to stay one step ahead of them. Do something on your own. Don't sit and wait for them to tell you what you got to do. You know what you got to do!"

"You got to stay two steps ahead of them," Cassandra said. "One ain't good enough. You got to learn to out-think them. When they call you back in court, there they are with their sheet saying, May Fay, she no good. You got to do it for yourself and for your children. Because what the man thinks about you ain't jack."

"You got to prove something for yourself," said Josephine.

May Fay listened without protest while her mother and cousin scolded her, and when they were finished, she lifted her bowed head and looked like a child about to cry.

Maxine said, "I did everything that I have to do. In two weeks I'm going down for a job."

"That's not what I'm saying," Cassandra said.

"I'm talking about as far as what I got to do," said Maxine.

"For *them*," said Cassandra. "But what does Maxine want?"

May Fay, who had pleased her cousin by returning to school, said, "She ain't as hard on me as she is on Maxine."

"I don't run her as hard as Maxine because Maxine is still full of joy," Cassandra said. "It's not to be mean. If I stay on you hard enough, then maybe you appreciate."

"But you shouldn't have to do that," said Josephine. "She got those boys out there that love her and need her. That should be enough. That would be good enough for me."

"It's kind [of] hard for an ex-convict to come out and try to get a job," Maxine said. "It's hard."

"And people spread you so much all over the news," said her mother, protectively.

"I'm not really hesitating about nothing," Maxine said.

"See, they've never really been outside by themselves without each other," Josephine said.

Cassandra, unmoved, would not let up on Maxine. "You keep saying that's the only thing you don't have."

"I'm talking about as far as what I got to do." Maxine said.

Maxine began to laugh. "You made me laugh," she told Cassandra.

"I think Maxine have a hard time expressing," said May Fay.

"Real hard," said Cassandra. "That's why I say she use the laugh to cover it up. See, Maxine ain't been where you been Fay. I haven't been where you been. Until she learn how to let go of all the joking, she'll be crying inside."

I asked Maxine whether she could do what she needed to do to get her sons back.

"Sometimes I have doubts that I can get them back," she replied. Then, she added, almost reflexively, "I got to do what I got to do to get them back."

May Fay began saying, "As long as I have faith . . ." and Cassandra, as if listening to her testify in church, called out "hello," instead of "amen."

"That's all it takes," said Josephine.

"Hello," boomed Cassandra. "Self-confidence in yourself."

But do they have that confidence? I asked.

"Fay do," Cassandra said. "Fay is a totally different person."

Getting Them Back

In the spring of 1995, a year after their first and what would be their only reunion, the Melton children were scattered. May Fay's third child joined two of her siblings in a foster home, after leaving her paternal grandmother's home. Cassandra's four children were split between a foster home and a paternal grandmother. Two of Denise's children remained with her cousin in the suburbs while the third was with a grandmother. Diane disappeared for weeks after the birth of her eighth child. Her oldest son was in a group home, which she did not visit. Five were with foster parents who wanted to adopt them. The other two were in foster homes with no assurances of adoption.

Maxine's sons lived with her godmother, Claudine Christian, in the countryside south of the city. They had been in three different foster homes until the private foster care agency prevailed upon Christian to take the boys. Maxine was pleased because her sons would no longer be split up.

"If I could take them back now, I'd take them back," Maxine said. "I need a house, money, some type of income. Before August, I should have my boys back."

Meanwhile, the boys got new clothes for school and clothes for church, and Christian had to remind them that dress-up clothes were for Sundays and not for playing outside. They lived in a house set on twenty-eight wooded acres. There were two geese, chickens, six cats, stray dogs, and a recent litter of thirteen pigs that the boys raced home from school to see born. The boys struggled to catch up in school, and when their mother came to visit, Christian reminded her to help the boys with their homework.

The children called Christian "momma," which is what they called Maxine, too. They were excited when Maxine came to visit, but did not ask about her in the weeks when she was gone. Maxine's godmother was unsure how long the state wanted her to keep the children. She had grown protective of them and was fearful that if they returned to the West Side of Chicago, they would slip back into the lives they led when they first came to her. She said, "The kids are part of me now."

Maxine's landlady was selling the house on North Keystone Avenue. A neighbor offered her $12,000, but she was holding out for $20,000. The house was empty. The front steps were gone, and the yellow curtain hung limply in the broken front window. Someone had scrawled over the doorway, "Heaven help us all."

I drove past Keystone one afternoon with Maxine and Josephine. They glanced at the house and then looked away and said nothing. We talked about Maxine's plans, and I asked whether she had thought of moving downstate, to be closer to her sons.

"I don't want to go there right now," she said. "I got things to do here. I don't have no way to take care of myself down there. I got to get myself a job."

Why not get a job there?

"That's something I didn't think about," she said.

Maxine had completed her parenting classes, but said she gained little from them. Mostly the women sat around and talked about their men.

Her sons, she said, were doing well. She was pleased that they were in school. They brought their problems to her. She wanted them with her, but, she said, she "thought all the time" about how, for the moment, they were perhaps best off where they were.

One afternoon, when I went to Cassandra Henderson Melton's house, I knocked and waited, but no one answered. It was cold and gray and beginning to snow, and finally Maxine came to the door. She wore laceless sneakers as slippers. She dragged her feet along the floor. Her thick black belt was open and dangling. Her face was covered with white cream.

She let me in and slumped in a heavy chair. We talked while May Fay and Cassandra watched a *Geraldo* segment about drug dealers. Maxine turned to the television and looked down, and when I asked whether this sadness was what she often felt when she lived with her sisters and the children on Keystone, she nodded yes, it was. Her sons needed her, she said, although their need could be overwhelming. I asked what she would do when the boys came home to her and she felt as low as she did right now. She looked down at the floor and, in a weary voice, asked, "What am I going to do when I get them back?"

THE LAFLAMMES, PART II

Angelica

An Appeal

A WEEK AFTER they surrendered Megan, Cindy and Jerry LaFlamme along with their new attorney, Barbara Ruhe, appeared on CNN's *Sonya Live*, a national television show. They were joined by Angelica Anaya-Allen, who spoke on behalf of Gina Pellegrino, who remained in hiding.

The LaFlammes told their side of the story, Anaya-Allen told Gina's very different side of the story, and Barbara Ruhe told how in her view Judge John Downey had misapplied the statutes and made "a terrible mistake." Anaya-Allen insisted that Downey's decision was "in the best interests of the child."

Jerry LaFlamme, who was uncharacteristically voluble, accused Gina of "going on welfare" and of growing up in a "welfare environment." Cindy took his hand. The host, Sonya Friedman, asked whether she was trying to calm him down. "No," Cindy said. "I took his hand to support him."

Anaya-Allen suggested that if the LaFlammes were going to malign her client, she could offer "information about them."

Friedman noted the threat of innuendo.

Anaya-Allen insisted that her client was a "hard-working young woman" who had quit her job and applied for public assistance "because she felt it was very important to spend that time bonding with her daughter, learning how to take care of her daughter, and making herself a full-time parent for her daughter from that point."

Jerry LaFlamme pressed on. He argued that the taxpayers of Connecticut would have had to pay nothing had the child been left with them. With Megan's removal, he said, the state now bore the cost of housing, feeding, and assisting both Gina and the child.

Anaya-Allen conceded as much. Gina, she said, was receiving "support services as a young mother taking care of her first child." Then, in a curious admission, she explained that Gina, "of course, is going to need to learn about being a parent, and she is receiving help with that process."

Friedman, a psychologist, asked Anaya-Allen whether she might recommend to her client that the LaFlammes be allowed to visit the child. Anaya-Allen replied that based upon "psychological advice" no such visits should take place so that "the child should spend her time bonding with her natural mother."

Friedman turned to Ruhe. She asked what the case meant for adoptive parents. Ruhe offered a nightmarish scenario. "What it means is that there's no finality. In Connecticut, at the moment, adoptive parents are frightened, the agencies are frightened, the Department of Children and Youth Services is very concerned, because what it says is that there is no end to a termination," she said. "Now we're being told that there is no end, and we're very concerned that birth parents will come back and say, 'Well, you know I forgot I had this baby' or 'I was being held hostage by gypsies' or 'For some reason I couldn't come to court.' "

———

In Barbara Ruhe the LaFlammes chose an attorney whose name evoked the raising of eyebrows and the weary sigh. Ruhe understood and to a certain degree reveled in the difficulty she caused people. She was an advocate, which was to say that she was less concerned with the details of statute than in what she believed to be the virtuous fight. This fight concerned the rights of adoptive parents and of children who became wards of the state. Ruhe and her husband were the parents of two adopted children.

Ruhe became a member of the Connecticut bar on the same day in 1976 as did Judge John Downey. She and her brother shared office space in downtown Hartford, close enough to see the dome of the state capitol. When she spoke about the LaFlammes and about her other cases that drew press attention, Ruhe did so with the sort of quiet intimacy that at times veered into folksiness, as if she could not imagine how it was that she, a "country lawyer," had found herself in the middle of all the fuss. Then she would offer an aside about how "bureaucrats respond to pressure," which served to bolster the reputation she wished to cultivate as a player of consequence.

"I remember Cindy's mom called me late in the afternoon and she started explaining this problem to me, and I just said to her mom, 'That makes no sense. That's impossible. That's insane,' " she said of the call she took the day before Megan's removal. "I tried desperately to piece it together. I couldn't even comprehend what had happened. I talked a little bit about it with my brother, and I thought about it that evening and called Cindy back early the next morning. I said, 'I thought about it. The whole thing makes no sense to me. Maybe the only thing you can do is go public. How do you feel about that?' Cindy said, 'The TV stations are already here.' When it started to go public, Bill Bloss [the LaFlammes' original attorney] was not comfortable with that. And he did not have some of the political connections that I did. I was known by various people in the legislature. I was sort of a known entity."

Ruhe's brother went to her house to pick up a dress because she had come to work dressed casually for what she assumed would be a holiday weekend and suddenly found herself preparing to go on camera. All press inquiries and interview requests were to go through her. On the day of Megan's removal Ruhe began explaining, in her practiced way, what was at stake in the issue of this child.

For Ruhe the "mess" had everything to do with fielding interview requests—"We had radio stations call. We had AP calling. We had the TV stations calling. They wanted to know what was going on. People started calling the governor and the attorney general." The case, in her view, was simplicity itself. "It was," she said, "about ownership of property." The property in question was the child, who in Ruhe's view was being treated as chattel.

Ruhe was a believer in the sanctity of the psychological bond and was quick to point out judges—John Downey among them—who honored blood as the primary bond between parent and child. She wanted the state to make termination of parental rights easier and more clearly defined, so much so that if a parent had, say, no contact with a child for sixty days, that alone was grounds for termination. She wanted the time period shortened during which drug-addicted, homeless, or out-of-work parents could show that they were able to take care of their children. And if they failed, she wanted the children taken away and given to someone else. "If the family is salvageable, you salvage, and if it ain't, you move the kid sooner," she said. "I truly believe there is a child for every family."

Ruhe was adept at the pithy sound bite and at infusing her views on the state of children and failing parents with great urgency. She possessed a flair for the dramatic statements that played well in print and on television. Of Megan growing up with Gina Pellegrino, she warned, "We're gonna wake up and she's gonna be dead."

It would be unfair to suggest that the angry mood that immediately followed Megan's removal was a result of Barbara Ruhe's distillation of the issues. Still, Ruhe wanted people to know what had happened to the LaFlammes—she would no doubt insist that the issue was not the LaFlammes, but the child—and to be upset. She was pleased that in the days that followed, callers jammed the telephone lines on radio talk shows, people began wearing little pink ribbons that read JUSTICE FOR MEGAN MARIE, and supporters of the LaFlammes began collecting signatures at shopping malls, insisting that the state attorney general appeal Judge Downey's ruling.

The pitch of the debate became so fevered that Gina Pellegrino's father issued a public call for restraint after his daughter, he claimed, received a death threat telephoned to the shelter where she had been living. Threats, he said, were also made against the lives of Angelica Anaya-Allen and Judge Downey. "All my daughter wants is to be left alone to raise her baby in peace," he said. Gina had moved out of the shelter to the home of a friend but moved back to the shelter, her parents told *The Hartford Courant*, after the death threat. Gina's mother insisted that in the week after Megan's removal, the family had received dozens of harassing phone calls. While Gina's parents were not prepared to take in their daughter and grandchild, they still rushed to Gina's defense. They argued, for instance, that the published report of Gina's arrest the year before for possession of a marijuana pipe and breach of the peace was the result of nothing more than a fight in her high school bathroom with a girl taunting Gina about her handicapped twin brother. "Somebody should have sympathy for Gina," pleaded her mother. "She has been crucified."

It was in the midst of this mood of accusation and of declarations of injustice—there were no public calls of sympathy for Gina Pellegrino just yet—that Linda Pearce Prestley, an assistant attorney general, took a call from her supervisor, Susan Pearlman, asking if she wanted to assist on the state's appeal of the case. Although the state had not initially intended to appeal Judge Downey's ruling, the attorney general, Richard Blumenthal, announced the week after Megan's removal that he would indeed appeal to the state supreme court and, in the meantime, would ask Downey to reconsider his decision.

"We will give the judge another opportunity to decide what's best for the child," he said. "Adoptive parents should not have to feel the kind of turmoil that's been in this case." Blumenthal also said that his office was supporting the LaFlammes in their appeal of Downey's ruling barring them from a role in the original trial. Blumenthal was joined in his appeal by the commissioner of the Department of Children and Youth Services, Rose Alma Senatore, who Blumenthal said ought to decide where Megan should live during the appeal.

Prestley remembered hearing about the case months before when Paul Bakulsky, who argued the state's case before Judge Downey, called for advice. She recalled thinking it "preposterous" that the birth mother could possibly regain the child but had learned no more about the matter until she heard reports of the child being taken from her home and word of all the petition signatures being delivered to the attorney general. She insisted that it was not the petition drive and angry editorials that prompted the appeal; rather, the decision reflected the attorney general's own view of the case.

The political and public relations considerations aside, Prestley and Pearlman recognized that their first and urgent task was to get Megan back from Gina. "Once we knew we were going to appeal, we knew we had to get that baby back with the LaFlammes," Prestley said. "It's possession. The baby needed to be with the people she was ultimately going to be with." So four days after Blumenthal filed his appeal, the state went before Judge Downey and asked him to reconsider his decision. The following day, July 15, Downey announced that his decision stood. Five days later, the attorney general asked the state appellate court for a stay of Downey's ruling, thereby providing the legal basis for taking Megan from Gina and, if the Department of Children and Youth Services saw fit, placing her back with the LaFlammes.

Meanwhile, Megan's life with Gina, in the department's view, was proceeding satisfactorily. The only moment of concern came the day after the removal, when a caseworker took a call from Marion Fay, Megan's law guardian, who on behalf of Angelica Anaya-Allen wanted to know why the LaFlammes had packed medicine in Megan's bag. The caseworker relayed a message from Cindy LaFlamme explaining that Megan had an ear infection. All parties were advised that Megan was running a temperature of 101.

The following week, the caseworker Jennifer Hauser went to see Gina and the child. She picked them up at the foster home where they lived. Gina asked if Hauser could drive her to Dunkin' Donuts, so that she could return her uniforms, now that she had stopped working. They talked about all the attention the case was receiving and how this had overwhelmed Gina. They talked about where Gina and the child should live. Gina said that her father wanted her to move back home, but Gina and Hauser agreed that considering how her parents' support of Gina had evaporated as the case wore on, it might be best for Gina and the child to stay where they were. Hauser noted in the case diary that in the home where she now lived, Gina and Megan had a room of their own. The woman in whose house they lived reported seeing the beginnings of a bond forming between them. Gina did not want the child to be called Megan anymore. Megan, she said, "was not the name for an Italian daughter." She renamed the child Angelica, after her lawyer.

Two days later, Hauser called the LaFlammes to see if they were well. She reminded them that the rules of confidentiality forbade them from discussing the case publicly. Hauser noted in her report that "Cindy did say they were still very upset about the loss of Megan and they miss her very much."

I asked Barbara Ruhe what she would have done had she been Cindy LaFlamme and been ordered to surrender her child. Ruhe said she would have fled the country rather than give her back. Ruhe's vision of fleeing notwithstanding, Linda Pearce Prestley was quick to point out that because the state at first had no intention of appealing Downey's ruling and because the LaFlammes had no legal standing, they had no reason to believe they had any choice but to surrender Megan.

Still, Cindy LaFlamme quickly came to see that she had been "grievously wrong." That, at least, was the way she put it in a deposition asking Judge Downey to reconsider his decision. The deposition was filed on July 7, less than a week after Megan's removal. Through the stilted wording of the document Cindy tried to explain why she had given up her child. She said that she had told the department's caseworkers that if the court ruled in Gina Pellegrino's favor, "my husband and I could not bear to act as mere foster parents." She went on to say that "that decision was made while we were under great stress." Cindy was concerned that Downey should not misinterpret what she told the caseworkers about her willingness to surrender the child immediately if the decision went against her and Jerry. Cindy assured Downey that she would allow Gina to visit Megan. She asked that she be allowed to come to court and offer evidence on her and Jerry's behalf. She admitted that she had made a "serious mistake." She said she could live with the uncertainty that she might, indeed, still lose her child.

In their depositions, the department's caseworkers took the LaFlammes' side. They had concluded, they said, that it would be best for Megan to be returned to the LaFlammes. The caseworkers confirmed Cindy's account of her decision to surrender Megan. If the LaFlammes were going to give her up, said the caseworkers in their depositions, the department would need a new home for Megan. And the department did not want her placed in foster care, which meant that the only other recourse was to place her with Gina Pellegrino.

Downey remained unswayed. The appellate court, however, was
—7 not. On July 20, the court granted the state's request for a stay of
Downey's decision. It ordered that the child be placed in the care of
the Department of Children and Youth Services. The department
was at liberty to choose where it thought she should live. Jennifer
Hauser called Cindy and Jerry LaFlamme and told them to prepare
for Megan's return. Jerry hurried out to buy juice.

The same day, the judiciary committee of the Connecticut legislature
held a day-long hearing to consider whether the state needed to reconsider its laws on adoption and termination of parental rights. The
call for hearings came from six Republican legislators who, as members of the minority, were eager to show that they were as sensitive
to the issue of children and adoptive parents as Richard Tulisano, the
Democratic chairman of the judiciary committee, who had already
announced that he wanted the state to clarify its law on termination.
"No one should be subjected to what this couple has been put
through," said the house Republican leader, Edward Krawiecki. Although he framed his appeal in terms of the LaFlammes' loss and
pain, he then added that it was, of course, essential that the laws "protect the best interests of the child."

The hearings, however, were a desultory affair. The LaFlammes attended but declined to testify because Judge Downey had forbidden
the parties to discuss the case and, as Cindy explained to a group of
reporters, she did not want "to say anything that might jeopardize our
chances." Cindy wore a pink JUSTICE FOR MEGAN MARIE ribbon on her
dress. She said she was "thrilled" that the legislators "recognize that
there is a problem here." As for the child, she said, "she's ours whether
we have her or not. In our hearts she will always be ours."

Angelica Anaya-Allen told the reporters that the anger directed at
her client was unfair and a result of ignorance of the details of the
case. "People should realize they do not know what a judge knows,"
she said. She explained, however, that because she too was under a
gag order she could not discuss those details. As for her client, she
said, she was "certainly capable of being a fit parent for her child, and
she does love her." She added that reports that Gina was homeless
and living in a shelter were "not necessarily correct."

The legislators had already conceded that there was nothing they could do to change the outcome of Megan's case, although that appeared to be the original intent. At least that is what the LaFlammes believed. The day after Megan's removal they took a call from Tulisano, who expressed sympathy—he too was an adoptive parent— and asked whether they kept records and notes of their case. Now, conceding that the legislature could offer no relief for the LaFlammes, Tulisano and the Republicans assumed the high ground and sought to ensure that no court could "jeopardize" future adoptions, "which is what seems to have happened."

The committee was left to hear testimony on the question of how long the state should wait before moving to terminate a parent's rights. Rose Alma Senatore, the commissioner of the Department of Children and Youth Services, told the legislators that to suspend judgment, to allow a failing parent to appeal beyond the statutory twenty days that Judge Downey initially applied to Gina Pellegrino was bad for children. "It is critical that there be a point in time where all parties can be assured of finality," she said, "and that the child's placement can be considered permanent." Her view was echoed by Richard Blumenthal and by Barbara Ruhe, who then took the argument a step further and asked the state to convene a special legislative session to reinforce the deadline provisions in the law as quickly as possible. Angelica Anaya-Allen, underscoring the legal reasoning behind Downey's decision, testified that courts should retain jurisdiction over children until their adoptions have been finalized. "If a parent decides they are able to care for their child," she said, "and it hasn't been adopted, they should be given a chance."

The committee recessed with the vague promise of future deliberations. The public debate, however, was altogether more acrimonious. *The Hartford Courant*, the state's leading paper, came out quickly and angrily on the side of the LaFlammes. In an editorial the paper argued that the best interests of the child were served by returning her to the LaFlammes. "The bonding that takes place between an infant and those who are its primary caregivers—whether natural or foster parents—is the foundation for a child's emotional life," the *Courant* declared. "Severing that bond produces deep scars." Conceding that Gina Pellegrino had a "need" to be reunited with her daughter, the *Courant* suggested that "there could have been ways, short of the emotional abuse involved in simply wrenching the child from the home she knew" to allow Gina to "come to terms with her loss." The *Courant* went on to insist that the state, as too often happened, placed the needs of adults above those of a child, resulting in a decision that "is nothing short of state-mandated child abuse."

The *Courant* was not alone in its denunciation of Downey's ruling. The Bristol *Press*'s editorial-page editor wrote of the moment that he became a parent, which was the moment a social worker handed his adopted son to his wife. "The judge," he wrote of Downey, "took Megan Marie from her real parents and gave her to somebody else. That may be legal. It *is* wrong."

The rage at Downey and sympathy for the LaFlammes, however, was soon matched by equally passionate arguments on behalf of women like Gina Pellegrino whom in the eyes of her supporters no court could deny the right to rear her child. The *Courant* devoted columns on its letters to the editor page arguing that the child's best interests could only be served by growing up with her biological mother.

"To separate Gina Pellegrino and her child condemns them both to a lifetime of pain and suffering," wrote the director of the Council for Equal Rights in Adoption, a New York–based agency that advocated on behalf of biological parents. "It would be child abuse to separate Pellegrino and her baby. . . . A couple suffering from the pain of infertility may believe that separating a mother and child answers their needs. They should consider the substantial pain created by separation for the child and the birth mother."

The arguments on both sides were predictable in their zealousness and, by extension, their utter conviction of certainty. There were frequent references made to "evidence" and "psychological" proofs to lend credence to calls for either keeping this child where she was or taking her away.

The presence of the zealots at the center of the story might have been tolerable had the details of the story been a matter of public record and had the story not been propelled by the enduring image of Megan being strapped into her car seat and driven away from the weeping LaFlammes. As it was in so many child welfare stories that became widely known and told, the central and defining event was the moment people learned that something bad appeared to have happened to a child, be it the news of Joseph Wallace's death, Ken Herzlich's footage of the removal of the Melton children, or the sight of a child like Megan Marie taken from "the only home she had known." That moment becomes the story, in the sense that there is a need to resolve that moment, to make it right or, at the very least, ensure that something just like it does not happen again. But in the view of Martin Guggenheim, of New York University Law School, the moment was deceptive.

For Guggenheim, the law and the courts had two responsibilities, only one of which the layman saw. The first was to rule in a particular case. The second was to "make law for the society" through those rulings and judgments. The latter, he explained, was the "policy" consideration, the implementation of statute that reflected the rules by which a society chooses to live. The layman, he argued, saw only the particular case before him. In Megan's case, Guggenheim said, "the moment looks ugliest, looks least acceptable when we identify with that parent who is losing a child. We identify with that moment: 'Whatever else you do, don't allow this relationship to be broken up.' If that's the concentrated moment, then every right-thinking person would say, That's wrong. But it's not the only moment. And if we don't enlarge our vision, we get a distorted picture."

By "enlarging" that vision, Guggenheim did not mean merely understanding more of the details preceding that moment. Rather he meant accepting that there were considerations essential to a society that were as crucial as that moment was painful. He went on. "The wise policy makers have to ask, 'What is good for children in the long run?' The question is, 'How can I do both well?' because if the rule always is anytime a child has been with a caregiver for a couple of days she must remain, that would have devastating consequences for our society. There are too many people who go into the hospital, who get ill, who have mental breakdowns, who need to be in rehab for drugs or alcohol whose children should be theirs."

Guggenheim has gained a national reputation for his work representing parents whose children the state has taken. These were the sorts of parents who either placed their children in the child welfare system or saw their children removed, and who then could not seem to get them back even when they believed they had satisfied the conditions set down by the state. Guggenheim was among those who saw the child welfare system as an institution that, even if not intentionally, nonetheless "placed obstacles in the path of poor people of color and of poor people generally that can be insurmountable." He railed against caseworkers who justified keeping his clients from their children with such vague but powerful pretexts as "not making the kinds of strides" the worker wanted to see or because those clients were "unable to manage." To the bureaucrats of the system, Guggenheim insisted, his clients were "unworthy." "There's an understanding in this system that the clients are failures," he said. "That is what clients deal with every day of their lives. My clients are always treated badly by everybody."

It was not surprising then that Guggenheim was sympathetic to the appeal of a young mother who lost her child to the child welfare system. But in the case of Gina Pellegrino, Guggenheim's interest had nothing to do with whether or not the Department of Children and Youth Services had somehow frightened Gina when she made her first calls to the hospital in the days after she abandoned her daughter. Rather it had to do with what he believed was the bond that still existed between Gina and the child. It was the same bond that existed between his clients and the children he worked to win back for them.

"I don't care how much we protest to the contrary, the norm remains that the best deal for kids is 'My mom and dad are my biological mom and dad,' " he said. "Because, rhetoric not withstanding, the most basic parent-child relationship is the biological. And however much we pretend to the contrary—and I am an adoptive parent—we attach stigma to all other relationships. And we have enough data to suggest that children raised by non–birth parents have more to overcome. All I'm saying is that all things being equal, birth parents are the best resource for children."

As for cases such as Megan's, he said, "sometimes what's good is that the birth parent, who in the post-birth trauma abandoned her child, is the best resource for that child if we can reunite them."

For Guggenheim what happened in this case was essentially what happened in the child welfare system over and over. "We tolerate separating children from caregivers all the time," he said. "We do it when a woman goes into the hospital and says to her sister, Take care of my children for me. We do it in a thousand ways. Poor people do it by going to foster care. We do that a thousand times a year in this city,

and all of us say that's just right. What's different about the Connecticut case? Nothing, on the child's perspective. Nothing on the
Goldstein, Freud, and Solnit notion [of the "best interests of the
child"]. What's the difference? The expectation of the LaFlammes."

He continued. "Were Gina to have given birth thirty miles further
to the west across the border in New York, here is what would have
happened: By law, the child could not have gone into an adoptive
home before six months expired because you can't abandon your
child in New York until you have abandoned your child for six
months. It's just a matter of definition. So what happens to children
left in hospitals in New York State is that they enter foster care for six
months. At the end of that period, rights are terminated. In New York
Gina shows up after four months and she gets her child with a rose
and a hug and goes home with her. And everybody says that the caregiver raising the baby during that time was a good egg doing a good
civic duty."

But who was to know the relationship was finite? I asked.

"If not finite," Guggenheim said, then with "no promises. Take care
of the baby. If mom appears, you did your good deed and now we are
restoring the baby to her rightful nest. So my point is, Was this a story
about a child going to live with parents who would keep her for the
rest of her life? No. If we say it that way, then it's a tragedy."

But the LaFlammes believed, I reminded him—because the state
assured them that they could believe—that the child would be their
child forever.

"Maybe the solution in this case is there should be a cause and action
against the state for pain and suffering," Guggenheim said. "So sue."

But this story had not taken place in New York. It took place in
Connecticut, where the laws on abandonment and the procedures on
termination were different. Guggenheim's point was not to compare
one state's practice with another. Rather, it was to underscore the
idea that in the hierarchy of claims to a child, the first claim belongs
to the biological parent, a bond severed when the child was placed in
the arms of an adoptive parent, and at that moment—and not after
additional screening and bureaucratic review—was made the child of
someone else.

"The question we have to ask is, How much tolerance do we have
for birth parents to make a mistake, to be unsure?" he said. "We rec-

ognize that social engineering is extremely dangerous. We don't perceive ourselves as social engineers when we reconnect birth children and birth parents. When we do something else, we are engineers. Justifying the refusal of a mother to have her baby is much more difficult than justifying the result that says, I'm putting these people back together.

"I think there's something deeper to it. Even as an adoptive parent I do. Not that I love my birth child more than I loved my adopted children. I don't. I know I don't. But I'm also keenly aware that I have the privilege to raise somebody else's child. I didn't need anybody's help to raise my birth child other than God's help. And that's different. So I don't ignore the fact that when Gina gets her child, all the judge is doing is reinstating something. He's not creating something. He's not breaking something."

———

After the Connecticut Appellate Court issued its order staying Judge Downey's initial ruling and ordered that the child be placed in the care of the Department of Children and Family Services, the caseworkers and assistant attorneys general met to discuss their course of action. The department decided to place the child back with the LaFlammes that day. As a courtesy, they called Angelica Anaya-Allen to tell her of the plan to go to Gina's home for the child. Perhaps, the caseworkers suggested, Anaya-Allen would like to meet them there, to assist Gina in what would doubtless be an agonizing moment.

Anaya-Allen asked the department to fax a letter to her, detailing the plan. A caseworker then called Anaya-Allen back. Anaya-Allen said that Gina had gone shopping. She said she would call when Gina came home. "In the meantime," the caseworker noted in her file, "Cindy and Jerry LaFlamme were anxiously awaiting the return of the child."

The caseworkers waited for Anaya-Allen's call. It did not come. Several hours later they learned that Anaya-Allen had filed her own appeal, asking the appellate court to keep the child where she was. The court granted her request. The caseworker was left to call the LaFlammes and tell them that Megan was not coming back to them after all.

Speaking for the Child

O N AUGUST 5, 1992, just over a month after the LaFlammes surrendered Megan, the lawyers for the parties gathered once again before Judge Downey, this time to argue whether or not the LaFlammes
should be allowed to visit the child during the appeal. When he issued his ruling the month before, Downey ordered that no visitations
take place for the first forty-five days of Megan's life with Gina, so
that mother and child might have the chance to bond without interference. Now that the period was ending, the Department of Children and Youth Services, along with the attorney general's office and
Barbara Ruhe, came to court to argue that it was in the child's best interests to be allowed to see the LaFlammes, so that if their appeal
succeeded, she would be returned to the home of people who had
not become strangers to her.

Angelica Anaya-Allen disagreed. Having secured the child in
Gina's home during the appeal, Anaya-Allen argued that mother and
child should be left alone. She was joined by Marion Fay, who, along
with Sara Martin, was the attorney for the child. Fay and Martin
based their objection to visitation by the LaFlammes on Cindy and
Jerry's willingness to surrender Megan in the first place. That decision, they insisted, suggested something less than a passionate commitment to the child they claimed they loved. Fay, who had agreed
with Downey's original decision terminating the then-unknown Gina

Pellegrino's parental rights, changed her mind after Gina appeared. Now, as the lead attorney for the child, she was lockstep with Anaya-Allen in her opposition to any role for the LaFlammes in the child's life. In fact, so adamant were Fay and Martin in their belief that the child was best served by being left undisturbed where she was, that they joined Anaya-Allen in fighting to keep the state from producing its star witness in the visitation hearings, Albert Solnit, the commissioner of the Department of Mental Health, the co-author of the *Best Interests of the Child* trilogy, and a leading exponent of the psychological bonding theory.

Albert Solnit was then a few weeks shy of his seventy-fourth birthday. Despite his stature and reputation, he was adept at putting people at ease. His office at the Yale Child Study Center was covered with art and tapestries he had collected from his travels. He had a shock of white hair and remained trim and hardy. He was given to wearing bolo ties. Later, when we talked about the case, Solnit made it clear that he did not believe the child should ever have been taken from the LaFlammes. Megan, he said, saw the LaFlammes as her parents and nothing in their behavior suggested that they posed any threat to her. That, in essence, was the beginning and end of the discussion of placement.

"By the time Gina reentered the picture after four months with the LaFlammes, at that point it was too late for Gina," he said. "Putting away the state's deadlines, developmentally, once you've had a child for four months, it's too late. The child has begun in the first two or three months to adapt, and to be adapted to—what we call 'mutuality.' And they have begun to form an attachment, a relationship that is built out of day to day practicing in how to get along." Solnit then spoke of the risk a child faced. "This risk is that the match of the baby to the biological mother coming on the scene will not be as good, and that that mother is going to need several months to reattach. We're talking about doing the same thing all over again. And I don't think it's fair."

In late July, Rose Alma Senatore, the department's commissioner, sent the department reports on the case to Solnit and asked that as commissioner of the Department of Mental Health he offer an opinion. Not surprisingly, Solnit wrote that the child should not have been taken from the LaFlammes: "Whatever weight, rational or mystical, is given to the blood tie, the removal of Baby B from the only primary parents she has ever had, her adoptive parents, is a demonstration of the State using its power to the disadvantage of an infant in order to alleviate the discomfort of many of our courts when they must decide to terminate parental rights." He went on to cite the words of Richard Blumenthal, the attorney general, who had told the legislature's judiciary committee that "many judges have told me that they more easily impose a life sentence on a criminal than terminate a parent's rights." The child, Solnit concluded, "requires that the State return her permanently to her adoptive parents before her relationship with them [essential for her healthy development] is so badly fractured that there is a risk of irreversibly damaging Baby B emotionally and psychologically."

Solnit started off badly in court. On the day he was called to testify Solnit arrived early at Judge Downey's courtroom. He took a seat in the back and started to read his newspaper. Because family court is almost always closed to the public and because witnesses are not allowed to be in court unless they are testifying, Downey looked across his courtroom and angrily scolded the man in the back reading the paper. No one read newspapers in his courtroom, Downey snapped. He demanded to know who Solnit was. Solnit identified himself. Downey ordered him out.

Before Solnit would be allowed to testify, Anaya-Allen and the attorneys for the child began their attack on his presence as a witness. The issue was not the letter to Senatore. Rather, they argued that because Solnit kept an office at the Child Study Center, and because the Child Study Center had issued a report on its evaluation of Gina, the LaFlammes, and their relationship with the child, Solnit's testimony would be tainted by his inevitable knowledge of that report. Presumably, only Downey knew the report's critical conclusions about Gina, and its support of the LaFlammes as the child's psychological parents, because Downey sealed the report after reading it. Still, the knowledge of the report's contents, the attorneys argued, could not help but sway Solnit's otherwise expert view on the wisdom of visitation.

Anaya-Allen, who coincidentally was a distant relative of Solnit's, had every reason to keep him from testifying: Here, after all, was one of the framers of the idea that disruptions in a child's life and in a child's relationship with her psychological parent be kept to a minimum. But Fay and Martin were assigned by the court to represent the child. Surely, I assumed, they would at the very least want to hear what a witness and expert of Solnit's stature had to say. Perhaps his testimony might be of use in serving their client, the child. But that would have meant that Fay and Martin felt they needed to hear and learn more before deciding how best to represent the child. Their written arguments, however, suggested they did not.

In a brief submitted to the appellate court arguing against allowing the department to take the child from Gina, they argued quite broadly that the LaFlammes desire to regain Megan may not have been merely a matter of the heart.

"The LaFlammes reportedly realized one day after the child was returned to her mother that they had a tremendous bond with the child," they wrote. "This realization coincided with an unprecedented onslaught of publicity, promulgated by the television crews waiting outside the LaFlammes' house at the time the baby was picked up by DCYS." Even if the LaFlammes were to regain Megan, an adoption would come "despite her attachment to the loving, capable and caring woman who gave her life and shares her blood."

Neither attorney would speak to me about the case. I was left to speculate not only about how they had come to the conclusion they reached, but how they viewed their job as the attorneys for the child. I was, however, able to learn something of Fay, her work and her reputation, from Robert Solomon, a professor at Yale Law School. As it happened, Solomon had written a paper on representing children in light of Megan's case. It was a subject with which he was familiar in his work at the school's law clinic. His interest in the case, and his work on the paper, Solomon explained, was prompted by questions raised over whether Marion Fay had represented Megan well.

Over lunch in a New Haven sandwich shop, Solomon told me that Fay "was not the worst" lawyer representing children. "She does something for her clients," he said, "as opposed to people who do nothing." She was, at the very least, light-years ahead of one lawyer who, Solomon said, was so profoundly uninterested in his client that he called her on the phone and asked to talk but, having never bothered to read the case file, did not know that his client was deaf and mute.

Marion Fay, he said, had been a social worker before entering the University of Bridgeport's law school. This suggested to Solomon that Fay possessed both good intentions, as well as a hunch that she "knew" what was best for her clients. This troubled him.

"My sense of her is that she spends time on the cases and some people do not. But she does so largely from a social work aspect and not from the aspect that she has a client she is representing," he said. "The sense I have is that she sits in a room with other social workers and other lawyers and makes decisions, and those are not necessarily her client's decisions. My sense is that Marion is making social service determinations."

What then, I asked, should lawyers who represent the interests of children do?

The question raised what for Solomon and other legal scholars was the great difficulty of representing children: no clear sense of what the job was supposed to be. In their *Best Interests* trilogy, Joseph Goldstein, Anna Freud, and Albert Solnit recommended that in child welfare matters adults not overstep the limits of their expertise: Judges should rule on the law, but they should not attempt to be social workers, a job for which they had as little training as social workers did in law. An attorney's job was to represent the child, not to determine what the child needed. This meant listening to a client, if the child was old enough to make her wishes known. And if the she was not, it meant gathering enough evidence to make a recommendation, but not a judgment.

"The attorney for the child errs on the side of being inclusive rather than exclusive," Solomon said. "It would be hard for me to imagine why you would exclude a psychiatrist as opposed to vigorously cross-examining him if you thought there were problems with what was being said."

One of the unpleasant givens of the child welfare system is that children are represented by lawyers who, all too often, are either too inexperienced or too unsuccessful to make a living any other way. The pay for private, court-appointed lawyers—this as opposed to lawyers from the Legal Aid Society or from law school clinics—is pitiful. In Connecticut the pay for court-appointed lawyers in family court was the lowest of all courts: In the summer of 1992, when Megan's case was being considered, the fee was $22 an hour for preparation time; for court time the fee was $50 for the first hour, $35 for the second, and $20 for the third with a $160 ceiling per day. The lawyers were often so young and so eager to build up their practices that, Barbara Ruhe told the judiciary committee at its hearing, at the age of forty-three she was probably the senior private attorney practicing in the field. Representative Tulisano, the committee chairman, citing the paltry fees, added "you get what you pay for."

"In Connecticut," Solomon said, "there is an economic reality, as in most places, that the people who are taking these cases are either doing it *pro bono* or because it's the only money they're going to make. That's a problem."

The money aside, there was another quality to those who chose to represent children that troubled Solomon. "It's a cop out," he said. "They don't really like the adversary system, and they don't really want to be lawyers. They like representing people who are worthy, and no one's more worthy than a child, especially a child in an unfortunate home situation, or what's perceived to be. Instead of lawyering, you sit there and you're a philosopher king or queen and you make decisions—what's best for this kid. You like that people are going to listen to what you say because you're the attorney for the child. And people do listen. When you walk into a courtroom and represent the kid and then you articulately say, 'Here's what should happen, judge,' people listen to that. That sounds pretty good."

———

Solomon was not suggesting that representing children was an impossible field or that it was impossible to find good people to do it. He pointed, as an example, to the lawyers in the Juvenile Rights Division of the Legal Aid Society of New York as especially good practitioners. Yet even for the experienced lawyers in that office, the burden of keeping track of so many children meant that at times they felt as if they barely knew their clients and how best to represent them. Eager to see how a lawyer for a child went about his work, I spent a morning in Queens County Family Court with Lance Dandridge, who had been with the Legal Aid Society of New York for eight years. Dandridge's reward was an office at the courthouse littered with five-year-old Nassau County telephone books and an assortment of collapsible umbrellas; the place had all the institutional charm of an abandoned warehouse. Dandridge was thirty-four, and the pants on the blue suit he wore almost every day were fraying at the cuff. He possessed the sort of even temperament that made the work possible. His day consisted largely of hurrying from courtroom to courtroom, a heavy stack of briefs and reports under his arm. Sometimes his appearances lasted no more than a minute or two as the court moved a case another incremental step along the bureaucratic process. Sometimes a caseworker was on vacation or a witness did not appear or another lawyer was stuck in another courtroom, and Dandridge was left to check his watch and calendar and see where he was needed next.

It was not the pace that troubled Dandridge. And he and his work were well regarded by his superiors. Rather it was the feeling that he was forever being asked to make critical decisions about the needs of clients and families he barely knew or understood. Between appearances he talked about cases. He talked, as those who work in the child welfare system often talk, of children growing up in awful circumstances that the adults in charge were all but powerless to do anything about. "I find myself thinking about my decisions all the time," he said. He remembered a four-year-old boy he was assigned to represent and with whom he actually had the time to talk. Dandridge had learned that with young clients it was unwise to ask where they wanted to live—that was placing too great a burden on them, and the replies to such a direct question were not always revealing. He also avoided such questions with adolescents, whose views of their parents and home were "fluid." He tried to get a sense of his clients' lives by asking seemingly innocuous questions, like what they liked to do for fun. He met the four-year-old on the day the boy was removed from his mother's home. The boy did not want to talk about home or about his mother. So they chatted about nothing in particular until the moment the boy spotted his mother coming out of a courtroom, turned to Dandridge, and said, "Please don't send me back."

Dandridge recognized that to his clients he was another strange adult who wanted to know things about them. Sometimes they told him the truth, and sometimes they did not. Sometimes he saw that no matter how good his intentions, he was an interloper in the relationship between his clients and their parents. He spoke of a teenager who told Dandridge that his mother forced him to steal so that she could have money to buy drugs. Dandridge was sure that his client had turned against his mother and had decided his life was best lived out of her home. Then he spotted the two of them talking in a courthouse stairwell. The mother was pleading with her son to change his story. The teenager later came to Dandridge and said, "I want to go back, and everything I said before wasn't true." Dandridge did not believe that it was his place to say to his client, 'Look son, I know best.' Besides, he had heard two different versions of the truth and could not be sure what in fact had happened in his client's home. In this family, as in the homes of so many of his clients, there was only clutter, accusations made between parent and client and between caseworkers and parents. There were histories of drug use and new people moving in and out of the home, and new siblings and new addresses and almost never a clear sense of what the best course was for his client. The work did not paralyze Dandridge. But the impossibility of knowing, and the danger of deluding himself into thinking that he understood a family, humbled him.

"I don't know if you're ever completely sure that you're not doing too much," he said.

Marion Fay, Sara Martin, and Angelica Anaya-Allen did not succeed in convincing Judge Downey to prevent Albert Solnit from testifying. Nor did they succeed in delaying consideration for visitation until a psychologist evaluated the child and adults. Both Anaya-Allen and Fay insisted that their request for the evaluation was not an attempt to further delay the LaFlammes' seeing the child, as Linda Pearce Prestley, the assistant attorney general, and the LaFlammes' lawyer, Barbara Ruhe, charged.

Solnit took the witness stand and, guided by the direct examination of Barbara Ruhe, offered his opinions: It was essential that the child be allowed to see the LaFlammes as quickly as possible; further delay in visitation could only hurt the child; and contrary to the perception that visitation would somehow confuse the child, such meetings would in fact strengthen the bond between Gina and the child.

"The baby," Solnit testified, "will be able to view the birth mother as a person associated with a good beginning and also a person who helps her overcome the challenge of the loss of the primary adults." The loss, he explained, had already occurred. He could not envision a situation in which a child was not somehow affected by being taken from the people she saw as her parents. He discounted the suggestion made by the attorneys for the child that all appeared to be good with Megan in her new life with Gina. He would have wanted to see evidence of bonding as presented by someone who knew what to look for and who was not necessarily convinced of an attachment because the child smiled and appeared to know her new name. A new person was attending to the needs of a child who was still at an age when she needed all her needs attended to. She had gone, Solnit explained, "from one set of adults, who have a particular way of meeting that child's needs . . . to a person who is a relative stranger." By relative, Solnit explained, he meant someone with whom the child had become familiar during visits but who, in the child's eyes, remained a "secondary person rather than a primary person concerned with the day to day, hour to hour care."

Children, he explained, needed months to change, to get used to someone new. He offered as an example the idea of "stranger anxiety," when at about the age of eight months a child suddenly grows fearful of people she does not see all the time because she has begun to identify certain people as the essential people in her life. Everything was different in Megan's life now, he said. But that did not necessarily mean that things had to go badly for her, that is, if the adults in her life could see themselves not as competitors for the child but as people whom she needed.

"I think it would be highly desirable from the child's best interest," he said, "that we think of the child as having an extended family now, in which the biological mother and the pre-adoptive parents somehow find a way of working together."

Ruhe asked if he thought overnight visits or weekend visits might be appropriate.

"I indeed would hope that they would take place," he replied, "not only for the baby, but because in that sense the young biological mother might have a little respite, a sense of being helped with her work, of becoming a mother and taking care of her child. And that the pre-adoptive parents would have some help in feeling that they too are represented by the biological mother when the baby is with her."

He continued. "We have seen babies grow up very healthy when they have three of four adults who are primarily important to them."

Solnit was attempting nothing short of changing the terms of the debate on this child. It was no longer a question of who should prevail. Solnit had stated what he believed would have been best; Downey had thought differently. That was done. Now it was essential to acknowledge that the state had made this child's life chaotic and that no ruling could eliminate that chaos. It was necessary to accept that things had been "spoiled" for Megan. By accepting that damage had been done—that at the very least her view of the adults around her was uncertain—it might then be possible to create a new world for her, not better, but a world where Megan's many needs were met by the equivalent of what Solnit called "a Chinese village."

Solnit wanted Downey and the other adults to see that even if the child was not growing up in a culture in which the important people in her life lived close by, it was still possible for those adults to surrender part of their dreams for the child—and of their places in her life—and make her "spoiled" life a good life by their assuming new and diminished roles.

Angelica Anaya-Allen, however, would have none of it. "My client, unfortunately, does not believe that the foster parents are capable of harmoniously supporting her position as the primary care giver," she told Solnit as she began her cross-examination. She alluded to the comments the LaFlammes had made about Gina.

Solnit replied that while acrimony was a problem, it could be overcome if the adults could get beyond their rage and understand that what mattered most was insulating the child. He did not use the example of a bitterly divorcing couple, but he could have. Perhaps, he said, counseling might help.

Anaya-Allen then began posing a series of questions that might best be described as the "what ifs" of adoption—the sorts of questions that anticipated all that could go wrong for a child if she did not grow up in the home of her biological parents. Anaya-Allen wanted to know, for instance, whether Solnit saw "any benefit" in being reared by biological parents.

Solnit replied the key advantage of the biological tie was the nine months a mother had to prepare for a child. But in this case, he said, "there were some qualifications" because the mother insisted she did not know she was pregnant.

Anaya-Allen then asked how the child might react if she one day learned that her adoptive parents had "fought to have her removed from her biological mother's care, when a court had determined that there was no basis to do so."

"That little girl would know how much she was wanted by those adoptive parents," Solnit replied. He conceded, however, that she might still grow up even as "normal children in biological families have to wonder if they couldn't have been raised by a more romantic or more adventuresome person."

Finally, she asked whether it might be possible for a child that had been moved as this child had to actually benefit from the experience.

"I've never seen a child who didn't lose," he replied.

———

Marion Fay deferred to Sara Martin in questioning Solnit. Martin picked up where Anaya-Allen left off. Her cross-examination was an attempt to extract from Solnit a concession that perhaps Megan had not suffered after all. But first she once again raised the suggestion that the LaFlammes' attachment to Megan was not quite as passionate as it appeared. Had the LaFlammes acted in the child's best interests, she asked, when they surrendered her without so much as a transition period. Solnit, reminding Martin of the legal advice the LaFlammes received and of their standing in court, dismissed the suggestion. With that Martin turned to damage that might have been inflicted on her client when she was placed with Gina.

How, she asked, could Solnit be sure this child had in some way suffered if he had no supporting empirical evidence?

"I don't know this child," Solnit replied. "I know it from hundreds of children that I have either studied, advised about, or heard about from my students whom I supervise. There has never been an instance—and I've been practicing for more than thirty years, more than forty years actually—in which an expert couldn't detect the cost to the child in such a disruption."

"Not to be repetitive," Martin said, "then you are saying that it is impossible for the child not to have suffered?"

"That's correct," Solnit replied.

Martin then turned back to the LaFlammes and the damage *they* had inflicted when they surrendered Megan. "Would the child . . . also blame the LaFlammes for allowing this wound to occur?" she asked.

"Your question sort of says to me, isn't there something bad, wrong, weak, pathological about the LaFlammes," Solnit replied.

"Well, you, no sir, I, I . . ." Martin began, hastening to qualify.

"You really are," said Solnit. And with that he reminded her that the issue was "what happens from now on."

Martin wanted to know how long it took for someone to become the "primary adult" in a child's eyes. Solnit replied that it usually took "six months minimum and we don't see clear evidence of this capacity in most children until eight months."

"But what can be achieved in thirty-five days toward that end?" Martin asked.

"You can begin to be a replacement," Solnit replied.

Martin then appeared to make the mistake of asking a question for which she did not already know the answer.

"In your expert opinion," she asked, "do you want to disrupt the bond that has been formed between the child and the biological mother, for the best interest of the child?"

"No, I don't want to disrupt it," Solnit replied. "I want to enhance it."

Other witnesses followed. Among them was Cindy LaFlamme, who, seven months after Judge Downey ruled that she and Jerry had no standing in the original case against Gina, would at last have her moment in court.

"Nobody wanted me to testify," Cindy later said. "I got up there. Barbara asked me one question. I cannot remember it. It was a leading question. And I took off on Downey. I said, 'I am a citizen, and you say I have no legal rights to be in this court; you would never see me; you would never look at me. How could you pass judgment on me and my husband without knowing us?' I told him that he held it against me, that he made it known that I worked. I told him that. He thinks a mother should be home. He said that in court. I told about the visit with the black and blue mark on her eye. I told him about coming home with pee running down her leg, dirty and disgusting, and that she was starving. He kept calling us foster parents, and I reiterated that I was not a foster parent. I would never be a foster parent. I told him that I had a bank account for her, that we had life insurance and savings bonds. I told him that I had plans for this child. This was her future. She had a future. A foster parent does not do that. I looked at him and I said, 'Do you understand?' And of course he didn't say anything.

"I told him that if I was taken prisoner—and I don't know why I said this—before I ever, ever would stay in that prison for twenty years, I would have committed suicide."

How could you have said that? I asked of her bringing up Downey's capture and long imprisonment in China.

"Because he was a coward. And I wanted him to know that he was being a coward by not reopening this case. I was on the stand for forty-five minutes. Everything I said I said it from my heart. I didn't plan it. I didn't write it. I kicked him once, and that was the only time I kicked him, except for the fact that he ruled wrong.

"He did ask, 'Do you still view this child as yours?'

"And I said, 'I am her mother. I will always be her mother whether I gave birth to her or not. Being a mother is being with her when she's sick. Growing inside of someone, that just makes that person an incubator.' He looked like he was shocked."

Did you realize that you were not helping your cause, I said. Why did you say these things?

"Why did I say it? Because it was true."

———

Cindy appeared after Downey had ordered Gina and the LaFlammes to meet with a psychologist, to see, as Albert Solnit had suggested, whether they could reach some sort of accommodation on the child. The meetings had not gone well.

"Jerry was really mean to her," Cindy said. "He told her how irresponsible she was for getting pregnant, for leaving her. He told her she was a tramp. He was terrible to her, really and truly was. And at one point, none of us could figure out what he said, but he made her cry. And I knew when he did, I just bent my head and said, shit. I looked over at her and she was crying. I moved over and I put my arms around her. I put my forehead on hers and my nose on hers—she was the kind of person you didn't touch—and I said, It is okay if I hold you? And she said it's okay."

Gina, said Cindy, lashed back at Jerry. She said, "It was none of your business. I made a mistake. I was scared. I was alone. I didn't have anybody to turn to. You don't know what it was like."

At one point Gina looked at Cindy and said, "It hurt."

"What hurt?" Cindy asked.

"Giving birth," said Gina.

Cindy said, "I know it did."

A week after the first of the six weekly sessions, Cindy came into the den. Jerry was watching television. She said, "I've got to come up with something. Get me a pad of paper now." Jerry got a pad and pencil. Cindy began to write.

Jerry asked, "What are you doing?"

"I'm drafting a contract," Cindy replied.

"For what?" Jerry asked.

Cindy recognized that if she was going to see Megan, she would have to convince Gina that she meant her no harm. "If she didn't trust us, she wasn't going to consent to this," Cindy said. "Her and I could talk without screaming, without losing it. There was a tension there, but we could still talk." The problem was Jerry. "It was terrible because he is not an understanding or forgiving person. He's not hard, but he is to a certain extent. She was messing with him. She took his child away. The first couple of times we actually got to the courtroom, I looked at him and he had this look on his face like he wanted to smash her. I said, 'Jerry, keep staring at her till the look goes away.' He said, 'I can't.' I said, 'Keep looking at her.' He kept staring at her, and finally the look mellowed. Then when we were in therapy, I'd give him a little kick on his foot, like 'Shut up.' "

Now Cindy explained to Jerry that the contract would outline the terms for visitation. The LaFlammes, she wrote, would consent to Megan calling them Cindy and Jerry. But they would not stop her from calling them mommy and daddy. Cindy wanted her to call them nothing at all. The LaFlammes would supply toys, food, bottles, and whatever else was needed for the visits. And, she wrote, "We would recognize Gina as her mother."

Cindy presented the contract at the opening of the next session. At the end of the hour the psychologist asked whether Gina would sign the contract. Gina agreed.

It is to John Downey's credit that he allowed Cindy LaFlamme to say what she did to him and still grant the LaFlammes the right to visit the child. He ruled that there would be two hour-long visits a week. The visits would take place on neutral turf, at the Milford Mental Health Center. They would begin immediately.

A Room of Her Own

By NOW, in early September, Gina Pellegrino had left the shelter. She and her daughter were living with her boyfriend, Jermaine; Jermaine's sister; and the sister's daughter. The caseworker, Jennifer Hauser, visited every week and in her case record noted that Gina was pleased because Jermaine had "accepted the baby." Jermaine was out of work. He had been painting houses but had been laid off. Gina told Hauser that he "was a nice guy who treated her well."

Because Gina had no car, and because Judge Downey had ordered that the department provide transportation for Gina, Hauser assumed the role of chauffeur—but more in the line of an older sister than that of an employee. She picked up Gina and drove her to court, and took her to appointments with the psychologist and the LaFlammes. The picture of Gina that emerges from Hauser's case reports—she declined to talk to me about the case—is of a teenager caught, as teenagers always have been, between melancholy and giddiness. There is the excitement in showing off for Hauser the clothes Gina bought for herself and her daughter at a consignment shop, especially the matching bathing suits. There is the occasional sullenness, the silent car rides and hurried phone calls and unexplained aloofness. There is also the crying, or rather the notation of tears hastily dried.

What's wrong? Hauser asked one day when she had come to pick up Gina for a trip to the mental health center.

Gina offered the teenager's eternal response: "Nothing." Then, just as predictably, when Hauser asked whether the problem was Jermaine, Gina, veering between the desire for silence and the desire to tell, replied that, yes, the problem was Jermaine, that he "wanted more money to go to Chick's for lunch," and that he "should just get a fucking job." They talked for a while, and Gina calmed down. Later, at lunch, Hauser asked Gina whether she wanted to take her leftovers home to Jermaine. "Gina," she wrote, "seemed happy."

When Downey returned the child to Gina, he required that Gina receive psychological counseling and parenting skills classes, and that she and the child remain under the department's supervision. The caseworkers had to press Gina to begin her therapy, but were satisfied that she had learned the rudiments of parenting under the tutelage of the woman who ran the shelter. Jermaine, however, was a source of concern. The caseworkers twice noted bruises on Gina's arm that appeared to be grab marks. Gina, with Anaya-Allen present, told the caseworkers that Jermaine "would never hurt her." Still, the department noted that it was "concerned for her safety and the safety of the child." That issue aside, the workers concluded that "the child is developing normally and is in good health."

For Gina, the prospect of the visits was an intrusion on the life she was trying to build. "I didn't really want to stay where I was," she said of the shelter. "I wanted to be able to prove I could do this." Then she learned that the LaFlammes "wanted visits with Angelica, with my daughter," and that "all kinds of psychiatrists said it will be detrimental if you don't let the child see the LaFlammes."

The visits began during the first week of September. They were held in a room with an observation mirror. A psychologist supervised. Gina attended. "I think they felt like we were going to run away with her," Cindy said.

The LaFlammes had been warned by the psychologist who conducted the sessions with them and Gina to expect the child to ignore them. She might get angry, he cautioned. She might hit them. The child was shown a photograph of the LaFlammes before the visit to remind her of them.

The LaFlammes fought each other to get into the room first. The child did not hit them, but she did ignore them. Cindy sat on the floor and waited. After a while the child came to Cindy and sat on her lap. Cindy read a book to her. Jerry sat on a chair, and Cindy motioned for him to sit on the floor. "It was very, very bad leaving," Cindy said. "It was so bad that we wanted to take her. Looking forward to the visit was very exciting. Coming home was very empty." At home they did not much feel like eating or watching television.

———

Whatever hope Albert Solnit may have had for the LaFlammes and Gina Pellegrino to find some sort of accommodation in the interests of the child soon evaporated. Instead, the relationship between the parties began to resemble the dynamic of a messy divorce, with all the claims and counterclaims of lateness and derelict parenting. Cindy LaFlamme was sure she could tell when Gina was having problems with her boyfriend because she seemed agitated and spoiling for a fight. The visits remained confined to the room at the mental health center. And in its acrimonious way the schedule slipped into a routine. The caseworkers noted that the visits went well. Cindy and Jerry were pleased that the child came to them easily. The caseworkers continued assisting Gina in attending to the details of her life, like driving her by Burger King on the way home from a visit so she could give her boyfriend his wallet. Cindy was weary of people stopping her on the street and asking how she was doing. "We're trying very hard to get our lives back to normal," she said. "And it's not working."

Infinite Patience

T HE CASE THAT Attorney General Richard Blumenthal was preparing to argue before the Connecticut Supreme Court focused, in the narrow legal sense, on three arguments: that Judge Downey was wrong in applying the law as he did in allowing Gina Pellegrino to appeal his termination of her parental rights; that terminations were not subject to the same rules as other civil matters because they were a category unto themselves; and that Downey had abused his judicial discretion when he dismissed the state's case for terminating Gina's rights.

The argument, of course, transcended these points. Blumenthal was prepared to argue, as he had before the judiciary committee, that the true issue in this case was one of finality—that in the matter of children who become the responsibility of the state, there had to come a point where the state made a decision about the future of a child and stuck with it. Such a point had come for this child. Her mother's rights had been terminated. The state had made its decision to place her for adoption, based upon the evidence of abandonment. Angelica Anaya-Allen, on the other hand, would argue that the law intended the state to be infinitely patient with parents who wanted their children back.

Anaya-Allen was joined in her argument by the Connecticut Civil Liberties Union. In a brief filed in support of Gina Pellegrino, the union argued that the harm of an "erroneous termination is so severe" that "the court must have the power, when justice requires, to reconsider its decision to terminate parental rights."

The larger question, as the legal scholar Martin Guggenheim had put it, was one of tolerance—how much parental failure was a community willing to tolerate before it decided to separate forever a child from a parent. In early September the judiciary committee met again, this time to draft recommendations to the state legislature on amending the state's adoption laws in a way that would clarify when a parent had exhausted her options for regaining a child.

The committee's proposals, which came with the support of both Democrats and Republicans, were a rebuke to Judge Downey and his ruling that extended Gina's appeal period and which granted him ongoing power over Megan's fate. The proposals were an attempt to bolster what had been the state's view on adoption since 1972, when Connecticut rewrote its adoption laws to ensure that biological parents could not reclaim a child they surrendered for adoption, even if the adoption was not final. The change in the law came in the wake of hearings prompted by what was the celebrated adoption case of its time, the 1972 New York case of Baby Lenore. In that case a biological mother surrendered her daughter for adoption but then, five months later, after the child was placed for adoption, changed her mind and asked for her child back. The New York courts supported the biological mother. The pre-adoptive parents, who were a month short of finalizing the adoption, fled to Florida, where the law did not give undue weight to biological ties. The Florida courts awarded permanent custody to the adoptive parents. The United States Supreme Court let the decision stand, and states like Connecticut hurriedly passed new laws, ensuring that the travails of Baby Lenore and her pre-adoptive parents were not repeated within their borders.

Now, the judiciary committee, eager to act on the case of Baby B, recommended cutting off all termination appeals at 120 days, allowing judges to oversee termination cases for four months—but only to ensure that a child was well, and not to reopen a case. The committee also recommended counseling for women considering surrendering their children.

At the same time, however, the state's supreme court was narrowing the definition of the grounds for termination, even for parents whose behavior was so horrific that it placed a child at great physical risk. In late August, the court ordered a new trial for a mother whose rights were terminated after she injected a quarter-gram of cocaine as she went into labor. The child, a girl known in court records as Valerie D., was born with cocaine in her blood. The Department of Children and Youth Services took her immediately and moved to terminate the mother's rights. As it happened, the case was heard by Fredrica Brenneman, who had been critical of Judge Downey's decision to re-open the case against Gina and who spoke of the need for finality in judgments and in her belief in the "process."

Brenneman was familiar with the mother, known as "Jean Doe," and her history of neglect and drug abuse; Jean Doe had started using drugs when she was eleven years old; the state had already taken her thirteen-month-old daughter when, a month before she gave birth to Valerie, a parole worker found drug paraphernalia in the home she shared with the child's father. Both adults were arrested. In fact, Brenneman was scheduled to hear a neglect case against them when the mother's water broke. In her decision terminating the mother's rights, Brennaman wrote, "This ground would apply without question to parents who, an instant after birth, injected cocaine into the bloodstream of a newborn. The injection of the drug into the bloodstream of a baby about to be born should have no different consequences." Jean Doe appealed. Her lawyer, coincidentally, was Sara Martin, who had assisted Marion Fay in representing Megan. Arguing the state's case was Susan Pearlman, who was also working on the appeal of Judge Downey's decision.

The appellate court upheld Brenneman's decision. The Connecticut Supreme Court, however, did not. The law granted the state's protection to children already born, not those still in the womb, wrote Justice David Borden. The legislature may have contemplated acting against mothers who risked giving birth to drug-addicted children. But it never went so far as to explicitly extend the protection of the state to the unborn.

His decision was a rebuke not only of Brenneman, but of the appellate court, which had upheld the termination on the grounds that the state could justify granting its protection to the viable unborn under its wrongful death and wrongful injury statutes. The unanimous appellate court decision, written by Flemming Norcott—who would soon join Borden on the supreme court and who would hear the state's appeal of Judge Downey's decision—had been blasted by women's rights groups who saw it as a judicial assault on women's right to privacy. Borden also dismissed Brenneman and Norcott's argument that there existed an additional ground for termination: no ongoing parent and child relationship. How could there be such a relationship, Borden argued, if the state had taken the child at birth and thereby rendered that relationship impossible?

It did not matter that the mother's behavior had been despicable, Borden wrote: The law protected the relationship between parent and child. The burden was not upon the parent to prove she was worthy. The burden was on the state to prove that when it stepped between a parent and child, it did so only along the narrow lines that the law permitted, and not simply because it judged that action to be best for a child.

Brenneman and Flemming had, in their decisions, essentially advocated less tolerance of failing parents. The supreme court—reluctant as high courts often are to allow lower courts to make new law—ruled that it was up to the legislature to decide what constituted intolerable parental failure. If the legislature wanted to make things tougher for failing parents, it was free to do so. That was not up to the courts.

Court of Last Resort

On the morning of October 2, 1992, the line inside the ornate, white marble lobby of the Connecticut Supreme Court began assembling two hours before the court was scheduled to hear the state's appeal of Judge Downey's ruling. Television camera crews parked outside. Friends of the LaFlammes tied pink ribbons to telephone poles along the streets of Hartford.

Shortly after ten in the morning, Chief Justice Ellen Peters, flanked by the other four justices at the dark wood bench, gaveled the session to order and admonished all in attendance that any outbursts would mean that the room would be emptied. With that she invited Richard Blumenthal to make his case for the state.

"The Legislature intended termination to be final and irrevocable," Blumenthal told the justices in his opening statement, "and this Court has so indicated in its other decisions as well. The rights of the parent are to be ended and set aside forever. . . ."

Chief Justice Peters interrupted with a question: Was there any circumstance in which a termination might be reconsidered?

Blumenthal said that the law made no such provision.

But what of those cases in which a parent was not present at her trial? she asked.

Fraud might be grounds for an exception, Blumenthal replied. Or failing to notify a parent that her rights were terminated. But that, he hastily added, was not the case here. The law required that notice be published, whether or not people read those notices. The state had searched for Gina Pellegrino and could not find her. The justices then raised questions about whether the state was truly diligent in searching for Gina, whether she had been given misleading advice by the caseworker Patricia LeMay. Those issues, Blumenthal replied, were not at the heart of the matter. The question was whether Judge Downey had the power to reconsider his termination of Gina's rights. And that, Blumenthal argued, was a power the law did not give him.

But what if you had a case in which a child was living with foster parents who had no intention of adopting him? asked Justice Robert Berdon. Say a judge terminated the mother's rights. Four months later he decided that the mother was ready to regain her child. Wouldn't it be in the best interests of the child to allow that judge the authority to reconsider the termination?

Not if she appeared after the four-month appeal period had elapsed, replied Blumenthal.

What of the child's best interests? Berdon asked.

"The interest of the child, your honor, is served by the principle of finality," said Blumenthal.

But didn't the legislature also intend to try to reunite children with their parents? asked Peters. Do you think that that is any less important than finality?

"Those," she went on, "are some of the competing values that this case illustrates."

That may be so, replied Blumenthal. But if there is no finality, there is no "bonding" between adult and child. "Finality means that bonding can begin whether it's a foster parent or pre-adoptive parent." And that bond, he added, was what the law intended once the state took a child from her parent.

Are you suggesting that terminations never be reconsidered? asked Justice David Borden.

No, Blumenthal replied. This was not a case of an incapacitated mother—someone, say, whose incapacity meant she could not be notified of the loss of her rights. "The mother, very simply, changed her mind without attempting to ascribe blame to anyone." She had no defense when her rights were terminated.

The justices then turned to a matter that had appeared almost peripheral: Why hadn't the state immediately appealed Judge Downey's decision to reconsider Gina's case? Why, instead, did the state amend its case against Gina Pellegrino, adding failure to maintain a parent-child relationship to the charge of abandonment? Chief Justice Peters was especially persistent on the point, one which appeared to have nothing at all to do with the question of the welfare of the child.

Blumenthal argued that the state did not believe it could appeal Downey's decision. Perhaps not, said Justice Berdon, but you could have asked the chief justice to appeal Downey's order. But that, countered Blumenthal, would have delayed the second termination trial. And that would have been unfair to the child.

Yet when you failed to appeal or to petition the chief justice, Berdon went on, the mother claims that you conceded that Downey maintained jurisdiction in the case.

The justices began to tip their hand. Peters and Berdon would not let go of the question of the appeal. Justice Borden tried offering Blumenthal a way toward a reasonable explanation. "You were hopeful that Judge Downey would, after the full hearing, reaffirm his initial decision to terminate?"

"Very certainly so," said Blumenthal. Besides, he added, we felt obliged to add the additional charges.

But by doing that, said Peters, you essentially brought a new case against the mother. And when you did that, the four-month appeal period started all over again. If there were questions about Downey's claim of jurisdiction, they were now moot.

The question was no longer one of finality, at least for Blumenthal. Now it was a matter of the implications of a procedural point. Blumenthal was left to insist, time and again, that it was the state's responsibility, to the public as well as to the child, to bring forward all it knew of the mother whose rights it wanted to terminate. "Amendments of this kind," he said, "are to be encouraged."

William Bloss followed, briefly. The justices were not much interested in the question of whether the LaFlammes had a right to be heard in court once Gina Pellegrino's case was to be reconsidered.

The LaFlammes had had no voice in the first termination trial because they were not yet pre-adoptive parents. That changed, Bloss argued, once the state gave them the child.

Peters would have none of it. "That assumes that your clients have a due process right in someone else's termination," she said. The matter concerned only the mother, and no one else.

Peters then called on Angelica Anaya-Allen, who barely had time to introduce herself to the court before Justice Norcott interrupted.

If you prevail in this case, what will that mean to the final resolution of terminations? he asked. Didn't the legislature intend that termination cases must at some point come to a close?

It did, she began, when Peters interrupted and posed this scenario: A mother abandons her child in the hospital. Six months later she comes to court to have her termination reconsidered. Would she have grounds to be heard?

She might, replied Anaya-Allen. It depends on whether she has a reasonable defense for her absence.

"But isn't finality of the utmost importance to the welfare of a child?" asked Justice Berdon. "At what point do we stop?"

At adoption, Anaya-Allen replied. Only then did the legislature intend to deny parents the right to try to regain their children.

"I thought part of the motivation behind this statute was the Baby Lenore case," said Justice Borden. In 1972 the New York court had said that that mother had the right "to change her mind" until her child was adopted. Wasn't that what Connecticut was trying to prevent? he asked. How can you say finality comes only with adoption?

Because, Anaya-Allen replied, the legislature assumed that until that moment there would be "uncertainty." Furthermore, she went on, the legislature wanted to give parents as much time as it could to "redeem themselves" so that they could "serve the greater public policy of preserving families."

Where in the law do you see that? asked Justice Robert Callahan.

Anaya-Allen, scrambling a bit, suggested that the legislature wanted judges to be able to review cases while the state was still contemplating a child's future.

Borden raised the question of how long adoptions took to complete. "Theoretically, at least, two, three, four or five years later," he said, "if that poor little child is not adopted, the mother can come in and reopen the petition to reopen?"

"That's correct," replied Anaya-Allen. "And that may be appropriate."

"Isn't that going to make adoption in this state pretty impractical?" asked Norcott.

No, replied Anaya-Allen.

But how do you explain the debate that led to the new law after the case of Baby Lenore? asked Borden.

"It's not clear that the Legislature intended, indeed understood" the decision in Baby Lenore, she said.

The justices turned to Anaya-Allen's original argument for reopening Gina's termination case. One by one Peters challenged the claims that Anaya-Allen had so effectively made to Judge Downey: that Patricia LeMay had misled Gina about the possibility of appeal; that Gina did not know she had only two weeks to file her suit to be heard.

Berdon asked whether Anaya-Allen was in fact arguing that courts had the power to reconsider their decisions whenever they wanted. "You're not really arguing that, are you?" he asked.

"Let me be clear about your position on this question," said Peters. Are you saying that all that is needed to reopen a decision is a "meritorious defense" without meeting any of the other legal burdens imposed by the legislature?

Anaya-Allen replied that it was.

"So from that point of view, it doesn't matter whether it's four months, six months, ten months, twelve months, twenty-four months, any time during that time frame?" Peters asked.

"That's correct," said Anaya-Allen, "prior to adoption."

No matter what excuse the person offered for his or her absence? Norcott asked.

A judge considers many factors before making such a decision, Anaya-Allen replied.

Are you saying that you're also factoring into that decision a judge's discretion? Norcott asked.

"That's correct," she replied.

"If we were to disagree with you," Borden said of the question of jurisdiction, "what happens to your case?"

She replied that the state amended its petition and accepted the judge's authority. That, she said, is our argument.

———

Sara Martin echoed Angelica Anaya-Allen's argument about finality coming only at adoption. Richard Blumenthal reiterated his claim that the legislature saw finality as essential to the welfare of children. And with that the chief justice thanked the attorneys and announced that the court stood in recess.

Cindy and Jerry LaFlamme returned home and, with Gina Pellegrino, resumed the twice weekly visits at the Milford Mental Health Center. The visits continued for two more months, until the first week of December.

Best Interests

FOR THE SAVIORS of children there is nothing so appalling as a decision based on an impulse other than what they believe to be best for the child. Charles Gill was such a person. Gill, a superior court judge in the town of Waterbury, valued children and was angered when adults treated them badly. Although he was not a family court judge, he did hear cases involving children and their families. Listening to Gill talk about children, about the way they were regarded as property, the way their rights paled before those of their parents, it would be hard to imagine him hearing, say, twenty-five child welfare cases a day.

Gill heard his mix of cases, but in the mornings (just after dawn), in the evenings, and during extended lunch breaks for speaking appearances and radio call-ins, he worked at his truer calling: as co-chairman of a campaign for a constitutional amendment safeguarding the rights of children.

Gill was fifty-three. He was a plump man with a kind face and easy manner. The world, as Gill described it, was good and bad. The good was the children, and the bad was the people who did not protect children and who allowed children to be maimed, beaten, abandoned, and ignored because we, as a society, did not honor them. Gill, who at twenty-nine ran unsuccessfully for mayor of New Haven and who later served two terms as an alderman, found his cause in 1989, with the creation of the National Task Force for Children's Constitutional Rights. He ran his campaign first from his house—a prior original owner, he told interviewers, worked on the amendment repealing prohibition—and later from a small basement office. "If we can't reach a consensus on our children," he said, "there's no consensus on anything."

The proposed amendment called for, among other safeguards, "the right to live in a home that is safe and healthy" and "the right to the care of a loving family or substitute thereof, which approximated as closely as possible such family." Gill wanted these, together with the right to counsel and the right to testify against a person accused of abuse out of sight of the alleged abuser, extended to all children fifteen years old and younger. He believed that "the worst thing we can do is leave them at home with the criminals who are their parents." He wanted these children taken from their homes. There were couples across the country, he insisted, waiting to adopt. And though no amendment could "force" people to love children, it could, he told *The New York Times*, act as "a shield to protect children from those people who don't love them."

I met Gill in his chambers. He had just heard the case of a sixteen-year-old boy accused of shooting his father. Gill was familiar with the father and son; they had already appeared before him when the father was charged with beating the boy. That day, Gill now recalled, he had had the uneasy feeling that he would be seeing them again. Now the boy, crew cut and skinny, stood handcuffed before him. Gill hid whatever compassion he felt for the boy as he ordered him held on $100,000 bond. In his chambers he first took a call from a producer for *Donahue*, which was still a popular television talk show in 1992. Then he returned to the subject of children. He asked me, "When does our obligation to children end and begin?"

In his many speeches—he spoke to as many as sixty groups a year—Gill invoked the names of wronged and martyred children: Gregory K., the twelve-year-old who wanted to "divorce" his neglectful parents because Florida's child welfare administration was reluctant to do so; and Joshua DeShaney, whose beating death at the hands of a father to whom he was returned time and again did not persuade the United States Supreme Court to find the state of Wisconsin culpable for his death. "He had a right not to be abused," Gill would say. The adults in the audiences would nod in agreement. He told story after story of children treated unfairly and badly, all of them proof positive of the need to ensure that the word "child" was at last written into the Constitution. He wanted to take his case to a wider audience; those on his mailing list were asked to write to Oprah Winfrey to get him on her show.

"You're looking," Gill said, "at a very angry man."

The United States and Somalia, he said, were the only nations in the world that had not signed the United Nations covenant safeguarding the rights of children. Nor was the United States among the seventy-nine countries that had provisions in their constitutions to protect children. That, for Gill, was evidence of a society that cared little for the young. Family preservation was a meaningless enterprise. "What are we trying to preserve?" he said. "I say they're not saving anything. Unfortunately they're using the wrong materials."

Gill and his wife had three children. He was pleased that he had managed to stop himself from being the kind of father who worked too long to be part of their growing up. His father was that sort of man, and when he was in his eighties, Gill's father told him, "The only thing I regret in my life is that I didn't spend enough time with you." Until he came to understand his lapses as a father, Gill said, he worked five days a week and until three on Saturdays, when he would go out for a few drinks. On Sundays he was tired. But Gill learned how much parents meant to children, so much so that he believed that no child deserved to be reared by parents who failed him. He explained that he was not doing the work of his campaign as a matter of choice; he was driven to do it. "I see all the adult baggage," he said. "The bottom line is that we are deluding ourselves. Who is for kids? And who is just kidding?"

It was not surprising then, that Gill saw the battle for Megan as yet another case of the needs of the child eclipsed by the state's regard for the interests of the adults. "I would have put the child's interests into that equation," he said. "And the child's interests are not in that equation."

The case reminded him of that of Baby Richard, the five-year-old Chicago boy who in 1994 the Illinois Supreme Court ordered removed from the adoptive home where he had lived all his life and placed with the birth father he had never seen. In Richard's case, a lower court judge had insisted that the case hinged on the best interests of the child. In striking down that ruling, the supreme court's chief justice, James Heiple, took issue with the appellate court judge's attempt to make what was essentially new law: The legislature had intended that the question of best interests was applicable only after a court determined that there existed grounds for termination; to make it a companion consideration risked what the United States Supreme Court had warned against in *Stanley v. Illinois:* The material circumstances of a prospective parent could not be the issue that decided placement. Just because someone could provide a better home did not necessarily mean that that person should be awarded custody.

When I mentioned this argument to Gill, his even tone took on a harder edge. "That is such liberal bullshit," he said. "The left is absolutely wrong on this one—that this is some class struggle, that this is the orphan trains."

The matter, he insisted, was not one of wealth or relative comfort. It was about being a good parent. The argument against imposing a best interests standard was just another form of opposition to his campaign. People, he said, simply did not understand what was happening to children in their homes and in the courts. "I know that I've spoken to people on the left and on the right and in the middle, and when you explain it to them, they can see the point—that kids are not respected as human beings in this country. Our political baggage has blinded us to what we should be doing. Kids have no power. They don't vote. As much as we say that kids are a priority, support for children is soft. We're not on the political agenda. On the right it's 'Keep your nose out of my family.' On the left you got 'This is a class battle; poverty is the real issue here.' "

But if the idea made such sense, why had no states ratified his amendment? Why was there no groundswell of support?

"The first resistance is always ignorance," he said. "People don't have a lot of knowledge about the child welfare system, or know about the law." And then there was the prevailing attitude toward children. If people saw a parent slap a child in the supermarket, they would do nothing, he said. "Change one factor and put a ninety-year-old woman in a wheelchair," he said, and those same people would call the police.

I told him about the story of the father kicking his child at the amusement park, of my desire to be very big and strong and step between them, and also of my sense that the child would have told me to leave his father alone. Gill, however, saw the incident as "an assault, a crime. We have societal values that it's a crime; we don't beat people up." The child's imagined response, he went on, was like that of a battered woman, protecting her abuser. He was speaking on behalf of those for whom the law had for too long kept silent.

But what would he have said to the father had he intervened, only to be told him to mind his own business because this was his child?

"When you say 'my,' it can be ownership or a trusteeship," he said. "The object of the trust has to be protected."

What, then, would be different were the nation to adopt his amendment?

"The nineteen kids in Chicago, Baby Richard, and Baby B would be living with people who love, nurture, educate, and protect them and let them develop to their full human capacities," he said. "Every one of those kids would have a lawyer saying, you have to factor the kids into the situations. Right now it's sort of a game; no one takes the child welfare system seriously. They give you so many chances."

But in the world redefined through his change to the Constitution, Gill said, "Parents would take more things seriously: If you don't properly protect your kids, you lose them."

———

That is what had happened to Gina Pellegrino, or rather what had almost happened to her. She had left her child and, temporarily at least, lost her. The child had been given a new home with people who loved her. The state had, in Gill's view, served Megan's best interests well. Or rather, it had done so at first. Then Judge Downey changed his mind and, in so doing, served the interests of only one person: the woman who abandoned her.

I asked Gill what he would have said to Gina Pellegrino had she come before him and pleaded for the return of her child.

"No," he said.

Why?

"Because I look through the eyes of the child," he said. "Who created this dilemma, and who should pay the penalty? The mom created this dilemma, and the child pays the penalty."

The statutes, he conceded, did not always allow him to see matters through "the eyes of the child." They would if he were presiding in, say, a Canadian court. In Canada, he explained, the law now required that best interests be considered in all custody cases. He cited the seminal Canadian case on best interests, one that bore striking similarities to Megan's. In the case of *King v. Low*, an unwed mother, fearing parental disapproval, abandoned her child. The child was placed with an adoptive family. The birth mother changed her mind and asked the court to give her back her child. The adoptive parents refused to surrender the child. The Canadian Supreme Court sided with the adoptive parents. It ruled that the court must choose what is best for the child. "Parental claims must be considered" but were to be "set aside when the welfare of the child requires it." The court went on to explain that best interests was "not to be measured by money." Rather, "ties of affection cannot be ignored."

Gill's argument resonated with the people who invited him to speak. Why shouldn't the state make the best interests of the child paramount? Why else was the state intervening if not to ensure that those interests were being met, if not by the parents then by the state itself?

And yet his proposed amendment was troubling. It placed the state squarely where the state, statutorily, has avoiding being: as the mediator between parent and child. It was placing children on equal legal footing with their parents—giving them rights that could justify the intrusion of the state for the most nebulous reasons: Who was to determine, after all, whether parents were "loving" and a home was "healthy and safe"? Gill, like all the many child savers before him, was advocating just what Goldstein, Freud, and Solnit had cautioned against: a greater commitment by the state to the relationship between children and their parents. Greater potential scrutiny, not less. And greater legal recourse to act against parents. To that, Gill replied that his amendment was an attempt to level the playing field, to ensure that children were guaranteed more protection from their parents than the law now allowed. He was sure—though incorrectly—that there was an ample number of beds in substitute homes for the children whose parents had, in the view of the state, failed to meet their best interests.

Final Decision

The Connecticut Supreme Court handed down its decision on December 2, 1992, almost a year after a worried Cindy had taken Patricia LeMay's call, asking to come to the house and talk about Megan. The decision was a narrow one. By a vote of 3 to 2 the court ruled against the state. The child was Gina Pellegrino's. The decision, written by Chief Justice Peters, rejected not only the state's arguments but also the LaFlammes' claim that they had a right to be a party to Gina Pellegrino's termination trial. This was not surprising: To have given the LaFlammes a claim to a child who was not, legally speaking, theirs would have run contrary to the United States Supreme Court's decision in which Justice Brennan affirmed that the state could not tolerate equal, competing claims by birth parents and "psychological parents" to the same child.

The court's rejection of the state's argument, however, was seen as more troubling, especially to Justice David Bordon, who wrote the dissenting opinion. Peters and the majority ruled that because the state had not appealed Judge Downey's original decision to reopen Gina's case, it had, in effect, accepted his jurisdiction in the matter—the jurisdiction that Angelica Anaya-Allen had argued he retained under the 1980 Adoption Assistance Act. By then amending its termination case against Gina—by presumably bolstering its case by adding the charge of failure to sustain a parent-child relationship—

the state only enhanced its de facto acceptance of Downey's right to reconsider terminating her rights.

The rationale was characterized in the press as "a legal speck" that allowed the court to keep the child where she was. Justice Bordon agreed. While he too believed that the LaFlammes had no place at Gina's termination trial, he wrote that the majority placed the state in an impossible decision. The state, after all, was required to bring all its evidence against Gina when it was asking the court to take the drastic step of terminating her rights. It was clear, too, that the state opposed the idea of Downey's continued jurisdiction. What was the state to do? Stick with an arguably weaker case against Gina Pellegrino and risk losing on those grounds? Or amend its charges against her and lose because, in so doing, is granted its tacit acceptance of Downey's right to still rule in the case?

Adding a twist to the legal axiom that "hard cases make bad law," Bordon concluded that this was an instance in which "hard cases often ignore good law."

I read into the decision a desire on the justices' part to keep the child where she was, that because she had been living with Gina Pellegrino for six months, it would have been cruel to move her once again. I was disabused of this notion by Wesley Horton, the state's best-known appellate counsel, whom both sides had spoken with in preparing their supreme court briefs. "This is an issue that had nothing to do with child welfare," he said. Rather, it had only to do with procedural matters. In Horton's view the court's decision was a rebuke of the attorney general's office for failing to follow the correct procedure in contesting Judge Downey's decision to reopen Gina's termination case.

While I granted Horton's point about the legal basis for the decision, I was still struck by how often Peters referred to the relationship between Gina Pellegrino and the child. Peters, who declined to discuss the case, raised questions about the department's behavior similar to those of Barbara Nordhaus of the Yale Child Study Center. Why, for instance, did the department not try to track down the man who placed the 911 call when Gina Pellegrino collapsed on the street when she went into labor? The police had that man's name, address, and phone number, and yet he was never interviewed in the search for the missing mother. She also noted how difficult the department made things for Gina when she called to try to find out about the child. Peters also wrote that while the state argued that there existed no ongoing parent-child relationship between Gina and Megan, the visits, though few in number, had nonetheless gone well. Gina, she wrote, had displayed an interest in and commitment to the child.

Peters was also concerned that Gina be given her day in court and cited a nineteenth-century Connecticut case in which the court ruled "the law condemns no man unheard." Horton's argument about the legal basis for the court's decision notwithstanding, Peter's opinion all but directly posed the question: Was this a mother whose child the legislature intended the state to take? The answer, implicit in the questions she raised, was that she was not.

Still, public sympathy remained with the LaFlammes: They were the "worthy" parents, which meant that they deserved the child. They had, in their commitment to her, earned the child whom Gina, for whatever reasons, had abandoned. As it was in the cases of Baby Jessica and Baby Richard, the child had become their child. It was, as Donald Cohen said in his imagined conversation with Gina: You had a child; the child is someone else's now.

And yet the court upheld Downey's view—and the prevailing legal and legislative view—that the child reverted to the parent of origin, so long as that parent was worthy. Gina wanted and fought for her child. She was not one of the unworthy mothers whom Angelica Anaya-Allen represented. She had proven herself sufficiently worthy not to lose her.

But what of the child? Twice in her opinion, Peters raised the question of her best interests—when Judge Downey originally waived the twelve-month period of abandonment and terminated Gina's rights in Megan's "best interests" and when he used the same argument to place her with Gina. But that was the extent to which the child's interests were raised; this was not, in the end, a case about the child, nor was it about whether the LaFlammes were or were not her true parents. It was about Gina Pellegrino and whether her disappearance from the hospital and her four-month absence were grounds for the state to take her child.

Ham-fisted as his argument was, Charles Gill had a point: Where was the child in all this? Was this fair to her? In declining to consider those questions, the court was reflecting the prevailing legal view that best interests mattered only after a finding of parental failure. To consider best interests earlier would be, as the court noted, to violate the spirit of the United States Supreme Court's ruling in *Santosky v. Kramer*, in which the Court ruled that it was not permissible to determine who would be the better parent, who could offer a child a better life. The best interests of Megan could not be considered, at least not yet. And that, for Gill and others, was the flaw at the heart of the way the state regarded children. The case should have been about Megan. The law, however, said it was not.

"We were a family," said Cindy LaFlamme. "And why break up this child's family that she had known for nine months? Gina made that choice not to have that child when she ran out the back door of the hospital."

The state did not believe it was breaking up a family. It did not discount the bonds of affection and devotion between the LaFlammes and the child; but those were not enough to make them a family. Gina and the child were a family. The state, then, was not punishing the LaFlammes, as it had the Meltons, by removing "their" child, because Megan was not their child. Still, the state recognized that it had treated the LaFlammes unfairly, that it had promised them a child and reneged on that promise. The LaFlammes did indeed consider suing the state, as the law professor Martin Guggenheim suggested they might. The department, however, "settled." It gave the LaFlammes $27,000 to pay for them to go to Russia and bring home a child.

In December of 1993, a year after the supreme court ruling, the LaFlammes flew to Moscow and then took an eighteen-hour train trip to Kirov, to the orphanage where his mother had left him. He was eight months old. He was so rarely taken out of his crib that his development appeared delayed. He cried on the train trip back from the pain of his infected and untreated ears. Still, he ate voraciously. They had hoped to adopt domestically but wearied of the wait. They learned that there was a Russian child for them to adopt two months after they placed an ad in the New Britain *Herald*, seeking a birth mother.

They returned to Connecticut from Moscow on December 24. Their families and friends met them at the airport. *The Hartford Courant* ran the story of the adoption on its front page on Christmas Day, providing a seemingly heartwarming conclusion to what the *Courant* had decried as so cruel and unjust a story.

Cindy LaFlamme, however, would have none of it. She had a child, but she had lost a child. She never saw Megan again. Still, Barbara Nordhaus told her that one day, when she was grown up, Megan would seek her out, if only to know something of that time in her life.

In the winter of 1996 Cindy and Jerry LaFlamme were living in a new home, in a town not far from New Britain, where they had lived upstairs from Jerry's aunt. They had at last bought a home of their own. It was an altogether more cheerful place, a two-story home with a front lawn and a backyard and space between the houses. Sunlight poured through the big windows in the living room. Cindy had chosen pastel colors, light blue and beige, that made the room feel airy. The room was filled with toys.

There was a tent and drawing table and framed photographs of a child on the shelves on the television. Cindy and Jerry owned all the popular kid videos.

Upstairs, the child was waking. Jerry went to the child's room. He returned a few minutes later. The child was tall and blond. The LaFlammes called him Jerry, short for Gerard Konstantine. They had named him for his father and had decided to keep as well the name his Russian mother had given him before she abandoned him. He was three years old. Jerry handed him to Cindy, who snuggled with him. Then Cindy both said and signed the words "I love you." The child had suffered from ear infections so severe that when they first saw him, a dark discharge oozed from his ears; he was still having difficulty speaking and hearing. He was a sweet, ebullient child. His father sometimes liked just lying on the floor next to him. Sometimes the child had trouble controlling himself; he had broken Cindy's nose once when he reflexively lurched his head backward while she was holding him on her lap.

There was nothing of Megan in the house, at least nothing displayed. Cindy had kept some toys and clothes. But those were tucked away. Still, she was there, a silent presence. And though the LaFlammes at last had their child, he did not, and could not, replace the child they had lost. He was, Cindy said, his own person. He was not a substitute.

The Child

THE CHILD HAS Gina Pellegrino's face and black hair. I saw her once, at Angelica Anaya-Allen's office, where she sat on the floor, playing while I went to another room to talk with her mother. She played with her toys and dolls under a chair that she made into a house. She said, "Do you want to come to Angelica's house?" She was a friendly child, talkative and at ease being left with her mother's attorney. She ate animal crackers. She seemed like a child without a complicated history. She looked fine. Her mother spoke to her with care and with attention to her feelings.

Was this proof that Judge Downey and the supreme court justices had been wise in their decisions, that Downey in particular had discerned a quality in Gina Pellegrino that convinced him that she was capable of being a good mother, and that whatever trauma the child might have suffered in being taken from the LaFlammes was acceptable? There was no way of knowing this. So too was there no way to reasonably assess Barbara Ruhe's bleak prediction that while the child appeared well adjusted now, the repercussions of her removal would become apparent in the years to come.

I am sure that I was looking for signs of a withdrawn or anxious child or for a mother who seemed less than up to the task of her care. I could discern nothing. But then how could I? There was a relationship between this mother and child that defied my understanding, just as there existed a relationship between this child and her first set of parents that the state was unwilling to understand or accept.

THE MELTONS, PART II

PART II

Missing Mother

Expecting

In EARLY OCTOBER of 1995 the Melton sisters returned to their mother's new home on the West Side of Chicago to await the birth of yet another child to their youngest sister, Cassandra.

In the twenty months after the police happened upon the apartment on North Keystone Avenue and removed the nineteen children, Diane, Maxine, May Fay, Denise, and Cassandra had lived in drug rehabilitation centers, the houses of friends, the home of a cousin, a halfway house, the Cook County Jail, and a women's prison as well as on the streets. May Fay had returned to heroin, and Denise, one of her prosecutors believed, to cocaine. The sisters received vocational training and talked, vaguely, of finding jobs. Nothing came of that. May Fay, who went back to school for her high school equivalency degree, started sleeping late and dropped out. Diane gave birth to a daughter. Now Cassandra was due.

The sisters' children, most of whom were sufficiently troubled to be categorized under the vague rubric of "special needs," were scattered among relatives and foster parents and a group home for troubled teenagers. One was living with his foster parents, a military family, in Germany. The sisters who still visited their children did so sporadically, sometimes arriving for their appointed visits bearing candy, cookies, and promises of Starter jackets and Air Jordan sneakers. Sometimes the mothers did not show up. One foster mother

229

found it wise to remind the children in her care that they should restrain their excitement until their mother actually appeared.

Despite having their children taken from them, despite their arrest and conviction for child abuse and neglect, the Melton sisters nonetheless believed for many months that they might still regain their children. They understood, or appeared to understand, that before this could happen they would need to find jobs and homes of their own, and prove themselves capable of planning for the futures of their children. Diane, May Fay, and Denise would have to pass their drug tests.

Meanwhile, all through the spring and into the summer of 1995, as the United States House of Representatives and then the Senate raced to end sixty years of public funds supporting the nonworking poor and their children, the unmistakable target was women like the Melton sisters—single mothers with many children whom they had begun having at an early age and whom they could not independently feed, clothe, and house. There was little pity left for the mothers and considerable contempt for—though too little anger at—the fathers, who too often did not even bother sticking around. The problem for the legislators was the children.

Cutting off the mothers meant, inevitably, cutting off the kids, too. And the children, unlike their troubled mothers and absent fathers, were accepted as innocents. It was a prospect that left Senator Daniel Patrick Moynihan of New York, who had been remanded to the periphery of a debate in which he had once been a player, to assume the role of a legislative Jeremiah, warning of children left to sleep on city grates. Even if the Moynihan scenario sounded too stark by half, the state would likely feel morally obliged to "do something" for the children. Ending the federal government's entitlement to public assistance for parents like the Meltons—women with no prospects, little education, and no employment record—would, in all likelihood, leave them increasingly destitute and even less capable of adequately caring for their children. If the recent past and certainly the present were any indication, the state would feel compelled to take many of the children. And while that sounded wonderfully decisive on first blush, the people who were on intimate terms with those children and their parents understood that that solution would not work.

The State of Illinois was now responsible for the many Melton children, as well as the children of Denise Turner. It was costing the state $21,789 a month in fees just to the foster parents and to the group home where Diane's fourteen-year-old son lived. That did not include the cost of the children's counseling and various forms of therapy, or their medical expenses. By early October, the state had spent $703,369.29 on the Melton sisters and Denise Turner and all their children. And that, an official in the child welfare system said, was "just for openers." The children were likely to continue being a financial burden to the state until they were eighteen years old because even if they were lucky enough to be adopted—only 1,300, or 3 percent, of the 47,000 wards of the state had been adopted the year before—the adoptive parents might reasonably insist upon the adoption being subsidized, so that they could afford to take in the children. The state stopped paying only on the increasingly rare occasions when the Department of Children and Family Services was prepared to return children to their parents. The year before, only 4,731, or 10 percent, of the children in the care of the state went back to their parents. At the same time a thousand children were entering the system *every month*.

The longer children stayed "in the system," the higher became the cost of boarding, feeding, clothing, and attending to those children's increasingly difficult needs. These were needs that, after repeated foster home placements, could only be met by group homes or expensive incarceration in "locked-down" group homes for children who were violent or who kept running away. The cost, for instance, of just housing Diane Melton's teenage son in a group home for troubled teenagers was $6,500 a month.

Implicit in the political rhetoric of "welfare moms" and "culture of dependency," was the assumption that the mothers whom the state no longer wished to support were, for the most part, women of connivance, cheats who had learned early on that by having more children, they could pad their monthly check. It followed, then, that these women could be motivated to alter their behavior, if only because there was no percentage in having another child.

But what if they were not motivated by the bigger check? What if tough love, or even retribution, could not stop them from having more children? It was by no means certain, for instance, that programs that cut benefits to teenage mothers for each additional child they bore—a plan first implemented in New Jersey—would curb teenage pregnancies. Yet lost on the floors of the House and Senate was any apparent understanding of the women whom this welfare reform bill was supposed to keep from producing yet another generation of public dependents.

It was simple and satisfying to talk of punishing mothers like the Melton sisters, which is just what the State of Illinois did. It was not, however, nearly so simple to determine what to do with their children. And given the scattershot history of the last 150 years of child welfare policy, it was increasingly clear to those closest to such failing families that the state could not begin to understand how to help the children if it did not understand the maddeningly complex pathology of their mothers.

The Melton children could not and should not have been left to grow up in the house on North Keystone Avenue. But that did not necessarily mean they were best served by their being taken immediately from their mothers. The Melton children were now living in circumstances infinitely better than those on Keystone. They had, however, been unusually lucky: The state was able to find them new homes. It was understood by people in the child welfare trade in Illinois that this good fortune was built on the enduring image captured on Ken Herzlich's video of the police carrying the Melton children out of their home. "But we have thirty or forty Melton cases a week, or more," said Patrick Murphy, the Cook County Public Guardian. "The other kids don't get lucky."

The Melton sisters had performed small gestures of affection. The children, as their replacement parents had since discovered, loved their mothers, too. That was not, in itself, a reason to give the Melton sisters "another chance," because there was no reason to believe that on their own they would ever be minimally competent parents. It suggested only that the relationship between these mothers and their children defied what had become the commonly held view that it was better just to get the children out of the house and start them on "new lives," as if the past had never existed.

"I don't care what you are, you love your children even if you don't know how to be a mom, or a TV mom," said Claudine Christian,

Maxine Melton's godmother, who was caring for Maxine's five sons. "The state is going about this all wrong. Nothing will ever fix the hole that's in those kids' lives. I could be the best mother in the world. I wish I could fix it all." Then, in a weary aside that would seem to defy logic, she explained, "They miss their mother."

Claudine Christian said that the five boys she was rearing for Maxine did not resemble the children who had come to her home a year before. Now she could actually take them to a restaurant and not worry about their running wild and throwing food. They went to school, where they struggled, futilely, to catch up. When the oldest, who was ten, got angry in class, he simply got up and walked out. "He gets mean with his brothers or breaks his toys," she said. "It's devastating for him to lose everything like that. It's been hard. It's been hard on all five boys." The oldest boy, she said, craved attention but would not permit anyone to comfort him. Sometimes she found one of the younger boys sitting and gazing into the middle distance.

I heard similarly troubling stories of the other children. The children received counseling, speech therapy, play therapy, physical therapy, and, in some cases, special education. One social worker familiar with the case said that now, a year after getting the children, the foster parents were no longer witnessing the rapid transformation they had seen in the first months, when the children were learning such skills as eating with utensils and getting dressed for school. Progress slowed and, in some cases, stalled. The joy in seeing the children in their own beds and in clean clothes and learning to use words had, for some, been muted. In its place came the frustration of decent people who naively believed, the social worker said, "if we just love them, they'll be fine."

"No Space for Me"

On October 4 Cassandra Melton gave birth to her fifth child, a daughter. Cassandra was twenty-two. Two of her children were living with their paternal grandmother, and two were living in a foster home. On the morning after Cassandra gave birth, I went to see Patrick Murphy. Now that the Melton children were living apart from their mothers, I assumed Murphy would sound triumphant, considering how harshly he had spoken of them when I last saw him, a year earlier. But Murphy surprised me with the weariness of his tone. Murphy's view of the future was laced with the new and acceptable verbs of social welfare, words like "cut" and "sever." But there was a sense of resignation about him. It was as if he were saying, We got the kids from their moms. Now what?

It was just before nine, and Murphy had already been at work for a few hours. He liked to get to the office early, he often told reporters, so that he could get home in time for dinner with his family. His office overlooked the Loop. It was long and paneled in wood, and lined with congratulatory plaques and citations. On a far wall hung a framed copy of the cover of a book Murphy wrote in 1974, *Our Kindly Parent, the State*. The book was a savage indictment of the child welfare system's intrusion into the lives of the poor and was written at a time when Murphy saw himself as a vigilant advocate for the less fortunate. Though he still thought of himself as a liberal on

234

social matters, those who had known Murphy over the years had watched the passion that he had once used to denounce the state come to include the very people the state was supposed to help. Some who once admired Murphy now saw him and his increasingly harsh views as the result of someone who had spent too many years too close to the horrors that parents inflicted upon their children and which the state only seemed to compound. It was, they suggested with sighs and nods of understanding, as if Murphy had been driven a bit mad by what he had seen and what he knew. Murphy was not sounding angry as he sat at his desk drinking his coffee. Instead he seemed like a man who had walked into a maze confident that he knew the way out and now, after many wrong turns, found himself staring up, once again, at a high wall of green shrubbery.

"It all sounds naive and simplistic," he said, "but you have to cut into it somewhere." Murphy, however, knew enough of the state of the families, and of the limits of the child welfare system, to admit that he was stuck on the question of what to do with the children. He talked, vaguely, of providing "services" to the mothers as quickly as possible, in the hope that they might be capable of responding to help. Beyond that he was no longer so sure. "Do you put that kid with a parent who is marginal, or a relative who is marginal, or a system that is marginal?"

———

Later, I recalled the afternoon in Cassandra Henderson Melton's living room, with Josephine, May Fay, and Maxine Melton. May Fay was still going to school, and Cassandra was as pleased with her as she was frustrated with Maxine. Cassandra believed that she was seeing in May Fay the confidence she so valued in herself. If Maxine was still foundering and offering the thinnest sorts of excuses for her inactivity, then May Fay had begun acting like a woman gaining some control of her life.

Cassandra had succeeded in steamrolling over the messiness and clutter in her own life. She was wise enough to recognize and understand all the impediments that stood between her cousins and the lives she wanted them to lead. All they had to do was be determined, as she was. All they had to do was take steps—go to school and get jobs and keep their homes clean and remember the good things they had learned about caring for children. Then they would not only have their children back, but would become, as she was, a mother whose children had reason to admire her.

I had come to believe that Cassandra and then House Speaker Newt Gingrich were very much alike, if only in the way they regarded mothers like the Melton sisters. Cassandra, like Gingrich, and for that matter, like other men and women who ascend to positions of influence, were motivated people. They were motivated to be heard, to be powerful, to be able to tell other people what to do. They could not understand the passivity, the drift of the Meltons. It was as if they assumed that everyone was like them, filled with purpose, able, at the very least, to make connections between threat and punishment. And if they were depressed, they nonetheless suffered as fulfilled people.

It is, however, an altogether different matter to be a poor person who also feels emotionally empty and adrift—a characteristic that Cassandra at least recognized, even if she could not understand why anyone would allow herself to live in such a state. Cassandra, in her own infinitely caring way, maintained as crystalline a world view as the altogether harsher and unforgiving view of Newt Gingrich. The Melton sisters made no sense to either of them. And that was why both Cassandra Henderson Melton and Newt Gingrich spoke as if they believed that by demanding that women like the Melton sisters behave as motivated people behaved, they could become good and decent parents.

It would have been comforting had the Melton sisters merely been evil. They were not. Evil is purposeful, which suggests that the behavior is motivated, even if out of malice. And evil, like hope, exists at the fringes of the child welfare system. Yet as parents, the Meltons presented a problem far more intractable than that of the abuser: They lived lives of such utter emptiness and despondency, lives so devoid of meaning and purpose and motivation, that to assume that they would respond to persuasion or to universally understood threats—"We are going to take your kids"—was foolish and naive.

When I told people about the Melton sisters, about the lives they lived and what they believed they had provided their children, the response I heard was almost always the same: incredulity. Surely, I heard again and again, these women are moved to act on *something*. They buy drugs, don't they? They're motivated to do that. In response I offered Patrick Murphy's explanation of drug use by the mothers whose children he represented: I go on vacation, Murphy would say, and for these women drugs is the only vacation they have from the misery of their lives; if I were one of them, he concluded, I would get high, too.

That response, however, went only so far. It did not explain why all the money and help and free advice that the state had for years provided for women who had lost, or who were about to lose, their children—drug counseling, therapy, parenting skills classes, family preservation—did not turn these mothers into people like Cassandra Henderson Melton, who so much wanted to believe that her cousin May Fay was now "a totally different person."

That May Fay was not, and was perhaps incapable of ever being, such a person was brought home to me by three teenage mothers I met at the Maryville Parenting-Teen Center at the Illinois Masonic Medical Center. Their assessment and treatment was done by CAUSES, a program founded in 1974 for the victims of sexual and physical abuse, but which now also worked with the children of neglectful and abusive parents who had themselves become mothers.

The mothers were wards of the state. The program's director, Richard Labrie, said that his program was not especially popular among those who wanted services for children provided quickly and cheaply. The twenty-two girls who lived at the center stayed at CAUSES through high school, which meant that some were there—receiving help in building new lives—for four years.

The mothers at the center went to school. Their children were in the program's day care center. The mothers received years of psychotherapy. "I wonder whether we're taking a look at what's really damaging, at being a year old and not being taken care of," Labrie said. "I'm talking about children who aren't picked up and held and responded to. I wonder what happens to them when they grow up and raise their own families."

They became the mothers in his program, at least the lucky ones did. The others ran the very great risk of losing their children. "I'll get a call from somebody we saw as a child five or six years ago, and he'll say, 'Remember me?' The first question is always 'Remember me?' " Labrie said. "Their child will be injured at home, and they'll say, 'I'm kind of feeling like I can't do this. Can I come back?' "

At CAUSES I met three teenagers who, to protect their confidentiality, I will identify by the initials P, B, and R. R and B each had two children. P had one. R was eighteen and had been in the program for two years. P and B were seventeen and newly arrived. I asked about their mothers.

B said her mother was fifteen when she was born. She had two younger brothers whom her mother placed in her care several weeks after they were born. "She'd say, 'Watch 'em, I'll be right back,' " she said. "She'd come back two days later." When her mother returned, she asked B whether the baby had cried, and when B said he had cried, her mother told her she could have called. "But if I tried, she probably would have got upset," she said. " 'What you calling me for?' "

P said her mother "was there and not there; she was doing her little thing, and I was doing my little thing." While B's anger was barely concealed, P still sounded like a teenager who believed she could drive very fast because nothing bad could happen to her. She and her son, who was two years old and named for his father, went to the movies together. They had just seen the movie *Jason's Lyric*. P's mother, when she was present, was "too strict," and P had decided she would be a different sort of mother. "I'm gonna let him go outside, let him watch TV. We gonna talk. We gonna kick it. We kicking now."

Then there was R, whose mother "stayed at home, cooked us dinner on Sundays," until she met a man and started staying out, like B's mother. Two of R's sisters went to live with her grandmother, and two went to live with their father. "I was left to stay there by myself," she said. "I used to ask her, 'Why you got to stay on the street?' She said, 'I spent eighteen years of my life taking care of y'all. It's time for me to get out.' When she first left, it bothered me. All my friends turned me down. They said they didn't have no space for me." The heat was turned off, and R was placed in the emergency shelter on Montrose Avenue, where the police first took the Melton children. R was surprised when she found herself pregnant, even though, she said, she "always wanted to have a baby."

B said she wished she had not waited until she was three months pregnant to tell her mother because her mother's response was, "I could have got you an abortion." Her mother was also pregnant. B's daughter and youngest brother were born three months apart. When her second child, a son, was born, B refused to look at him because, she said, "he was ugly." Still, Robert Spector, the psychologist who worked most closely with the girls, had hope for B. She was bright, and there was an intensity about her anger that, he believed, might be channeled, with time.

R concerned him. She had completed high school and was beginning to take college-level courses, but her affect was so flat that she seemed incapable of anything but a muted response. When I saw her with her children, she sat with the younger one looking like a teenager on a school bus, staring vacantly out the window, a knapsack on her lap.

I asked R what she had learned in the last two years about what mothers were supposed to do for their children.

"Keep the kids clean," she said. She spoke slowly, in an almost lifeless recitation. "Teach them good manners. Don't let them hang outside like after ten o'clock on school nights. Don't let them do whatever they want, disrespecting, stuff like that."

Later, Spector told me that many of the mothers in the program were, developmentally, younger than their three- and four-year-old children: They could not see the world in anything but the most childishly narcissistic way. This was not the self-absorption that Patrick Murphy railed about. Spector was describing mothers who were profoundly emotionally stunted, seeing the world only as it reflected upon them.

"They're being told to take certain responsibilities, which is like telling a four-year-old 'Grow up already,'" Spector said. Then, thinking of B's reaction to the birth of her son, he added, "Imagine at the moment of birth you've got a mother who can't look at you. With all that, you're hoping that somehow the program can speed up their adolescent development to get beyond wanting to have fun, to get them to be able to make a decision that suggests that their child's welfare has become the equal of their own. And I don't know if that's a fair expectation, given their past and given that they're fifteen."

I could imagine no more compassionate a listener than Spector. Yet his conclusion based upon so many hours with his clients appeared to confirm the suspicions of those who believed that the children of mothers like the Melton sisters were best off swiftly removed from home. This sort of reasoning has long been a part of the discussion on child welfare, from Charles Loring Brace's belief in the virtue of the orphan trains to Newt Gingrich's widely quoted if offhand remark that the children of failing families might fare best in orphanages. There is a seductive simplicity in believing that if the state could only muster the will to act decisively on behalf of those children, it could break the cycle of what Brace called "hereditary pauperism"—a generation of the unredeemable poor begetting yet another equally troubled and threatening generation.

That view, however, was challenged for me not by the one-time radical, Bernardine Dohrn, but by Richard Calica, the director of the Juvenile Protective Association. Calica was a Republican from Brooklyn who, even after twenty-five years in Chicago, had not bothered calibrating his speech or pace to the Midwest. In addition to his work with families subcontracted to his agency by the Department of Children and Family Services, he was also a consultant to Jess McDonald, the department's director.

Calica had read the case file on the Melton family. The depiction of life at 219 North Keystone Avenue reminded him of an experiment in which he was a subject while at graduate school. He spent three days in a sensory deprivation chamber. "Your ability to count backwards from ten to one goes out the window," he said. "You start floating around. I don't know if in this family it made any difference whether it was daytime or nighttime outside. No clock; no table to sit down to; no saying, This is the time we eat. That's not providing your kid with anything to grow into a functioning human being. What began to be apparent in this case was that the family—I guess I'll call it a family—seemed, as a group, devoid of at least the immediate capacity to attend to their kids. You do not let children roam through life as an undifferentiated horde."

Yet harsh and bleak as that assessment was, Calica surprised me when he said that he might not have taken the children on the night the police found them. He might have taken them a week later. But he would have waited. "I would have said, This is intolerable and the only way you keep your kids is that I'm going to put someone in your house immediately twenty-four hours a day, seven days a week, to make order out of this mess."

And if Maxine had said, Get out of my house?

"If the condition is you let me in or I take your kids right now, that's the forced choice," he said. "In that instance I would have been horrified enough to say I couldn't just walk away. I would have exercised the state's right to get involved with the family." But he still would have wanted to leave the children with their mothers. "My standard is the cessation of biological existence. As long as we're not talking about a kid dying, then I've got time. If you're not hallucinating that rays are coming in from Venus and I don't have any belt marks on the kids and the kids look well fed and I have no history of a delusional system that the devil is telling you to kill these kids, I'll keep the kids in your care. I'll wait to see what else is possible before I do a radical surgery job."

But why wait?

Because, he replied, "you're better off staying with your mom than staying with me."

Calica, who had earned a graduate degree in developmental psychology from the University of Chicago, had spent twenty years working with failing families. He was as knowledgeable about families like the Meltons as he was familiar with the questions they posed to the state: "How pernicious is this neglectful environment going to be for this kid? And do we have anything better to offer?"

He did not believe "we" did. This was not merely the result of a shrinking pool of skilled foster parents and too few institutional beds. Rather it reflected what he and others who viewed families from a classical psychological point of view believed was the essential and inescapable paradox in the relationship between failing parents and their children: The state could not extricate that parent, no matter how awful, from that child's life. She was going to be there, perhaps as a physical presence and certainly as an emotional one. Accepting that belief—one widely, though not universally, held—meant that a resolution for a failed child in which the past was wiped clean was all but impossible.

Was he then suggesting, I asked, that even if the state could provide a child with a new life with smart, thoughtful, and trained adults, that child might still be better off with a mother like May Fay Melton?

That, he said, was precisely what he meant.

But why?

"Because May Fay is where you come from," he said. "And you're always going to long for and wish to work out your relationship with

May Fay, not with me. And somehow, one way or the other, I have to deal with you and May Fay, and I'd rather deal with you and May Fay living together than taking you apart and spending all that money and all that time, because you're going to run back to her anyway. If I take you away, I have to deal with you blaming yourself for her failure. And it's going to cost me a gazillion dollars, and it's going to take pounds and pounds of time and energy and effort to overcome all the damage that's going to be done to you before you can finally see what Newt can see—that, jeez, this is a rather inadequate mom and we're giving this kid a big break. Kids don't view it that way."

Calica did not advocate infinite tolerance for parental failure—as Angelica Anaya-Allen had before the Connecticut Supreme Court. Quite the contrary. He believed that "all behavior is purposeful," which was why he was troubled by the Melton sisters' slipshod attempts to satisfy the requirements of the state. He saw in their stumbling and backsliding a "message" about the limits of their commitment to their children. For all his years with parents like the Meltons, Calica could still not fathom how a parent, no matter how marginal, could bear the idea of losing a child. Calica was the father of a teenage son. It was not surprising, given what he saw and knew, that he spoke of him with a particularly ferocious love. "I'd be willing to kill you if you came near my kid," he said. "And I'd be willing to die first instead of my kid. And it's instinctive." If his child was taken from him, Calica said, he would tell the agents of the state, " 'Do I have to kill you,'—to get him back—'or do I have to do the dance you want me to do? I'll do it.' "

Calica recognized that the state placed hurdles in the way of parents who wanted their children back and that these obstacles sometimes forced those parents to protect their own needs at the expense of the needs of their children. Yet he had seen parents "a lot sicker" than the Meltons—the homicidal Amanda Wallace among them—who "held on longer" in the hope of one day regaining their children. Where was the Meltons' longing for their children?

He did not need to see a reflection of his own devotion in the Meltons. But he needed to see "some capacity to understand that your child's experience in the world may be different than yours." Because only then could that parent be capable of giving something of herself to her children.

"I'm talking real broad here," he said of what he demanded of the parents with whom his agency worked. "My bottom line is that you have some level of guilt or shame. And that there's no immediate threat that you're going to kill your kid. That's all."

And what if that mother was a drug user like May Fay, Denise, and Diane Melton?

"I don't care that she's using drugs," Calica replied. "I care about what she's doing when she's using drugs to make sure her kids' needs are being taken care of. That's my question."

I told him how the sisters called their mother to come watch the children when they wanted to go out.

"That's cool," he said. "It's not, 'I'm gonna nod out with a cigarette in my mouth with no one here but you and me.' What matters is that you have some notion that you're going to protect your child while you're taking care of your own stuff."

Calica estimated that of the 250 parents for whom his agency provided counseling and, if needed, years of assistance in rearing their children, perhaps 25 failed to display even that minimal level of concern for their children. For those families, he said, placing the children in new homes was necessary. Even then it was often the case that the parents consented to this removal, a decision that struck Calica as a hint of decency: The parents understood that their children were better off elsewhere, this despite whatever hopes, dreams, and fantasies about their babies might have attended the birth of those children years before.

I had heard nothing suggesting that Diane Melton had made any effort, let alone any sustained effort, to try to do what she had to do to regain her children. But I recalled the way Maxine, and especially Denise and May Fay, talked about their desire, however vaguely articulated, to have their children back one day. May Fay had at least tried before she failed, which was more than could be said of Maxine, who nonetheless managed to visit her boys every so often. Denise, in particular, was proud of what she had learned in rehab, about herself and about her ability to stay with a routine task and about what that might mean once her children came back to her. This was what Calica needed to see, the possibility that there existed in these mothers the quality that all children needed—an adult who had an interest in their lives. His agency was in the midst of a extensive study on "resiliency," why certain children in horrible circumstances managed to flourish while others were crushed. He was not suggesting that this nascent capacity to parent might somehow redeem May Fay or Denise. Their children might, in fact, well need to live apart from such unreliable mothers. But even if they did, the mothers still had a role to play, an essential one. This was not a reward for the mothers. It was a necessity for their children.

By the time the state felt compelled to impose itself upon a family, the lives of the children were, as Donald Cohen of the Yale Child Center put it, "spoiled." There was no way the state could undo this. This was as apparent to Father John Smyth on the night he first saw the Melton children "dirty and confused" at the emergency shelter on Montrose Avenue, as it was to Claudine Christian a year later as she watched her clean and schooled and well-fed godchildren struggle with the sad and simple fact that they "missed their mother." Yet spoiled as things were, said Calica, "if you think you're incapable of forming attachments left in the hands of a neglectful mom, just wait till you see what happens to someone when you start changing caretakers on a regular basis, or an unpredictably irregular basis. Why would I want to attach to anyone when I don't know when there will be the next knock and 'Time to move'?"

What, I asked, happens to that child?

"They constantly long for the parent we took them away from, and most of them land back with these parents anyway," he said. "When they get older, they run away and they go back, and we ultimately leave them with the people we took them away from. The kids always long for their parents. Always. The only kids who don't want to be back with their parents are either psychotic, really mentally ill, or some small subset where the parents were so out of it. But most kids who have been beaten, tortured, burned, raped, mauled want to go back to the people who did it."

Why?

"The devil we know is much better than the devil we don't know. It's much better to be able to see your mom high on drugs or superdepressed and being in and out of your life irregularly than not to have any reality at all," he said. "Because then you create some fantasy that has nothing to do with the real world at all. At least you can say, 'Gee, maybe it wasn't just me. Maybe she's a little screwed up and wasn't able to take care of me, and it wasn't my fault. It may be her fault too.' She will be part of her children's lives whether she shows up or not because they will carry around whatever fantasies plus whatever reality they remember about their mom, as they will create the fantasy of the missing father. Each one of them will have a missing father, whether they knew that father or not. They will have a fantasy of what he was like, and what he looked like and why he left."

If there was, in Calica's view, a risk in leaving the children as they were at 219 North Keystone Avenue and a risk in rushing to take them away, how could the state keep the risks to a minimum?

"What's the best of a bunch of bad alternatives?" Calica asked. "And what's the most cost-effective solution from a psychological as well as a financial standpoint? In many instances it may be to support these seemingly undesirable situations with some kind of help—maybe job training or financial help or counseling or day care or developmental opportunities for the kids. But leaving them with their parents would be a better alternative. Or would it be better to take the kid and move him five times in the first year of his life from one well-meaning home to another? My answer would be leaving them with their parents."

———

It was all well and good to hear Richard Calica talk about the way children felt about their parents. But I wanted to hear it from the children themselves. In New York City I met with five teenagers who had come of age in the child welfare system and who now wrote for a newspaper called *Foster Care Youth United*. The paper, which was published every other month by Youth Communication, dubbed itself "the voice of youth in foster care." It was filled with stories about such issues as sexual harassment in foster homes and whether foster siblings were true siblings. It was also a forum where the writers could address such matters as "gaining strength from the past" and learning to trust a social worker.

At the center's newsroom—a room that could have passed for a college newspaper's office, with its computer terminals, tacked up notices and clutter—I met A and C, who were nineteen, G, who was eighteen, and Q, who was seventeen. We were joined by a sixteen-year-old, Y. We talked about their mothers and fathers.

"I grew up without my mother," said A. Her mother left when A was six months old. Her father's relatives took her in and then passed her along to other relatives. When she was nine, A moved in with her father. "At ten," she said, "I had my first and last birthday party."

When A was fourteen, she found her mother. "She didn't look for me. I had to look for her." Her mother did not want to see A. A's therapist convinced her of that. In her mother, A met a woman who "had been on welfare all her life. She had other kids with different fathers. My mom, she's very complex. She didn't have any friends. All her life she didn't have nobody. After her last boyfriend, she's not dating anyone. She's telling me, Never have a boyfriend. Never have a friend. All her life people hurt her feelings."

A visited her every weekend. She listened as her mother complained about her other children. A had a stepbrother who was mentally retarded. Her mother was, in her fashion, devoted to him and would not give him up. A said, "She kept on forgetting that I'm her daughter, too."

A's visits had not led to a happy resolution with her mother. "Me and my mother is an off and on thing," she said. "She told me she didn't want to see me. It hurts."

As for her father, A ran away from him when she was fourteen. He found out that she was smoking and that she had a boyfriend. She was then living with her father's old girlfriend. At two in the morning her father came into her room and dragged her out of bed by the hair, screaming, "I want to know who this guy is!" A begged him to let her go. "He punched me very hard with his fists. He kicked me. I was scared. The last thing I remember was being knocked out. When I woke up I was bleeding from my head. I wondered, Why did he let me live?"

Still, A went to see her father on Thanksgiving. He was living alone, in a single room. "I don't know. I just wanted to see him again," A said. "I felt sorry for him."

C remembered his father as a man who had little time for his family. C was born in Jamaica and recalled that his father had been part of his life, distant as that was, until he was nine. C was then living with relatives. He had lived with his parents until he was five, and then because his parents worked, he was sent to live elsewhere. He moved to New York with his mother and sisters. His mother, he says, favored his sisters. C said he would like to ask his mother, "Why didn't she treat me like a son?"

C told how his mother yelled at him and hit him. "I was like the bottom," he said. C's mother placed him in the child welfare system. C says she did this to him because "I didn't want to listen." He would say only that he had caused "problems" but did not want to tell what the problems were.

"I wanted my mother, like any normal kid," he said. "But I couldn't."

G, too, had had "problems." The problems began between G and her mother when they lived in Tobago, where G was born and where her mother left her when she came to New York. G's mother left her with a friend. But that arrangement did not last, and so G moved from home to home. "We fought like we hated each other," G said of her mother, before her mother left. "But I tell you something, when she was in New York and she was a thousand miles away, I cried at night."

Y did not cry for her mother. Y, who was the youngest and most sullen of the group, said that she did not much want to see her mother. Y had placed herself in the system when she was eleven.

Why? I asked.

"Mental and physical abuse by my mother," she said in a flat, bored voice. "Sexual abuse by my mother's father." She made a point of not calling him her grandfather. Y ran away from home seven times before she told an adult at school what was happening in her home. She did not go home that day. She waited at school after everyone else was dismissed. A caseworker came. "I went with somebody who came and took me," she said. She stayed in a foster home for four months, before an aunt took her in for what Y described as "three unhappy years." When Y first went into the system, she said, "I used to miss my mother. Then I got older and learned the way of the system." She would tell her foster siblings "the only reason I'm not hitting you is I need a place to stay."

Y saw her mother every other weekend. "I came in from Long Island to Manhattan. I just wasn't allowed to go to my mother's home. And I do better without seeing her. She puts too much stress on my life. Last time I spoke with her, I told her she was full of shit."

She had not seen her father in five years, since she was eleven. She does not know where he is. "All I know is that I look exactly like him."

Y admitted to some confusion in how to regard her mother. "My family's telling me that she's bad, and the system's telling me my family's bad," she said. "My mother thinks the system brainwashed me. I don't want her to have no part of my life. I don't trust people."

C and G, however, believed that no matter how awful a parent might have been, that parent, even if long absent, still exercised a powerful tug at a child. That, at least, was how they felt.

"That's who they knew when they were small," G said.

C said, "There comes a time in that child's life when he is going to miss that parent. They're going to miss seeing them."

Q disagreed. "The way I see it, I don't want to see my mother because she gave me up."

The state took Q from her mother when she was three years old. She had been in the system during the fourteen years since. She is not sure just how many foster homes she has lived in. She had long since learned to stop giving anything of herself to the people who took her in. "When I was taken away, that was from the person closest to me," she said. "You're being taken away from friends and neighbors." And with each successive placement, she said, "you have to start leaving all over again." At first, she said, she tried to feel something for the people who took her in. But that did not last.

"I always recognized things," she said.

What sorts of things?

"How bio kids wouldn't let me play. They said, 'Don't touch my mother. Don't hug her.' You stop caring."

Q said she did well in school, although she seldom talked. Her teachers believed she was depressed. She felt that people who asked her to tell them how she felt were intruding upon her. "It's too much to open up. Nobody wants to do that.

"You go around planting seeds, planting seeds of love. And you don't stay long enough to let it grow."

The enduring and unanswered question in the story of the Melton family, for me, was what would have happened had the police not taken the children that night. Would the sisters have responded to Calica's demand that they allow a stranger to help them make order of their lives? Would they have allowed that stranger or a series of strangers to assist them in rearing their children?

I asked Maxine and May Fay whether they would have welcomed that sort of help. May Fay, in particular, was intrigued with the prospect of someone assisting her with the work of taking care of her children. But then this idea came months after their removal and after she had already been in rehab and counseling. I could not know how she would have reacted that night.

Richard Calica was describing a relationship between the state and failing families that was altogether different from the one that had existed, in England and here, for centuries. The relationship he described was not adversarial. But neither was it something that approximated friendship. It was, in a sense, like the relationship between parent and child and carried with it all the dangerous implications of a parentalistic attitude of the state toward the poor. It was a relationship between two unequal partners, in which the dominant and powerful partner, the state, was understanding but not accepting of the failure of the subordinate partner, the parent. The state made demands that it expected the parent to meet. But the state was not brandishing a stick at the parent, first threatening it with a jail term for failing a child and then dangling the prize of that child before that parent's eyes as a reward if the parent performed as the state demanded.

The child remained that parent's child. It did not become the child of the state, even though the state had taken an interest in it. The state expected more from the parent than the parent had done, and if the parent railed against the state for imposing its values, the state could counter by reminding that parent that the standards she was violating were her community's standards. One need look no further than the recovering drug addict who lived across North Keystone Avenue from the Meltons to be reminded that among their neighbors the behavior of the Melton sisters toward their children was intolerable.

Left to wonder about what might have happened had the police who stumbled upon the nineteen children that night responded in a way short of immediate removal, and thinking about Calica's idea of a different relationship between the parent and state, I left Chicago for New York. There in the Sunset Park section of Brooklyn, I met two nuns who for eighteen years have been applying this same approach to the families in their supervision. The essential difference between the work done by Calica's agency and Sisters Mary Paul and Geraldine at the Center for Family Life was that the sisters confined their services to Sunset Park alone. They did so in the belief that the only way to assist troubled families was in the community where those families lived. Because then, as it was in Elizabethan England and in Jacksonian America, the responsibility for the adult poor rested not with strangers, but with people who knew, and perhaps understood, something about their lives and their children.

The Inevitability of Mother

THE CENTER FOR Family Life sat in the shadow of an expressway, on a street of sagging two-story homes. Sunset Park was a square mile filled with some one hundred thousand people, most of them Hispanic, black, and, in growing numbers, Chinese. It was a poor neighborhood, but not a blighted one. The center was housed in a mustard-yellow brick building that had once been a home for seminarians. The center felt old and cramped. It was a place of many small offices with white walls, endless coats of dark brown trim, and, on the bulletin boards, pictures drawn by children. The phones rang constantly. The center opened at eight in the morning and closed at eleven o'clock at night, after which emergency calls went to the apartments on the top floor where Sisters Mary Paul and Geraldine lived.

The center received visitors from child welfare agencies not only from across the country but from around the world—representatives came to see how the center managed to succeed with the families in its care. The sisters and their twenty-five social workers spent years attending to the interminable needs, demands, failures, and hints of success, as well as the despondency, addiction, and psychosis of, at any one time, 250 or so families in their care. The sisters would never say that the state was stuck with those troubled, wearying, and endlessly struggling parents. But that was precisely the case.

"It's not a question of whether we keep her in the picture. It's whether the mother stays in the picture," said Sister Mary Paul, the center's co-founder. "We don't have a choice about extricating that mother from that child's mind or reality." This meant that the parent, if he or she chose to remain a part of a child's life—and most did, with varying degrees of success—could not be willed away by a well-intentioned caseworker who wished only to save a child from that parent.

The sisters were a striking pair. Geraldine was fifty-six, a tall woman who was direct in her speech and manner. Mary Paul was tiny. She spoke in a small voice with which she dismissed questions of her age by saying, "We don't go in for that mushy stuff." The center's social workers found her magnetic. They were sisters of the Order of the Good Shepherd, which was founded in seventeenth-century France to assist poor women. The sisters had worked at residential treatment centers for teenage girls, and it was there, Sister Geraldine said, that they began to believe that the work with children in troubled homes was best begun well before the state needed to take them from their parents. "We ended up as the end of the road for many adolescents," Geraldine said. "I don't know how I could ever go back to that work."

Given the backgrounds and vocations of its founders, the center was not, strictly speaking, replicable. Yet Mary Paul insisted that while the center was an extension of their faith, the work did not have to fall only to women who had taken vows. The casework was indeed done by social workers. But the vision was Mary Paul and Geraldine's. It was an extension of their faith.

"These are not clients," Mary Paul said. "Our caring for them comes out a very strong sense of their meaning, of their importance. I don't look at them as clients. They are people I love and work with. We are engaged together. They are meaningful to me as mothers and fathers and children whom I encounter."

Sister Geraldine oversaw the center's many different programs—among them summer jobs for teenagers, day care, an evening teen center, a family learning center, and parenting classes. Mary Paul remained the first person at the center a troubled parent met. Families came to the center because the city had taken a child and assigned the case to the center. Families came to the center's attention because, say, a guidance counselor called to alert the sisters about problems in a home or because a neighbor called, as one did to report a ten-year-old sleeping on the top of a car. Half the parents simply walked in and asked for help.

The center was a division of one of the large, private foster care agencies with which the city contracted to handle its growing caseload. It received referrals from the agency, but in keeping with its philosophy it would only accept families who lived in Sunset Park.

Mary Paul began. "A person, on the surface of things, has failed her children miserably and seems to be denying the effects on the children." Mary Paul believed that she had to learn how this apparent failure came to be. So she sat with a parent at a table in the center's bright but threadbare family room and, in a manner that was both gentle and insistent, began her inquiry into what she called the "degradations" in that parent's life. She asked these kinds of questions: "Who are you? What has caused the madness in your own life? How do you place yourself in the world? To what extent do you live in fear of what you've missed in life?" Then she asked, "Do you still have any dreams left for yourself or your child that nobody ever asked you about?"

It took time to answer these questions, to get a sense of the life of newly arrived strangers. But, Mary Paul explained, "unless you are willing to look at that complexity you don't see the individual. You just see shadows. And if you don't see the individual, you're going to have the perpetuation into another generation because misery begets misery."

The state, too, asked questions and transcribed the answers in case records. "Case records superficially capture the 'problem' and not the feelings," Mary Paul said, "not the relationships, not whether there is something that has held that mother and child together in spite of anger, in spite of feelings of futility."

The center had worked with hundreds of families over the years. Sisters Mary Paul and Geraldine, echoing Richard Calica, said that virtually all the parents had some degree of commitment to their children. This alone did not mean that a parent should regain a child. "We're not saying you shouldn't separate a child from a parent," said Mary Paul. In the eyes of the sisters and their workers, these parents had something of themselves to offer their children. In more cynical eyes, it meant that the parents, even if they disappeared for weeks or months on end, would keep coming back, again and again, making the same promises of sobriety, work, and insight.

"You cannot change the psychological process in another human being," Mary Paul said.

———

At the center I met a woman whom I will call Anne. Her daughter was taken away from her the first time in 1992, after her husband told his addiction counselor he was afraid to leave his daughter alone with his wife. The counselor, who was required to report cases of abuse, abandonment, or neglect, contacted the city's child welfare administration, which sent a caseworker to her home. Anne and her family lived in an apartment empty of all furniture except for two beds—for the child and parents, placed side by side—a television, and an exercise machine. Anne threw away everything that she believed had not been given "with love." She tore a hole in a wall and took the handles off all the doors. Yet Anne was somehow able to protect her child, whom I will call Jane, from her psychotic episodes, which meant that the nature and extent of the risk she posed for Jane was by no means clear.

The caseworker interviewed Anne, her husband, and their daughter separately, and when he was finished, he left with the child. Jane spent eight months in foster care and then went home.

Anne lost Jane for the second time in the very office where she and her daughter now sat. That was when Jane was eight. Anne stood between her social worker and her daughter and said, "You're not taking my kid." The social worker told Anne that if she did not surrender the child, she would call the police. Anne refused. The police took the child from the social worker's office. "At that moment you think they're the ogres of the world," Anne said. "You can't imagine the fear it puts in a mother's heart. A complete stranger has your child. How would they know what a child needs?"

Anne was gone for four years. She lived in homeless shelters. Jane's father lived in a residential treatment program for alcoholics and drug addicts. Now, however, he was clean and working and supported Jane and his elderly mother. And for her part, Anne, after years of refusal, was at last taking her psychotropic medication. Anne, who was in her thirties and spoke in therapeutic euphemisms, had returned to assume the role of mother.

For the family's social worker, Gretchen Lord, and for the center, monitoring Anne's return to her child was like watching someone skipping along the edge of a cliff. This was not to suggest that Anne was about to fall—only that it would be foolish and naive to assume she might not.

I met Anne at a time when New York was contemplating profound changes in its child welfare system. Her story was a parable of sorts of what was possible and what was not in the relationship between parent and state as envisioned by Sisters Mary Paul and Geraldine. Since the widely publicized death of a six-year-old named Elisa Izquierdo at the hands of her mother in November of 1995, New York's mayor, Rudolph Guiliani, had made the fate of children a matter of great urgency. He appointed a new commissioner, Nicholas Scoppetta, to preside over a newly renamed and independent department, the Administration for Children's Services. The mayor and Scoppetta, himself a former foster child who has won wide praise for his knowledge of the field and for his leadership of a maligned, dispirited, and malfunctioning agency, introduced a plan for reform.

The plan called for the city to decentralize its vast central bureaucracy and replace it with satellite offices around the city. The approach, which has gained popularity at child welfare agencies across the country—in Los Angeles and Hawaii most prominently—has been touted as a way to reduce the single greatest cost in child welfare, to the state and to children: prolonged and indeterminate care in a succession of foster homes.

The proponents of such plans insisted that the work of salvaging families and helping children could not be done by strangers—by caseworkers arriving from distant offices, with sixty other equally troubled families on their caseload. The work, they argued, could be accomplished only when the workers knew those families and understood the manifold problems with which they lived, the relationships that mattered in the children's lives, and the needs of those children. And that knowledge, in turn, came only to people who spent their days in the neighborhood and who could offer the sorts of assistance—counseling, housing, rehab, and foster care—that were available locally. It was work still done by, among other unofficial agencies, institutions such as black churches. It was also work done with mothers like Anne at the Center for Family Life.

Anne came to the center the day after the caseworker took her child. She knew about the center because when she was young, her father, an alcoholic, came to the sisters for help after Anne's mother left him. Anne recalled how her father was told that he would receive no help rearing Anne's younger sister until he got sober. On the day she came to the center, Anne met with Sister Mary Paul and with Gretchen Lord, a former actress who had returned to school, had gotten a degree in social work, and had just been hired by the center. Lord recalled how Anne made many promises that first day about how things in her home would be better. At that moment, Lord believed she was talking to a rational person because Anne did not immediately veer off into the angry tangents that would, at times, dominate her conversation.

Mary Paul and Lord believed that the city was right to take Jane. But they also saw in Anne's shielding her daughter from her rage a sign of promise—evidence that this mother possessed a devotion to her child, limited though it was. On the day they met her, Lord and Sister Mary Paul told Anne that Jane was in a foster home in the neighborhood and that she could see her immediately and have a visit at the center every week.

"I felt that my absence from her life would somehow destroy her life," Anne said. "That she would hold it in—not understanding why she was in foster care."

When Lord first came to Anne's home, she said, "all the wallpaper had been systematically peeled off. Every little piece. The plates around the electrical sockets had been removed. There were no curtains, no shades, no furniture. There were no doors on the doorways. There was no privacy." That day, Lord recalls, she listened as Anne talked about "her fear, guilt, and anger about what had happened to the child."

Jane, meanwhile, was withdrawn to the point of silence. Jane responded with shrugs. When she did speak, she did so in baby talk. Jane was seven. Lord later came to see that Jane believed that it was good to talk like a baby because people did not get angry at babies. She would continue talking this way for years. Lord asked Jane to help her build a house out of cardboard and wood. The child did not understand that in other homes there were separate places for children and grown-ups and curtains on the windows. She did not have friends. After a while, in foster care, she began making friends. She appeared in plays, where, she said, she liked making believe that she was someone else.

Jane lived with a foster mother in the neighborhood, an especially easygoing woman who was patient with Anne. "She sensed Anne's fear that she would lose her connection with her daughter," Lord said. After two months during which Anne managed to compose herself on visiting days, Sister Mary Paul agreed to let her go to Jane's foster home and walk her to school. She met Jane at school at the end of the day to walk her back to her foster home. "Except she wouldn't want to separate from the child," Lord said. Lord discovered that Anne was staying for supper at Jane's foster home and explained to Anne she had to leave after returning Jane. "She had a very strong will," Lord said, "and would manipulate the situation."

Jane spent nine months in the foster home and then went home to her father and Anne. The father made this possible. He worked hard at his own recovery. Lord told the family court judge that despite all Jane had been through both at home and in being removed, she wanted to go home to her parents.

Jane remained at home for a few months. Then her father called Lord and said, "You've got to do something." The relationship between the parents had grown poisonous. Jane was depressed. "She would lock herself in the bathroom because her mother was acting strange," Lord said. "It was the image of her mother throwing things out of the window or getting rid of her bed. Just the sight of it was scary to her." Jane told Lord, "I don't want to go to foster care. But I'd like to go live with my friend." Then she said, "I hate my life."

Lord arranged for the family to come for what the workers call a "removal meeting" with Sister Mary Paul. Mary Paul explained to Anne that it would be necessary for the child to go back into foster care. She told Anne, "It saddens me so much that things have fallen apart." Anne stood in front of Jane and refused to let her go. Lord threatened to call the police. Anne would not relent. Finally, after Lord called the police and Jane, crying and frightened, allowed herself to be escorted away, Anne asked that her brother come to take her home.

Anne sank. She had once worked as a secretary. Now she lived in homeless shelters, where she met other women who had lost their children. "People didn't want to raise it," she said. Asking a woman about her child might lead to a fight. The women did not see their children very much. They felt helpless, Anne believed, because they understood that they would not get their children back. "I would take long walks," she said. "I had a lot of doctor appointments." Her life, she said, was like "a wheel that doesn't stop spinning."

Anne refused to take medication. Yet she almost never missed a weekly visit with her daughter. The center provided counseling for Jane and for Anne. In time, the counseling would extend to individual sessions with each member of Anne's family, as well as family therapy. Jane attended one of the center's after-school programs.

Anne visited Jane at the center. On nice days Lord arranged the meetings at a park, so that they would not feel quite so institutional. On other visits Anne and Jane met in Gretchen Lord's office. The office was decorated with pictures of the children who were under Lord's supervision.

Anne sometimes came to the center in the morning and lingered in the hallways and bathroom all day because she had nowhere else to go. The other social workers got used to seeing Anne, which was just as well because Sisters Mary Paul and Geraldine know that when any one social worker moved on, that could be hard on the parents and children who had grown attached to her. The families' attachment extended to the center as well, to the place and to the other people who worked there. It could take months to prepare a family for a worker's departure and months for the family to adjust to someone new. The center was the constant.

When Anne came for visits, Gretchen Lord would ask, "How was your week?" That would be enough to get Anne started. Anne would argue. Anne would digress. Lord would tell her, "I'm going to do paperwork. You need to talk with your daughter."

As is the practice with all the center's social workers, Lord met every week with Sister Mary Paul. "She would guide me in the moments when I felt I wasn't being any help at all," Lord said. These moments became more common as the symptoms of Anne's illness worsened. Anne would launch onto angry tangents. She would complain about, say, a bus driver who was not nice to her or about her welfare caseworker, a woman for whom Lord felt nothing but pity. She would appear not to hear or comprehend the simplest instructions.

"Sometimes I was just dreading it," Lord said of the weekly meetings with Anne. "There were times when I'd go to my colleagues' offices and say, I'm not being of any help to this person. Why am I doing this?"

Mary Paul would tell her, "I know it's hard, but this is where she visits her child. She needs us."

Lord tried to get Anne and Jane to do projects together. One time they made Jell-O. But Anne got upset and started to ask Jane whether this was what she did with her foster mother. "I think at times I would compare myself to the foster mother," Anne said. "The foster mothers are very strong-willed. You have to be to become attached to other people's children."

After school, foster mothers brought the children to the center for their visits and counseling. They opened the brown metal door and stepped into a small waiting room already filled with other foster mothers holding children on their laps. Upstairs, children played in the hallways. Later, cabs pulled up outside to take the foster mothers and the children back to their homes.

At any one time twenty-five families in Sunset Park had children in one of the center's foster homes. Unlike the arrangement elsewhere in the city, where a child taken from a home in the Bronx might end up in a foster home in Brooklyn, Mary Paul and Geraldine believed that their work with families in the neighborhood extended to keeping children near their homes, even when they could not live with their parents. The children stayed in the same schools and remained in close proximity to their friends and relatives. And, as often as was possible and advisable, they saw the parents from whom they were taken, as Jane did when she was first taken from Anne.

These mothers were called "the bio moms"—the biological mothers—and the encounter with them, Lord said, was the most draining part of the job. "These are damaged people," she said. "They were abused kids, and you become the idealized parent for them." She told of one parent who vanished for over a year, only to call on her child's birthday and tell Lord, "I want to be a parent." Then she disappeared again. Fathers called from jail and mothers arrived late for visits and then told their child's foster mother that the child was "not dressed as nicely as when I dress him." When the bio moms did not come on visiting day, the children got angry not at their mothers, but at their social workers. They said, "You should have found mommy by now." Sometimes the children said nothing. Their foster mothers reported that the children were wetting the bed and behaving badly in school.

One afternoon, a foster mother who, for reasons of privacy asked to be called Mrs. A, sat in her social worker's office with the child she was about to adopt. The boy was seven. He was chubby and friendly and had been with Mrs. A since he was two weeks old. He was born with cocaine in his blood. Mrs. A came to the hospital to take him and that is where she met the bio mom. The bio mom was a crack head with a round face and large eyes that her son inherited. Mrs. A, whose four children were grown up and who became a foster parent because she believed she was good at being a mother and longed to have another child in her home, said, "She needed as much help as the child." He was her first and only foster child.

For six years the bio mom appeared and disappeared as the mood struck her or as circumstances in her life allowed. "She always got lost," Mrs. A said of the excuse the mother generally offered for missed appointments and visits. She disappeared for two or three months at a time only to surface and tell Mrs. A "next month they're giving him back to me."

Mrs. A would call the child's social worker, Valerie Segal, who would assure her that the child was staying where he was. "It made me feel depressed, heavyhearted," Mrs. A said.

Segal would try to contact the mother and schedule other visits that might end with her nodding off as she sat with her son and Mrs. A in the little play yard outside the center. Mrs. A would try to wake her. Segal finally told Mrs. A not to bring the boy for visits until the mother appeared. On good days the mother was determined. She grabbed for the boy. This upset him. The mother would turn to Mrs. A and say, "Do you think that he's yours?" Mrs. A would tell her, "No, he's your child. Let him calm down. Let him get used to who you are."

As she told this story, the boy drew a picture of Batman, a fish, the sun, a snake, and a house. The figures floated around the page. The affects of exposure to cocaine in his mother's womb had abated long ago. Still, he seemed a young seven-year-old. Segal and Mrs. A talked about the termination of the mother's rights and how this came only after years of trying to bring the mother into the boy's life and how, in the end, it became clear that the mother had neither the interest nor capacity to sustain a relationship of consequence with the child.

Mrs. A and Segal met with the mother in the park, and when Segal told her of the decision to terminate her rights so that Mrs. A could adopt the boy, she did not protest. This was not surprising. Often the word of termination for a profoundly narcissistic parent comes as a relief; the parent is freed of the burden of the child. The father's rights had long since been terminated for abandoning his son. Because the center believed in making all adoptions open, Mrs. A told the biological mother that she would continue inviting her to the important events in the boy's life.

In December she came to the center's Christmas party. The family room was filled with children and foster mothers and bio moms who had their pictures taken with the children to whom they had given birth.

Mrs. A kept a picture of her son with his bio mom. In the picture the woman pressed her face next to the boy's. It was the same face. They were smiling. Mrs. A showed the picture to the boy.

Segal asked, "Do you like her?"

The boy said no, a little too angrily and a little too hastily.

———

Because the sisters believed in separating parents and children only as a last resort, they would try to keep the children at home, but with the understanding that the worker would be a continuous presence. Some parents, of course, refused this assistance, and if they did, the center would refer the case to the city's child welfare agency. But, the sisters said, many parents accepted the help and allowed a social worker into their homes and families.

Social workers like Lord and Segal visited. They called. They did virtually all that they believed had to be done to keep the family afloat—perhaps walking the parent to school because, say, the mother, feeling that the school secretary was mean to her, left before enrolling her child. A city caseworker is almost always cast in the role of monitor, scold, and cop. The center's social workers, on the other hand, would, if necessary, join the family, albeit as an outsider. For Lord this meant being, at turns, loved, hated, turned to, rejected, screamed at, and embraced.

When Lord first came into a home, she explained, she had learned to listen to the parent tell about her life. She guided her with questions: "How did you struggle in school? How did your parents punish you?" This line of questioning, she said, was designed to "give them permission to say that things weren't their fault." She would then connect the questions to the child. "When your father beat you for getting F's and you felt so ashamed that you dropped out of school, can you see how your daughter feels when you deny her things, month after month?"

In time, she would begin to encourage them to perform the important tasks of being a parent. She would say "Good parents get their children tested for HIV" or "Good parents take their children to the dentist." The parent, who might at first have tried to get Lord to take the child for her, might well say, "I thought about sending her by herself, and I should really go there to protect her." Lord said, "The child respects the parent in a way they hadn't."

The social workers told of parents who needed to learn to cook and budget their money and to help their children when they got hurt—like the mother who set off a firecracker that landed on her child and who thought the best way to treat the burn was with toothpaste. The workers talked to children about how to speak politely to their parents, and to the parents about not threatening their children with a return to foster care.

Those were the simpler cases. Sister Geraldine told of one family in which the mother was reluctant to let her in. Geraldine told her, "I am a mother lover, and I want to get to know you." Over the six years the woman, who was no more than forty, revealed to Geraldine a life of utter confusion and sadness. "You don't start on everything," Geraldine said. "You look and you listen." Geraldine was never able to determine precisely how many children this woman had, but believed it was well over fifteen, six of whom were already in foster care. Geraldine walked into a home where children slept everywhere, on couches and crowded on bunk beds. Geraldine brought mattresses and bags of clothing. The mother told her, "Look at all the bad things I bought for my kids. I'm a bad mother." She left the older children to take care of the younger children.

One day, in the middle of a family meeting that Geraldine was mediating, one of the teenage boys screamed at his mother, "Why did you have kids?" His mother roared back, "You are stabbing me. You are wounding me. Why are you wounding me?" The children resented their mother's frequent absences. The mother resented the children because she wanted to start a new life and the children were in her way. The mother believed that had she not been her own mother's "pretty little girl," her mother would have gotten rid of her. One day one of the girls told Geraldine, "I'm gonna be a nun like you and not have twenty kids like my mother."

The casework was depleting, unsettling, and filled with many moments of doubt. Sisters Mary Paul and Geraldine offered the workers not only a vision of what the work was supposed to be, but also the reassurance that even if the workers had, say, gone home for the night or for the weekend, the sisters would be available if a client called. The workers were paid roughly the same as the city's workers—$30,000 a year for those with a master's degree in social work. But unlike the city's workers, they were given great autonomy. And, in contrast to the city's child abuse caseworkers, whose turnover rate in 1992 was 77 percent, the center's social workers could actually talk of the moments that make their often maddening work feel worthwhile.

"In the struggle with the client they start to have insights," Lord says. "It's not so much that they thank you."

Even so, there were times when a parent who had demonstrated virtually no ability to care for her child nonetheless came to the center and managed to tell her child what he most needed to hear: "I want you to know that I never stopped thinking about you."

The workers and the sisters were not so naive as to regard this as anything more than a moment of rare and fleeting empathy. All it meant, said Mary Paul, was that one day, perhaps, "when the children get old enough, they can say 'I can have my parents as long as I don't ask very much of them.' "

Jane would be so nervous before she saw her mother that she would throw up. Anne looked forward to the visits. "It was hard when I had to leave," she said.

When Lord went on vacation, Anne was devastated. "I was heart-broken," she said. "I wanted to do well, to please myself, to please my daughter, to please the nuns, and to please Gretchen." But sometimes Anne would display the sort of anger that made Sister Mary Paul and Lord wonder whether she would get herself killed on the streets. She refused to be medicated.

To reunite Anne with her child, Sister Mary Paul knew, was a very great risk indeed. Still, it was one the center believed worth taking, when measured against the cost to the child of having her mother severed from her.

Anne's return home began on the day she most frightened Lord. "We were in the hallway, and I just felt she wasn't able to hear me," Lord said. "There was an intensity behind her anger." They happened to be standing in the narrow corridor outside Sister Geral-dine's office. Geraldine invited them in and closed the door. She spoke to Anne in a calm, soft voice. "She said how sad she felt after all this time working together that Anne wasn't able to take her medication," Lord said. "She put her hand on Anne's shoulder, and Anne began to cry and talk about how unhappy she was with her life."

Geraldine told Anne the story of another parent who had troubles much like Anne's and how that parent slowly began trying to take medication. "It was another voice," Lord said, "because at that moment I was the object of hatred."

Soon afterwards, Anne at last agreed to start trying medication. She entered a residential treatment program for six months. Through the next year and a half she kept up her visits. Jane's father, in the meantime, flourished in his recovery. It was to him that the child was returned. Were he not in the picture, it is highly questionable whether the center would have ever returned Jane to Anne.

Anne improved. Her visits got better. She visited Jane and her former husband in their home. Finally, at Thanksgiving, Lord said, "Dad and the child said they wanted her back."

———

When I met Anne, we sat in Gretchen Lord's office and Anne offered Jane a beatific smile. She reached to touch her. Jane tensed. She drew in her shoulders. She looked down and leaned close to the table where they sat, side by side. Anne tried to stop herself from touching her child, but could not.

"She's being cautious with me," Anne said. "She's remembering about being separated. Sometimes I see pain. She wants me near her, and then she'll say, 'Go away.' "

Still, Anne was taking great joy in once again being able to go shopping for clothes at Macy's with her daughter. Before the city first took her child, Anne used to take Jane grocery shopping. Anne liked that. Just now they shopped for household things for an apartment with a new computer, an eat-in kitchen, and a room of her own for Jane.

Anne talked of not allowing her "emotions to overcome the reality of the situation." She spoke slowly and quietly and measured her words. It was important, she explained, that the center helped her "keep [herself] at a level that is presentable and that is safe for the child." Sometimes, she admitted, she tried too hard. When Jane told her that she and her friends were going to get manicures, Anne ended up looking for her in all the nail salons on Fifth Avenue in Sunset Park because Jane did not seem old enough for a manicure.

"I kind of see a lot of love," Anne says. "She's a young lady. She's trying hard not to choose between her mother and father. She's remembering about being separated. But then she realizes that she's with her parents, and she's very calm and very relaxed and without worry."

Over her Christmas vacation Lord had a dream about Anne. In the dream Anne announced that she was going off her medication. A few weeks later, Anne called. She said she was feeling good. She did not like the way her medication made her feel. She felt she was doing much better. She told Lord that she was going to stop taking her medication.

Lord told this story and then sighed. All that was certain in the story of Anne was that it would not soon be over, not for Lord, or the center, or for Jane, who once told her grandmother in the midst of an argument, "The reason I get so sensitive is because I had to be separated from my parents."

The Philosophical Piece

SUCCESS IN child welfare is cause for muted celebration. It is measured incrementally and over years and, said Peg Hess, the associate dean of the School of Social Work at Columbia University, the work "is always disappointing." Failing families do not generally become model families. Children burdened by growing up in profoundly troubled homes do not easily, if ever, escape that past. Parents may wish to stop failing their children but will continue to do so, in different ways, just the same.

The Center for Family Life, Hess said, did its work exceedingly well. She had been studying the center for several years and believed that there was much the field could learn from its approach. Yet Hess did not delude herself about the prospects of a state agency's replicating the Center for Family Life. The center worked, she said, for the same reasons that terrific schools, companies, and other model social service agencies worked: It had two leaders, who happened to be nuns, with a clear and unshakable vision that was embraced by the people they hired. The center was not bound by the statutory and regulatory rigidities of a state child welfare agency.

Its work, as Sister Mary Paul had said, was based "on an understanding of relationships." But relationships do not materialize instantly. They evolve slowly, if they are to evolve at all. New York's plan for reform called for a five-year period of study of several pilot offices, an idea that struck many of those knowledgeable about child welfare as particularly wise: It would take caseworkers and their supervisors at least that long to establish relationships of consequence with their clients. Yet, even when those workers understood their clients, and even when the clients came to trust the workers, there was no assurance that such a relationship could salvage a family. The sisters and their social workers recognized that there were families so troubled that they defied the most compassionate and insightful assistance. They were the families like that of the child whom the foster mother Mrs. A was adopting.

And that was a child who had much working to his advantage: He was adoptable. Mrs. A had gotten him virtually at birth; he was, in the most profound way, hers. He was not the troubled teenager who set the bed on fire or the adolescent who ran away time and again or even the child who wet the bed and would not speak. He was not like most of the Melton children, who came into the system emotionally and developmentally stunted by their growing up in the house on North Keystone Avenue. As Patrick Murphy pointed out, the Melton children were also lucky: People wanted to take them in, in their case because of the publicity their story aroused.

The child welfare system, of course, was filled with many less fortunate children for whom a five-year period of study and evaluation of a community-based program meant nothing. They were in the system now, which meant that they did not have the time to wait for a relationship to evolve between their parents and the state in the hope that a team of workers might help hold their families together.

The mistake so often made by those who would reform the child welfare system comes when they look at an alternative—be it family preservation or the Center for Family Life—and proclaim it the magic bullet. Although a different relationship between families and the state was essential, it did not necessarily follow that with such a relationship would come good things for the children. Rather, it meant only that without that relationship the system would continue as it was, punishing the parents and as a result often making things worse for their children.

I would have liked to believe that Maxine, May Fay, and Denise Melton might have responded well to a social worker like Gretchen Lord, who was willing to hold their hands just as she held the hand of the troubled Anne. But despite their best intentions, the Melton sisters could well have become the sorts of parents of whom Sister Mary Paul had said "We're not saying we never separate children from their parents."

What then was a child welfare agency to do if it had not had eighteen years—let alone five—to establish a position of trust in a neighborhood and with it a group of foster parents who accepted its vision? What happened at the agency where the workers did, in fact, know a good deal about a family—knew the extent and nature of its problems, understood the complexity of its relationships—and still felt that they had to get the children out of the house because if they did not, the children would be hurt? What happened when the workers tried mightily to hold a family together only to see the children continue suffering at home? The sisters had argued for, and the teenagers at the foster care newspaper underscored the importance of, keeping children close to the homes and to people from whom they were taken. But what was the agency to do with the less desirable children—the ones who were suicidal or dangerously aggressive or beyond control?

In rural Indiana I came across the story of a home that was, if anything, the equal of the Melton house in filth and squalor. Ten children lived there with their mother and occasionally their father. The children ranged in age from a year old to sixteen. They had just been removed from their home for the second time in three years.

The mother, who was white and from the rural South, did not, in the view of the local child welfare authorities, understand that her children could not live in a house along with what the board of health estimated to be tens of thousands of roaches, could not play barefoot in the street late at night, and could not be left to fend for themselves when she was gone. The mother did not seem to understand this and got angry at caseworkers when they made demands upon her and threatened to take her increasingly violent children.

The most striking aspect of her case, however, was the amount of time that the county child welfare agency had spent trying to keep her children with her. The caseworkers kept a record of every phone call and visit. Over two years they visited or called several times a week. They came when the neighbors complained about the children playing in the street and that their mother was missing. They came because the children were, once again, absent from school. And they came because the mother called to complain that the children were not listening to her and she wanted her caseworker to come over and make them go to school. Things never got better.

Finally, when the house was becoming uninhabitable and the children were coming to school reeking of filth and displaying signs of depression so severe it bordered on the suicidal, the county's caseworkers took them. They placed the youngest ones in foster homes and the oldest ones in what had for a century been the county orphanage, but which was now a cluster of new, smaller buildings set on a campus. The workers arranged for parenting classes and therapy and frequent visits for the mother, all aimed at reunifying the family, which did occur, a year later.

The children were home for a year, and in that time the lessons presumably learned by the mother and her children began eroding, or so it appeared to caseworkers, who began hearing many of the same complaints they had heard before, except now the older children were more violent and more depressed. A year later, the state took the children again.

Even if there were faults in the way this help was provided, it was hard to imagine a social service agency spending more time trying to keep a family from being taken apart. In the end, nothing the agency could do would keep this family intact. But there was no way of predicting this. Reading through two years of case notes made it clear to me that the children could not stay with their mother. What also emerged from the thick files was a picture of the mother as a sad and hapless woman who could at once be oblivious to her children's clear distress and then arrange a yard sale so one of her daughters could join a class trip to Florida.

I happened to be in the county welfare office the day after the children were brought back in. Perhaps because this was a small office, where most everyone at one time or another had worked with this family, the mood was one of anticipated exhaustion: She's back. I spoke with the director, a woman well regarded for her work in the field. (She asked that I not use her name or her county's because, having been so forthcoming about the case, she understood that she risked incurring the wrath of her superiors in Indianapolis who, like child welfare officials across the country, sought to protect client confidentiality.) She shook her head and smiled ruefully at the prospect of yet another round with this family. The problem was not in determining what steps to begin taking: There were clear procedures. Rather it was with the question she characterized as "the philosophical piece": "What do we do with a family like this?" she asked. "Which is more damaging? Taking them away? Or do you just leave them there? Are we willing to pay for putting them in foster care or a facility and raising them till they're eighteen? Which is better for these children?"

She went on. "And once you've made that decision, the system raises the kids. If you're trying to break the 'lifestyle,' how do we break those cycles, or do we try?"

What was clear to the director was that as incompetent as this woman was at being a mother, she was still devoted to her children. And this, the director believed, meant that there was little wisdom in terminating her rights: The years that it might take to successfully sever her from her children would cause far more emotional harm to the children than the director believed acceptable. "As long as she was willing to visit, as long as she was giving the appearance of working with her problems, you didn't get to that stage."

For the short term, the director believed foster care was best for the younger children. For the older, and profoundly troubled children, there would be a year of treatment for depression in the county residential facility. But what of the future? How could she and her staff craft a resolution that kept the younger, more vulnerable children out of their mother's home, kept her in their lives, and at the same time satisfied the critics who would charge their tangled solution reflected not a decision made but a decision avoided?

Freed of the question of whether or not to terminate the mother's rights, the director was able to look at the mother in something other than an adversarial way. The director looked again at the state of the home. Perhaps, she concluded—because she no longer needed to prove the extent of the mother's failure—it was not in such awful shape as to be "life threatening." As for the charge of "educational neglect," that the mother had failed to send her children to school, the mother had argued that while she "brought them to the front door, they walked out the back." It did not seem worth trying to prove that the mother had failed to make sure they stayed.

The director was left to split the difference: The older children, she concluded, were not only devoted to their mother, but had, over the years, made her lifestyle their own. As for the younger children, she said, the system stood to have "more [of] an impact in changing their lives." So she decided that three of the children would remain in foster care, albeit with their mother as a visitor. Four of the older children returned to their mother. For the two most troubled children this came only after a year of treatment at the county residential facility. With their two other siblings, they went home with the understanding that their mother's inevitable neglect would cause less harm to children old enough to care for themselves. The three remaining oldest children went to live with their father.

The director recognized that the children of this family would, as a result of the state's action, grow up scattered and separated from one another and that this would be difficult for siblings. "The kids are in different places, different options," she said, "and the only constant is her."

Then she added, "In this business, nothing is absolute." The director spoke of her weariness with the debate on families that hinged primarily on whose rights were paramount—children's or parents'. This was a dialectic so meaningless that it was possible to cross the state line from Indiana to Illinois and discover that the dominant rights in one state were subordinate in the other. She believed that her work was about assisting both, at the same time, which meant that she began by asking: "What can we do to help these kids and this family survive in the best way possible?" And with that, she answered her own question about "the philosophical piece" of her work.

It was a pragmatic solution; it made use of all the means of assistance that the state has long had at its disposal—the home, the foster home, the orphanage. Still, I left wondering what it was like for a child to move from a home to an institution, even to a pleasant-looking place like the county residential facility. There the children got rooms and beds and the assurance that they would never have to leave, except to return home. The children were introduced to ordered lives built around school and sports and friends and supervisors, who were there to assist them but not to assume the role of replacement parent. I wondered what benefit, if any, the children saw in that life.

As it happened, I had also visited such an institution outside Chicago. It was run by Father John Smyth, who had seen the Melton children on the night the police brought them to the emergency shelter on Montrose Avenue. The shelter was run for the state by Columbus-Maryville, a large Catholic child care agency that also ran what used to be called an orphanage, in the suburb of Des Plaines. Two hundred and eighty children lived in three buildings set on a sprawling campus. They lived in groups of eight or nine in dormitory rooms. The children ranged in age from seven to eighteen; group living was not deemed appropriate for younger children. Maryville kept the children busy. There were school and sports and no end of after-school activities. The children were supervised by adults who lived in their dormitories and who maintained discipline on a point system through which privileges were extended and withdrawn.

At Maryville I met Nicole, who was eighteen and who had come into "the state," as she put it, because the aunt she lived with could no longer tolerate her. "I beat her up," Nicole said. "I spit in her cup." Nicole's mother died when she was seven. "Every day I went to live in another place, and then my auntie decided to take custody of me," she said. "I just couldn't accept the fact that my mom died. I can't accept it now." Nicole said she remembered nothing of life before her mother died. She lived in Chicago with her aunt for eight years. "In the beginning I listened to her," she said. "But then I got tired of it. I started hanging around with the wrong persons." Nicole's aunt took her to the Department of Children and Family Services.

"I was big then. I was trying to be big and bad, like I don't care. But I didn't want to be in no state. When they started telling me about it, I begged my auntie to take me back. I was crying when my auntie left and they took me. When you first get into the state, they got to do, like, a lot of paperwork on you. Then you get a physical. They asked me whether I needed a therapist. I said, Hell no, I don't need no therapist, 'cause I didn't. They took me to the shelter, and then I came out here. When I got out here, I said, I'm not getting out of the car. I don't know what's out here. I thought I was in the boondocks.

When you come out here, all you see is the cemetery and this big old place."

At Maryville Nicole learned that the one question not asked was why someone was there. It was okay to talk about home in therapy, in which she and everyone else took part, and in the occasional aside to a friend about what they might be doing at that moment, if they were home. Nicole tried to be good at first. Then, she said, "I started getting bad. I couldn't really deal with the consequences, telling me what to do. I started goin' off. When you go off, it's hard to explain. You might throw chairs, curse a lot. To really express yourself, you might hit a staff. I hit one staff." In time she began to see that her behavior brought her nothing. "Then I started being good, and I moved to another home, a less strict home," she said. "I can't be acting up all my life. I'm very different because I know my life's not gonna revolve around me all the time."

Nicole had been at Maryville for two years. She liked it. She did not always like the people who supervised her, the adults the children called "staff." Staff made them clean their rooms and do their homework and maintained control of the points that brought them privileges. They talked about staff the way other teenagers talk about their parents. When I mentioned this to a group of teenagers, they looked surprised and confused, as if they could not imagine how teenagers actually spoke about their parents.

Nicole leaned across the table where we sat and absentmindedly scribbled with a pen. The pen point was withdrawn and so she left no marks. But when I asked Nicole whether she might have once simply drawn on the table without thinking or caring, she jerked herself back defensively and said, "I didn't do ink." Then seeing that she was not being accused, she admitted that in the past she probably would not have given it a second thought.

"I'm still gonna do teenager things. But I got some sense," she said. "I know how to act because Maryville teach you that." Nicole had learned "how to talk to people. You're not gonna swear when you're at your job. You're gonna learn how to accept criticism from authorities." She learned how to act in the world. "Like when you go to dinner. They show you how you supposed to eat. You sit straight down for dinner. Sit straight. Bring the food to you, not go down to the food. When you have dinner, you sit with all the kids and you have a nice dinner and then all talk about what everyone talks about, how your day at school been. At Maryville, if you have some good grades— Like Father Smyth wrote me a letter yesterday. It said, 'I'm very proud of you, Nicole. Keep up your good grades.' It made me feel like somebody's looking at me, like I'm not doing it for nothing."

It would have been comforting to conclude that what stood between the purposeful life Nicole was building and the lives of the Melton sisters was the tutelage she was receiving in the rudiments of a successful life. But obviously there was something more. Just as the Melton sisters did not doubt their own mother's love—stunting as it could be—Nicole did not for a moment believe her aunt had stopped loving her when she placed her in "the state." "My auntie told me, 'I'll never stop loving you no matter what you do.' She would never stop loving me. I see her every weekend."

If her aunt could not control her, Nicole had come to believe that her aunt was somehow able to impose something of her own values upon her, which was more than Josephine Melton was able to impart to her daughters. Nicole did not have a child. Her friends did. Her friends, she said, "tried to peer-pressure" her to have a baby. They told her, "You can have somebody to love," she said. "That's really it, somebody to hold and love."

I asked whether her friends who had babies felt toward their parents as she did toward her aunt.

"No," said Nicole. "Maybe that's why they had kids. Maybe they thought their parents wouldn't love them. Or maybe they thought if they had a kid, their friends would like them more than they did. Or they thought they'll look so good when they're with the baby. They got all this attention when they got the baby, and maybe that's what they want."

Nicole did not have a child because while she could brutalize her aunt, she could not bear to disappoint her. "I knew if I had kids, my auntie would have tried to kill me," she said. "She would have been very offended."

That fear of disapproval, however, got Nicole just so far. She had come to see that she needed the other component that a parent could offer, a person whom she wanted to please and whose approval mattered. She found that in Father Smyth.

John Smyth was a tall, burly man who smoked, it appeared, without pause. His size worked to his advantage. It gave him a sense of command that he then leavened with a manner that was gentle and attentive. He had been an all-American basketball player at Notre Dame, where, he acknowledged with a wry smile, he had set and still held the record for personal fouls. He had been drafted by the old St. Louis Hawks of the National Basketball Association in 1957 but instead chose to enter the seminary. He was, like Sisters Mary Paul and Geraldine, a frustrating figure in that he was impossible to duplicate. Like the sisters, he believed that a parent should be a part of a child's life, even when the child lived at Maryville.

"We do not want to take the place of their biological family. We want to make their parents totally welcome, if the parents can," he said of the parents' capacity and desire to make their way to Maryville to see their children.

Nicole understood this. She went home to her aunt on holidays. But she wanted the notes from Father Smyth. Staff may have needed better training, she said; but the idealized Father Smyth was someone she could talk to.

"They would never try to take the place of your mom or dad unless you really wanted them. If you really want them to be your mom and dad and call them mom and dad, they won't mind," she said. "Father Smyth, he'll never want you to be separated from your family."

What was it like, I asked, living in a place you did not have to leave?

"That's a good thing," Nicole said. "You're not gonna keep shifting from place to place to place. I kept going to a family, and then when you start getting in good with your family, then you go to another place. At Maryville all you got to do is go by the rules and behave. If you keep acting up, Father Smyth is not gonna let you stay here. He's gonna bring in someone who really want to be here and be loved."

Unlike the Melton sisters, or even the teenager mothers at CAUSES, Nicole could envision a future. She would soon graduate from high school. "I graduate in June. Right now I work at Wal-Mart, a cashier. I make seven dollars an hour."

Nicole thought she might want to be a contractor, like her uncle. She also lived in terror of what might become of her when she had to leave.

"I might just fall apart," she said. "I don't have nobody to tell me what to do. Nobody will be there for me but myself. I want to be somebody. I don't wanna be no bum."

———

It cost the state of Illinois $35,000 a year to keep a child at Maryville, which was more than a year's tuition at Harvard. The state did not have the money to pay to keep all the teenagers in its care at places like Maryville. Nor were there enough beds at Maryville or at the other similar institutions around the state. Nor was there the assurance of replicating elsewhere the relationship that Father Smyth achieved with children like Nicole. Maryville, like Gretchen Lord's holding the troubled and struggling Anne's hand, like Claudine Christian rearing her goddaughter Maxine Melton's sons, was yet another option. The state could make use of any of these options in the interests of helping a failed child. So too could the state, if it was willing, make use of the various people who could, in their own ways, add something to that child's life.

Surrender

Denise Melton was the first of the sisters to surrender her children. Even after her months in a residential drug treatment program, even with the insights she gained about herself and the pleasure she came to take in completing her assigned tasks, and despite her dream of "being a family again," Denise told her lawyer in June of 1995 that she wanted her cousins to adopt the two children living with them. She wanted her third child to be adopted by his paternal grandmother. Denise told her lawyer, "We can still be all together and see each other."

"Truly," said her lawyer, Ellen Domph, "she believes that."

Two months later May Fay, too, signed an order surrendering her parental rights. Her four children were living with a foster family in the Chicago suburbs whom the Department of Children and Family Services hoped might adopt them. (They have not yet done so.) The state's attorney, meanwhile, was proceeding with cases of termination of parental rights against Diane and Cassandra. That same summer Maxine told her lawyer that she wanted her sons to remain with her godmother, Claudine Christian. Christian was devoted to the boys but was fearful that if she adopted them she would be unable to afford the cost of college tuition.

The news that the Melton sisters would no longer be the legal parents of their children was greeted with delight in Chicago. This was not to be a reprise of Joseph Wallace, dead at his mother's hands. Instead this was a child welfare story with a good ending: The children were freed from their mothers so that they might begin new and better lives. In July of 1995 the *Tribune* ran a front-page story under the headline " 'Keystone Kids' Find World of Good; All 19 Recovering from Life in Squalor." The story opened with a series of questions: "Can you see love? Can you watch it unfold? Can you capture it in a photograph?" Implicit in the questions was that you could, when love was good and real. It made no mention of what love might have looked like in less satisfactory conditions.

The story went on to tell of the happy lives the children were now living, most especially the son of Denise Turner, who suffered from cerebral palsy and whose mother was the lone parent convicted of physically abusing her child. (She was sentenced to five years in prison.) The story told of devoted foster parents attending to the heretofore unmet needs of the children in their care. It described new rooms and new clothes and the much-needed order upon which their lives were now built.

Throughout the story were reminders of just how awful things had been for the children on North Keystone Avenue, how they had lived in "subhuman" conditions, and how, in the words of Kathryn Gallanis, the chief prosecutor, their mothers "weren't able to affect the souls of these children." Still, the author wrote, "It is way too early to tell how this story will turn out." The author then posed a series of questions that went to the heart of the state's long, if unstated, mission on behalf of children: "Will the children grow into compassionate adults or remorseless criminals? . . . Will they raise their own children with love and kindness or duplicate the drug abuse, teen pregnancy, criminal records, illiteracy and welfare dependency of their parents and grandparents?"

The questions suggested a lesson to be drawn from the Keystone story: Had the children remained with their mothers, they surely would have become people just like them, and removing them improved the chances that they would not. It was a view that achieved its fullest and least equivocal airing two years later, in *Newsweek*, in a story titled "Chicago Hope." The story was a testimonial to Lynne Kawamoto, a judge "who bucked the system by putting children first." It suggested that many in Chicago had believed, and fretted, that the children would surely be returned to their mothers because since the 1980s the state still clung to the "ideal of family preservation." Kawamoto, the story told, was an altogether different sort of family court judge, albeit one with only a month's experience when she was assigned the Keystone case. In a curious admission, Kawamoto, who had been a prosecutor until her appointment, said that as she listened to the state's case against the Melton sisters and Denise Turner, she "struggled to keep a poker face, wishing she could be a prosecutor again."

Kawamoto, who declined to speak with me about the case and who granted no other published interviews about it, told *Newsweek* how she stayed up late during the final days of the trial, crafting her "passionate decision on a legal pad."

"It may sound harsh to say this," she said, "but can anyone argue that their lives would be better if they'd been returned home?" It was a reasonable question that fell short of the larger point. I do not disagree with the decision to remove the children from their mothers' home. But I take issue with the premise that the state could divorce the children from their mothers. Judge Kawamoto's solution was clear, but incomplete, for reasons that I will detail in the book's epilogue.

The story and Kawamoto's handling of the case were attempts to resolve at last the dilemma at the heart of the state's relationship with failing families: Place the burden on the parents to improve themselves, and if they cannot, they will lose their children. But who does that resolution satisfy? The adults who have taken an interest in the children or the children themselves? What good comes of saying to children from a home like that on North Keystone Avenue that their mothers have wronged them and will not be their mothers anymore? If Kawamoto was right, then she stood in refutation not only of decades of research and thinking on the emotional needs of children, and not only of the experience and insights of people ranging from Richard Calica to Sister Mary Paul, and not only of the yearnings of the teenagers at Foster Care Youth United, but of the observation of Maxine Melton's godmother, Claudine Christian, who told me how the boys in her care "missed their mother."

Ironically, the *Newsweek* story seized upon the story of Maxine's sons as a harbinger: "The lives of the five brothers living with Claudine Christian may offer the best insight to how the Keystone children have fared."

I did not doubt that the children were enjoying lives and futures far better in the care of Claudine Christian than they had had with their mother, aunts, and grandmother Josephine in the house on Keystone. Nor did I doubt Christian when she told *Newsweek* that "they're just happy little kids." Christian believed that the children were "over mom," although one of the boys had "a lot locked up in his mind from what happened before he got here."

What was missing from Kawamoto's reasoning and from the call for decisiveness in the name of "putting children first" was the idea that Maxine Melton's presence might actually be of benefit to her sons. Christian, who had asked that I not come to the house for fear of what the arrival of a white stranger might arouse in the boys, spoke to me about them several times by phone.

In one conversation she told how she had witnessed a transformation in her goddaughter, Maxine. Now that Maxine had given up her futile struggle to regain her children, she was left without responsibility. Her visits, which had been every other week, became less frequent and more chaotic. "It's like having six kids," Christian said. "She does not talk to them. She does not read to them. They go out in the yard and run around and play and wrestle. Then she sends them to me, and she'll go to sleep. She yells at them when they start getting on her nerves. She'll say, 'Sit down. I'm tired of you. Games are over.' "

Surely the children were best off not living with a mother who treated them this way. I asked Christian, however, what she thought might have happened had Maxine been allowed, or even encouraged, to play a role in her children's lives. I wondered whether Maxine would have ever been capable of performing in any consistent way the simplest tasks for her children, like feeding them meals three times a day and making sure they were clean. Christian, who knew enough of the hard life on the West Side to have escaped to rural Illinois and who knew enough of her goddaughter's growing up to understand her faults and limitations, believed this was possible, if only because hidden beneath Maxine's despair was a desire for purpose.

"Things become a habit," she said. "It will get to be a habit." But now, she went on, "these girls are free. Look at them. They're right back. They walk around holding their friends' kids' hands. They should be holding their own kids' hands. It's the same as before. The only thing that's missing are the nineteen kids."

The Cook County state's attorney and the Department of Children and Family Services worked hard to put a positive spin on the tale of the Melton children. Again and again the children were described as "doing great" and "adjusting well," dismissing reports of one child burning down his foster parents' home as an "accident" and downplaying another foster family's decision to adopt one child in their care but not a more disruptive sibling. I am not suggesting that beneath the happy tales lay darker stories of troubled children, only that in my talks with social workers and with Claudine Christian the picture that emerged of life for the children after Keystone was often one of struggle. That this struggle began with their mothers' failures was not in dispute. But even after their mothers were gone, the struggle continued.

The five Melton sisters had twenty-three children, sixteen of whom the police removed on the night of February 1, 1994. (Three of the original "Keystone 19," as the newspapers dubbed them, were the children of the Melton sisters' friend, Denise Turner.) One child was born that night to Diane Melton. Cassandra and Diane each later bore another child. Diane also had four other children already in the custody of the state.

Seven of the Melton children were eventually adopted; eleven live permanently with relatives. The other six children have moved from foster home to foster home. Three were those children of Diane already in the child welfare system on the night of February 1; another one of Diane's children lived with his father. One child had been in nine foster homes. Most had been in five.

On the surface, the fate of most of the Melton children suggests some success: eighteen, or three-quarters of the children, were either in adoptive or long-term foster homes. In fact, it is almost impossible to overstate the remarkable fortune of the Melton children compared to most wards of the state. Not only had they been placed in lasting homes shortly after their removal, but most were living with their siblings.

Yet on closer examination, the state's success with the Melton children offered very little in the way of comfort and assistance for other failed children. Long before Judge Lynne Kawamoto began drafting her decision in the case against the Melton sisters, most of the children the police took from the house on North Keystone Avenue were in their new homes. The homes, as it happened, were often those of the very relatives whom Josephine Melton always believed had snubbed her and her daughters. It was to these relatives the state had turned in the frenzied days and weeks after the story of the house of North Keystone Avenue broke.

Would that all the state's children were so fortunate. They are not. Their relatives or friends do not or cannot open their doors as did the relatives of the Melton children. Strangers cannot fill the gap. In 1995, 1,046—or 2 percent—of the 44,917 wards of the state of Illinois were adopted. Even with the subsequent federal and state subsidies aimed at boosting the number of adoptions, by June of 1998, still only 5 percent of the wards of the state—as compared to 30 percent of the Melton children—were adopted.

Epilogue

AT THE END of the Melton story the question was not whether the state saved these children. Rather it was whether by acting as it did, the state had learned how to act on behalf of all the children in its care. It had not.

Judge Kawamoto allowed her justifiable outrage at the conditions in which the Melton sisters allowed their children to live to guide her thinking on what the children needed. What she did not accept, and what others are profoundly reluctant and at times unwilling to accept, was the inevitability of the Melton sisters enduring in their children's lives. This was not merely a question of their presence—as visitors or as custodial parents. Kawamoto and the agents of the state could rescue the Melton children from their mothers' home. They could not erase those mothers from their children's lives.

Kawamoto's handling of the Melton case brought to mind what the psychologist Barbara Nordhaus had said about the caseworkers' "rescue fantasy" in the story of Megan Marie: If the worker could just get the children into the right foster home, or if she could only get the mother to complete her rehab, or if she could only find the family a clean and decent place to live, this could be a "family" in the way that she envisioned a family.

Kawamoto's opinion, like Judge John Downey's in Megan's case, reflected the desire to achieve an ideal: to make things right, to re-create families as they are supposed to be. That desire rests upon the premise that the protection of a relationship between parent and child is contingent upon the worthiness of the parent. Parents should be worthy of their children. If the parent, however, fails the test of worthiness, then the relationship no longer deserves the protection of the law; the state may move to sever it.

John Downey accepted Gina Pellegrino's claim to her child even though no relationship—save for the act of childbirth and the nine hours that followed—existed between them. He rejected the LaFlammes' claim to the child even though a relationship had begun developing between them and the child, a relationship established by the state on the very reasonable belief that the child had been abandoned by her mother and left unclaimed by her father, and was secured in a new home with people who believed that the child would remain their child forever. That expectation guided their behavior and feeling toward her. Gina Pellegrino's worthiness lay in the fact that she gave birth to the child and that she wanted her back. The LaFlammes were, in a sense, unworthy because the child was never theirs. The child then was supposed to go home to her mother, which to Downey's thinking, was just what she did.

Even with their palpable failures as parents, the Melton sisters enjoyed a position in the lives of their children that Gina Pellegrino had not achieved with her daughter: They knew each other. The sisters and their children spent weeks, months, and years in each other's company. And it was in each other's company that the children came to define themselves in the world. The problem was that those relationships with their mothers were likely to produce in the children so little sense of purpose and so little order and meaning that the children stood a very good chance of becoming people like their mothers.

The question with which the state for so long grappled, and which Kawamoto's decision did not resolve, was this: How was it possible to avoid that undesirable fate for children while accepting the fact that their mothers—their drug-addicted, unemployed, uneducated, and unmotivated mothers—were central to the children's lives before they ever met the new and better people whom the state found to rear them?

Judge Kawamoto proceeded against the Melton sisters with a series of legal steps (fact-finding, disposition, sentencing) aimed at answering one question: Do the children go home to their mothers? Faced with so stark a choice, Kawamoto, angered by what the prosecution told her about life on Keystone and unswayed by the defense's "dirty house" argument, was left to conclude that no, the children could not go home. If they were not going home—and, *Newsweek*'s view aside, it was hard to find anyone with knowledge of the case when it first broke who thought they ever would—then their mothers would have to be removed from the picture.

Kawamoto did not, strictly speaking, put children first. She put punishment first in the belief that such punishment not only reflected society's revulsion at the Melton sisters' behavior, but might goad the Meltons into becoming worthy parents.

By setting out to build a case against the mothers, the state could not be expected to build simultaneously a case for preserving what it could of the relationship between those mothers and their children. The children became the instrument of punishment: Do as we ask and you can see them and maybe get them back; fail and you lose them. The Meltons were going to fail, or more specifically, they were going to fail to meet the demands the state made of them. Time and again the failure of parents like the Meltons has shown itself to be all but inevitable. It is a failure demonstrated by drug programs begun and dropped; parenting classes attended and forgotten; court dates assigned and missed; visits scheduled and skipped; jobs found and lost. Were those failures not so likely and not so numbingly common, family preservation programs would be flourishing instead of failing to keep children out of foster care.

Even allowing for Kawamoto's passion, what would have happened had she been permitted, or been encouraged, to proceed not toward the resolution of a single question but with options that still kept the children from ever returning to the lives they had led? What might have happened had she been allowed or, perhaps been forced, to proceed with the stipulation that the mothers were going to remain part of their children's lives, not because it was a noble thing to do, but because that would be good for the children?

What if Kawamoto had then looked at the record and noted that while the Melton sisters were often absent, they never left the children unattended. They did not abandon them. They fed them. They did not abuse them—only Denise Turner abused her son. They were unacceptably poor parents, in the eyes not only of the social workers who met them, but of the relatives who for so long rejected them and the neighbors who observed them. But what might have happened had Kawamoto seen the case as the child welfare director in Indiana saw her own "dirty house" case and said, We are stuck with these women. Now, what can we do for the children?

From the moment the police discovered the Melton children, the state proceeded in its encounter with their mothers as an adversary: Something was wrong. Who committed this wrong? What punishment does this wrongdoer deserve? Accepting the inevitability of the mothers, however, would have meant no longer being able to proceed against them as an adversary; to do otherwise would have been counterintuitive. Instead such acceptance would have meant proceeding with an approach based not on punishment, but on reward. Rewards, however, are not easily imagined for mothers like the Meltons.

This approach does not mean accepting the behavior of failing parents. It means being demanding of them, saying as Sisters Mary Paul and Geraldine did—and as Claudine Christian wished she could have said to Maxine—this is what we expect of you and what your children need from you, which is why we need to keep you a part of their lives.

It means the state saying—as the sisters and social workers at the Center for Family Life had said to the troubled Anne—this does not assure you that your children will return to you; but it does hold out the promise that they will look at you not with fear or confusion, but with something that approaches affection and perhaps even respect. You may not necessarily live with your children. But you will be of consequence to them. If the parents are capable, this means that the children can be freed both from blaming themselves for being taken from their parents—witness Diane Melton's teenage son shoveling the filth so that the place would not look so bad that the police would take them—and from the enduring and damaging fantasy of how much better life would have been with the mother from whom they were taken. As I heard from Richard Calica as well as from teenagers at Foster Care Youth United, it means that by the time the children are eighteen, they will have come to see that perhaps their parents really were dreadful parents and that the state did them not an injustice but a favor in putting them in new homes.

———

I did not believe that Judge Kawamoto would have been content with merely removing the children from their parents' home. She wanted better lives for them. Who wouldn't? Kawamoto did, however, have two great advantages in securing such lives for the Melton children: As Patrick Murphy had pointed out, these were lucky children in that the publicity surrounding their case made securing permanent foster homes, and potential adoptive homes, far easier than was typical. And most of the children were already in permanent homes. Much more common is the story of the child who remains in foster care because his mother cannot seem to do what she has to do to regain him—often this begins with overcoming a drug addiction— and because no one else wants him.

This meant that the most powerful weapon a judge like Kawamoto possesses—termination of parental rights—can, in most circumstances, achieve only part of the desired result, as Martin Guggenheim, the New York University Law School professor, had concluded in his study on terminations. That conclusion led Guggenheim to coin the term "legal orphans," children freed for adoption whom no one wants to adopt and who therefore remain in foster care as wards of the state.

For all that Kawamoto was praised for her boldness, the truth was that across the country, states were often quite decisive on behalf of children: States took many more children from their parents than they sent home; they were taking them younger and keeping them longer, which was why, even with the slowing rate of removals, the number of children living apart from their parents remained essentially constant. And when the agents of the state feel themselves under assault—as happens when a tragic child welfare story breaks— they take children they might have left at home, as evidenced by the surges in removals after the death of Joseph Wallace and after the Melton story aired.

But what did the celebrated decisiveness accomplish, other than separating the children from their parents? Did it set the children on the course for better lives? Or did it condemn them to different sorts of awful lives? The vast numbers of children who age out of the child welfare system only to end up on the streets, or in prison, or without work, and with children of their own, suggest the latter. By 1995 and 1996, however, the perception that family preservation had failed and the highly publicized deaths of several children at the hands of their parents—the 1995 killing of Elisa Izquierdo in New York most prominent among them—helped propel a change in policy away from reunification toward adoption.

This shift culminated in December of 1997 when President Clinton, who in 1993 had sought an additional $1.3 billion for family preservation programs, signed into law legislation that paid the states $4,000 for each child adopted beyond a specified minimum and $6,000 for every child adopted who had "special needs." For its part, Illinois had preceded Washington by several months with its own new adoption legislation. The state demanded that the private agencies with whom it contracted place for adoption each year six out of every twenty-five children on its caseloads; failure to do so meant that the state would not reimburse the agency for taking in more foster children. By the end of 1997 the state was expecting to have filed 6,000 termination cases—an increase of 4,800 over 1992.

No matter how noble the sentiment of this new legislation and of Kawamoto's decision, there were dangers in the lessons being drawn from them. They were based on the assumption that new homes were, in fact, available for these children and that the children would remain in those homes until their parents were prepared to take them back or until they turned eighteen. It further assumed that there were enough institutional beds for those children who did not have lasting, alternative homes and that there was the money to pay for them. Finally, it assumed, that that new home would assure a life in which the scars of the past were made to disappear. Yet even so harsh a critic of failing parents and of the child welfare system as Patrick Murphy admitted that the state was offered not the alternatives like Claudine Christian that were presented to Judge Kawamoto, but "a parent who is marginal, or a relative who is marginal, or a system that is marginal." Even though he had twice testified in Washington in favor of the new legislation, Murphy was still troubled by the impact of its passage. "I hate to be a doom sayer always," he told the *Chicago Tribune.* "My concern is the pendulum in 1980 swung over to family preservation, now it's swinging way back over."

The new laws were trumpeted as reflections of bold thinking on child welfare. They were nothing of the kind. Instead they merely perpetuated the cyclical approach of the last 150 years, with alternating cycles favoring removal and reunification. As Murphy and others wise about the child welfare system and failing families recognized, the change in policy was merely another rigid approach to a problem that demanded what Murphy called "wiggle room."

The answers for failed children are all about wiggle room. They are answers, not an answer but answers, that begin with the premise of "it depends." It depends who they are as people and who can best help them grow up without too many lasting hurts and scars. But "it depends" sounds like such a paltry and unsatisfying solution to so sad and sometimes horrific a situation. The resistance to the idea of untidy resolutions comes in part from the nature of the debate on child welfare, which has for so long been dominated by ideologues who see only their answer, their solution. And those answers have proven to be infinitely more compelling to policy makers, to the press, to politicians, and to the public than solutions that begin with the idea of "it depends," which does not promise a miraculous wiping away of the past.

Still, it is all well and good to argue about the importance—and inevitability—of keeping failing parents a part of their children's lives. But how does this translate into the daily business of running a child welfare agency or sitting on the family court bench?

First, it means making it easy for the children in care to be near not only to their parents, but to the people and places with whom they are familiar—cousins and siblings, aunts and uncles and friends, as well as schools and churches. Secondly, it means making it easier for their parents to see those children. It is naive to assume that parents who have already failed their children are suddenly going to find the will and capacity to accomplish even so simple a task as getting on the subway and finding the foster home where their children live.

Helping make the parents accessible means minimizing for the children the trauma of being taken from their homes. For the parents it is a statement by the agency that their relationships with their children are of such consequence that the state is going to do what it can to make sure the parents do not lose those children, and those children their parents.

This approach can only happen when the distances between parent and child—both physical and emotional—are kept to a minimum. I have sat in New York's family courts and listened as parents much like the Melton sisters whined about having to travel by subway from Brooklyn to the Bronx and then to Staten Island in order to visit the various foster homes where their children lived. I say "whined" because listening to these parents, I heard only the desire to be excused for failure. The parents offered familiar excuses: rude caseworkers, scheduled urine testing, oversleeping, rehab, sick relatives, cruel boyfriends. There was no point in threatening the parents to "get their act together." They were not going to get their act together, or if they could, it would take a very long time with a great many stumbles before it happened. The parents spoke of their troubles. For them, these troubles eclipsed the sorrow they had inflicted upon their children. It was, as Robert Spector, the psychologist who worked with the teenage mothers at CAUSES, had said: Developmentally, the parents saw the world in a profoundly infantile way; no one else's needs equalled their own. It is wiser and more prudent, then, to implement a program that says to the parents, we know you are looking for excuses to fail, but we are not going to let you fail or put you in a position to fail because your children cannot survive on your excuses. They need something, anything of you.

By keeping the work of child welfare confined to the neighborhoods where people live, an agency is also far more capable of being flexible with the families in its supervision. It means knowing enough of the families to judge when a parent needs a caseworker's constant visits, or an extra set of hands with the cleaning and cooking, and when even that sort of help is not enough to keep the children at home.

Sisters Mary Paul and Geraldine established the Center for Family Life upon just such an idea. And while the center is not necessarily a model of what all child welfare agencies could be, it is a template for the way agencies should be organized and money spent. I am not alone in this view. Child welfare agencies across the country are experimenting with or talking seriously about decentralizing their operations and opening satellite offices in the neighborhoods where families most need assistance.

It is clear where the help is needed; it always has been. Pockets of rural poverty and cases of suburban abuse and neglect aside, child welfare is, and has always been, a city problem because it is the cities that have the greatest concentrations of poor people. So too has it always been less a race problem than a problem of class. The revulsion that Charles Loring Brace described over the plight of the children of German immigrants in Lower Manhattan in 1850 sounds very much like the reaction to the bands of poor children who lived on the streets of seventeenth-century London and like the outrage in 1994 in Chicago over the Melton children.

The neighborhoods from which child welfare agencies draw their populations are not difficult to identify. In Illinois, where Jess McDonald, the department director, had been talking for years about just such a reorganization, the department had identified the boundaries and demographics for the neighborhoods most in need. One of them included West Garfield, where the Melton sisters lived. The numbers were empirical evidence of despair and struggle: Of the 172,000 children who lived in the general vicinity of North Keystone Avenue, 42 percent lived in households headed by women and 45 percent were poor. Thirty-eight hundred children, or two out of 100, were found to be neglected or abused in 1993—the year before the police took the Melton children. Two-thirds of those children were neglected; 15 percent were abused. Of those children, only a tenth were removed from their homes within six months after the department first investigated. But 90 percent of those children were still in placement six months after they were removed. Less than 40 percent were living in foster homes in the neighborhood. Almost two-thirds lived with a relative; a quarter were in foster care. Three-quarters had been living away from their parents for more than a year; almost half had been in care for over two years. Only 435, or 5 percent, had returned home in the previous year; 2 percent, or 129, had been adopted.

It is also clear what this population shared in addition to poverty: drug addiction, joblessness, dependency on a government check, and effective illiteracy, in that what relatively little schooling they received had not prepared them for the sorts of jobs that would allow them to support their children. That is the extent of their common experience. All the rest varies with the particulars of circumstance, character, intelligence, and capacity to act. The poor are, of course, no more monolithic a group than were the Melton sisters. I did not believe, for instance, that Diane Melton had the interest, let alone the ability, to care for her children. Maxine's resistance to drugs put her at an advantage compared with May Fay and Denise. (The same, I came to believe, was not true of Cassandra, who did not share what little spark existed in Maxine.) Denise was an angry person who had begun to understand how to make use of that anger to propel her to act. May Fay had the sweeter disposition and greater self-awareness but little will to act. Although the last hundred years have supplied, with a few notable exceptions, a paltry amount of data on what is best for failed children, what is strikingly consistent in the studies conducted since the late 1800s is that some approaches work for some children and some work for others. Orphanages have been appropriate, as have foster homes and helping parents to rear their children at home. Even the orphan trains helped some children.

I have often wondered what the nuns and social workers at the Center for Family Life would have done with the Meltons. I spoke about the Meltons with Mary Paul and Geraldine and their response was to counsel patience. They were not inclined to rush to act. Rather, as was always the case in their approach with new clients, they would have had many questions to ask. But they would have kept them in Sunset Park, if need be, with the children living in the homes of foster parents who accepted the limits of their relationship with those children and who accepted, too, the unpleasant reality of the arrival of a mother like Denise Melton, at the door, ready for a visit. Perhaps Maxine might have been able, after assisting her godmother in rearing her five children, to one day take them back, having learned the rudimentary lessons of being a parent that, as

Claudine Christian put it, "become a habit." Perhaps Denise and May Fay would have never quite overcome their addictions, which means that it would have been unwise ever to send their children back to them. Even so, I recalled the pleasure Denise took in hearing her children tell about their days at school and singing their ABCs with her. I suspect that Mary Paul and Geraldine would have seized upon that as evidence for Denise of what she, and she alone, was capable of offering her children—even if it came on their way home from school, as she returned them to their foster home. I suspect, too, that they would have heard in May Fay's concession of how she had failed her children a desire to make amends, to be of use to them. As for Diane, I am sure they would have invited her to the center Christmas party every year, in the hope that she might want to at least see the children who were permanently living with someone else.

Most every new idea for reforming child welfare comes with the assurance that the new method will be cheaper. In truth, there is no way of knowing this because there is no way of determining just how much a program would cost for a particular child in a particular place. The annual budget for the Center for Family Life, for instance, was just under $3 million. The center gets its money from New York City and from private foundations. Tempting as it might be, it is not necessarily helpful to use one agency's spending patterns as a model; the costs differ, as do services.

Fred Wulczyn of the Chapin Hall Center for Children in Chicago, who specialized in budgeting for child welfare services, explained that the argument that a decentralized approach will prove more expensive is hard to prove because it is difficult to draw reliable conclusions based upon the data now available. Wulczyn, who worked on a New York State task force that studied a managed care approach to child welfare, went on to say that foster care, or any sort of placement outside a child's home, represents the single greatest expenditure to the state for child welfare. Washington assumes roughly half the cost of foster care for federally eligible children—children who until 1996 would have been eligible for AFDC. About three-quarters of the almost $4 billion the federal government allocates each year to child welfare services—other than training and administration—goes to foster care, which even with the passage of welfare reform legisla-tion—and serious talk of making child welfare payments as capped block grants—remains an open-ended entitlement. A state or city gets the money that it claims from Washington with the understand-ing that the claims can only be made for money to be spent on foster care, not on services.

The cost of keeping a child in foster care is roughly $30 a day—although there is considerable variation across the country. That is the base cost. But because so many children come into the child wel-fare system diagnosed with special needs, the cost for the counseling, therapy, and any number of other programs the state deems that a child needs can escalate rapidly. It is not unheard of for the state to spend $100,000 a year for a troubled teenager who lives in a special group home and who needs considerable help.

Because Washington has been and remains reluctant to end that entitlement to children, the cost to the state is unlikely to go down unless the state spends less money on foster care or rather has to sup-port fewer children outside their homes. The number of children coming into the system goes up when parents get poorer or more desperate. The National Center for Children in Poverty at Columbia University projected in early 1997 that in the wake of the passage of the welfare reform bill in August 1996, the number of children re-moved from their homes would grow as parents reliant on the gov-ernment check found themselves facing the prospect of harder times.

"In my view, when I'm feeling frustrated, if you're going to change the system, then you have to buy something else," Wulczyn said. "If five years from now we look at current practice and see that we spend seventy-five percent of our money on foster care, we're going to be pretty disappointed. So ultimately if you're going to change the system you have to change what you buy."

What you buy depends on what you would like to see happen. Conservative thinkers look at a place like the Center for Family Life as evidence of what is possible when the private sector is free to pur-sue its own vision without the imposition of government. The prob-lem is that the charitable organizations who help underwrite the cost of child welfare have been saying for years that they cannot go it alone, that the government's money is essential. And if Washington and local governments are to continue funding child welfare departments, they also have a right to demand that their money is well spent. The difficulty, though, comes when that money is so rigidly allocated. It is equally difficult when the bureaucracies that oversee those allocations insist upon controlling just how the money is spent for fear that if they do not, the money might not be spent wisely.

There is, however, another way to oversee spending: the increasingly popular idea of pegging funding to outcomes, to the meeting of certain clear and reasonable goals. The method of reaching those plateaus is up to the individual agency or department, or perhaps even to a local field office. Despite the enduring debate about the needs of children and despite the varying perceptions of the parents of those children, there are some goals that most people who work in child welfare can agree upon, whether for fiscal or humanitarian reasons: reducing the number of children in foster care, while at the same time making sure that those children's lives are monitored. As Fred Wulczyn argues, if a government wants to reduce or at least control its funding of child welfare, it has to reduce the amount it is spending on foster care. And the only way to do that is to place fewer children or to keep them in care for fewer days. But the child welfare agencies also recognize, if only out of fear of a political and public opinion disaster, what awaits them if they allow vulnerable children to grow up unsupervised and unprotected. How then to accomplish both goals simultaneously when the perception has for so long been that the state has to make a choice?

As it happened, part of Wulczyn's work in New York has been spent on a two-and-a-half-year experiment in which several private foster care agencies were allocated the same amount of money they would have ordinarily received, but which they were allowed to spend as they saw fit. The experiment was an attempt to see whether by allowing greater flexibility in how they approached individual families those agencies might find ways to not only reduce the number of children in care, but—and here was the crucial element—make sure that the children were doing well enough at home to avoid having to come back into care. The program was called HomeRebuilders. The agencies could plan their casework on the basis of the needs of each child, rather than on the guidelines of a distant child welfare bureaucracy.

The point was not to spend more money for services that might assist a family to the point where a child might safely be returned home.

Rather it was to spend the same money differently. The money was allocated as a lump sum to be spent on what the agency believed that child might require, not on the traditional method of a per diem allotment that went for "hots and cots"—meals and a bed in a foster home.

The results were not so much striking as they were illustrative about what was possible, given the families who made up the child welfare population. At the end of 1994, the experiment reported that 79 percent of the 1,800 children in the experiment remained in foster care a year after their removal; the percentage for a comparison group of 1,300 outside the experimental program was 85 percent. The difference—200 more children returned home—was not vast; and that was important. The program could safely say that it did, in fact, get some children home more quickly, but that the condition of many of the families still did not allow them to be reunified. The program was a modest success: Fewer children remained in care; the state was better able to assist them and their parents; it was able to spend the money it might have spent merely housing and feeding them on helping them with services ranging from therapy to cash assistance to detox. HomeRebuilders did not try to portray itself, as had the boosters of family preservation, as the salvation of the child welfare system. When an agency was allowed to spend money according to the needs it identified, that agency proceeded slowly—witness the 6 percent difference in children returning home—but progressively, in that it was able to spend the money in a way that assisted families according to their need and capacity.

The state does not necessarily have to spend more money. But it has to allow those who best understand the particular needs of individual children and families to decide how best to spend it. This is neither an open-ended entitlement nor a capped block grant. It is money that comes based upon performance. And when the performance, as defined by the stated goals, falls short, then the state has a responsibility to demand that the agency account for itself or risk, as happens with substandard school districts routinely, the state itself assuming the control.

———

It is difficult for any society to accept the limits of what it is possible for the state to accomplish on behalf of children, to accept that not every child can have a growing up that feels suitable. That acceptance is too often regarded as defeat, as "giving up on children." It is nothing of the kind. It is, instead, a realization that what the state can best do for children is not necessarily to shield them from their parents or punish the parents for their failures.

Sometimes the state must take children from their parents, temporarily or permanently. But sometimes children will be better served by what might be called muddling through, taking on the sometimes interminable work of cobbling together a childhood, sometimes with several people who can assist in doing for those children what their parents cannot. This can happen in a child's home, in a foster home, or even in an orphanage. Those other adults, however, do not and cannot replace the parents.

It is ironic that the history of the state's relationship with children was for centuries one in which children mattered so little that few thought it wrong for them to work and to live in the corrupting world of adults. Then, in a very brief period beginning at the end of the nineteenth century, the view of children shifted dramatically. They became, in the words of the social historian Viviana Zelizer, "priceless." That view, along with enhanced stature of their mothers— who had heretofore mattered little in comparison to the fathers of the children—attained for mothers and their children the unfortunate position of sainthood. I say "unfortunate" because it meant that for the mothers, deviation from that lofty position meant a fall from grace. Once fallen, a mother would have to demonstrate her worthiness if she wanted to keep her child.

The word "mother" here and throughout this book is intentional: The state's encounter with failing parents is largely about its relationship with mothers because most often it is with their mothers whom failed children live. This is not to say that fathers do not appear in family court or battle to keep their children. But the families in whose lives the state feels compelled to intervene are for the most part headed by poor women who appear to the agents of the state not to be able to independently care for and protect their children. That child welfare stories are often stories about failing mothers, then, adds to this drama the moral component of a fallen woman's attempt at redemption. To slide, to fall and fail is to be as Eve was— tempted, sinful, and banished. The problem with sainthood is that it is assumed to be a life without complications. It is left to the people who labor at the often grim task of child welfare to see just how awful and complex are the lives they supervise and how naive are the demands that they keep the parents on the straight and narrow and keep the children safe.

Once it takes a child, however, the state faces a dilemma of its own making: trying to determine whether the offending parents are worthy of their own child. In basing inevitably complex decisions on the most basic of moral judgments, the state—family court judges, child welfare caseworkers, and administrators—set themselves an impossible task. It is easy to say that, in hindsight, a child should not have been left with a psychotic and potentially homicidal parent. It is infinitely more difficult to decide what is best for a child who loves his mother but whose loving mother cannot seem to keep that child fed, clothed, educated, and safe. Does she deserve the child? Is she worthy? Has she so violated our standard of worthiness that she loses the child?

These are noble questions. They are, however, the wrong questions. They are questions that reflect a desire to save the child, and, if possible, to redeem the mother. The child cannot be saved. I do not mean it cannot be helped. I mean saved—delivered from his parents and secured in a new home where he begins a new life in which his parents are made to disappear.

This book is about two families whose children the state felt compelled and justified to take away. The implications of the state's actions are felt every day in the state's confrontation with parents like the Melton sisters. But the state's failure to deliver in any consistent way on the vague promise it makes to the child it takes into its care reflects a problem that transcends an inefficient, inept, and uncaring bureaucracy. The state's failure lies in the myths we share about what families are supposed to be.

We need families to project images that are familiar and safe, images that remind us that there are havens in an otherwise threatening world. I do not disparage these myths. I do, however, question the validity of rendering that mythical view of the family into an ideal to which we ask all families to aspire. Because when families do not meet that lofty aspiration, they risk becoming families that the law—the manifestation of our social will—does not respect. Neither the Melton nor the LaFlamme families ultimately earned that respect.

The state took the Melton children and Megan Marie from their homes because it did not believe that, strictly speaking, their parents were worthy of them. The state believed that it was not then taking these children from true families: The LaFlammes were not quite a family according to the legal definition of their bond; the Meltons were not a family because the Melton sisters had not behaved toward their children the way parents in acceptable families are supposed to act. Both accusations were, in a narrow sense, true.

But it was also true that these were families. They were families because they existed as families in the eyes of the children. The state, believing what it felt was best for those children, chose to ignore the relationship between parents and children that preceded the children's relationship with the state. It does so every day, just as it has been doing for well over one hundred years. And it will continue doing so until the state is willing to accept the complex, sometimes maddening and incomprensible relationships its agents find when they walk through the door and into a family's home.

The story of Megan Marie did, for the protagonists at least, end with the supreme court's decision that left the child with Gina Pellegrino. Those still familiar with the case now say that Gina is a good and attentive mother. For this child, then, there may be a happy ending. But it is an ending to a story that should have never taken place. It is an ending that does not reflect wisdom. Rather, the state, like the child now known as Angelica Pellegrino, got lucky, as it did with the Melton children. The state took a needless risk when it acted on her behalf. Its actions are not justified by Gina Pellegrino's proving to be up to the task because when the state acted, there was no assurance that she would be. The case concluded with the law's view of relationships between parents and children not defined by blood essentially unquestioned.

But then, in the late summer of 1998, a federal district judge, Kimba Wood, ruled that a New York foster family did, in fact, enjoy a legal interest in that child after the biological parents' rights were terminated. As happened in the case of Megan Marie, the child's biological mother abandoned him at birth. Like Cindy and Jerry LaFlamme, the foster parents in this case proceeded with the expectation that the child would be theirs forever. Shortly before the adoption was to be made final, a caseworker removed the child, charging that the child was not well supervised in the pre-adoptive parents' absence. The parents, left without legal standing, could not appeal the ruling, nor could they so much as visit the child for three months. The city eventually found that he had not, in fact, been neglected and returned him to his pre-adoptive parents, who sued. In her decision, Judge Wood wrote that there was, "a constitutionally protected liberty interest in the stability and integrity of the relationship between such a foster mother and such a child." Essential to that relationship, she wrote, were two factors: the time the child had been with his family, which in this case was for a year and since shortly after his birth; and the expectation that the relationship was to be permanent.

The LaFlammes might not have met Judge Wood's standard; Megan, after all, was not with them for a year. But Wood's decision went to the heart of their case: The LaFlamme family—Cindy, Jerry, and Megan Marie—were a family because their life together was defined by the expectation, not the wish or desire or hope but the expectation, of permanence. It was a reasonable expectation, given Gina Pellegrino's abandonment, disappearance, and loss of parental rights. Life was proceeding for the LaFlamme family based on Gina's action and the state's response to it. It was Judge Downey, after all, who had terminated her parental rights. It was he who still presided in the matter when her appeal period passed. And it was he who then acted, on the thinnest of legal rationalizations, to undo what he and the Department of Children and Youth Services had done and attempt to restore the child to what he regarded as her rightful home.

The child was safe with the LaFlammes. The only problem with their home, in the eyes of the state—and, in particular, the eyes of Judge John Downey—was it was not the rightful home. It was a good home. But it was not, in his view, where the child was meant to be— a home in which parents rear their child with the assurance that, barring death or gross and enduring failure, they will not lose their child.

The story of the Melton sisters did not end when the police took their children or with the surrender of their parental rights or with the state's termination cases. It did not end there or at any other point because child welfare stories offer no tidy resolutions. The stories endure for the protagonists long after the legal proceedings conclude. Often, they simply start all over again.

So it was that in the first week of October of 1995 Cassandra Melton brought her new daughter home to the West Side of Chicago. The child shared this home with her mother, her grandmother Josephine, and her aunts. It was a red brick house down the block and across the street from the boarded-up house on North Keystone Avenue, where her nineteen cousins once lived.

Acknowledgments

This book would not have been possible without the assistance of a great many people.

My agent and friend Barney Karpfinger first suggested the idea, and, as he has for years, provided boundless encouragement and support. No author could ask for a better advocate. My editor Philip Turner was invaluable in honing the manuscript. Early on, Peter Smith provided important and enthusiastic guidance. Ann Godoff, as always, proved a wonderful shepherd.

Miles Corwin, Celia Dugger, Peg Hess, and David Remnick were extraordinarily generous with their time and energy in reading and improving the manuscript. LynNell Hancock, Mike Hoyt, Suzanne Levine, Brenda McGowan, Carol Sanger, and Tom Turley provided important insights on particular portions of the book.

My parents, Herbert and Lorraine Shapiro; my sister Jill; brother James; and sister-in-law Mary Cregan were wonderful boosters. So too were my in-laws, Joseph and Estelle Chira. Others who provided more help than they might know were Terry Anderson, Diane Corwin, Paul Fishleder, Esther Fein, Sam Freedman, Walter Gadlin, Amitav Ghosh, Ari Goldman, Lisa Gubernick, Paula Heeralall, Leslie Howell, Kami Kim, Tom McDonald, Amy McIntosh, Eileen Norris, Carol Phethean, Elisabeth Rubinfien, Dan Sneider, Jeffrey Toobin, Bill Utter, Carey Winfrey, and Peter Yawitz.

The Freedom Forum provided me with a grant that helped launch this project. My colleagues at Columbia, in particular James Carey, were generous as well with their grant.

I want to thank the doctors and nurses at Babies Hospital at Columbia-Presbyterian Medical Center and at Mt. Sinai Hospital. Special thanks goes to

Acknowlegdments

Myron Schwartz and Charles Miller, as well as to Terry Coffey, Jean Emond, Laura Flanagan, Ken Gorfinkle, Ria Hawkes, Naomi Hawkins, Genevieve Lowry, Cathy Mazzella, Marni Rubin, Jackie Simpson, Karen Suchoff, Jakica Tancabelic, Laura Tralongo, Max Van Gilder, Michael Weiner, and most especially, to the remarkable Leonard Wexler.

In writing a book about families I have spent a great deal of time thinking about my own family, my daughter Eliza and my son Jake. They are my everyday wonders to behold. At the heart of my family, my work, and my life is my wife, Susan Chira, for whom I give thanks, today and forever.

Sources

The main source of material in this book came from personal interviews. The subjects of those interviews are for the most part identified in the book. There were some additional interviews that proved very helpful, particularly on the subject of the law. Those included interviews with Jane Spinak and Carol Sanger of the Columbia University Law School, Sylvia Law of New York University Law School, and Joseph Goldstein of Yale Law School. I took Jane Spinak's course on family law when I first began my research. My finals, so to speak, came in extended conversations with Joseph Goldstein, one of the authors of the *Best Interests* trilogy, who put me through my paces.

My brother, James Shapiro, an English professor at Columbia, provided valuable insights and materials on the history of the family in England.

Bruce Dold, Tom McNamee, and Jerry Stermer provided invaluable background on the workings of the Illinois Department of Children and Family Services. John Savittieri, Ellen Domph, and Martin Shapiro were helpful in learning about the Melton sisters. Ed Smith and Sokoni Karanja offered valuable insights about the city and its neighborhoods. In Connecticut, Susanna Rodell brought me up to speed on the workings of the state's child welfare system and on the case of Megan Marie in particular. Steve Sabato of WFSB-TV generously provided me with videotapes of Megan's removal and of the supreme court hearings. In New York, Al Desetta and Pat O'Brien introduced me to children who had grown up in foster care. Marcia Robinson Lowry explained the intricacies of the suits she helped bring against child welfare systems. Jody Adams kindly allowed me to observe in her courtroom. David Ilford offered important insights on the psychological impact of foster care on children.

In addition to the following list of source material, I gleaned a good deal of background information from the pages of the *Chicago Tribune, Sun-Times, Law Journal,* and *Reader,* as well as from *The New York Times, The Washington Post, Time, Newsweek,* and the *Atlantic Monthly.* In Connecticut, *The Hartford Courant* and the *Connecticut Law Tribune,* in particular the coverage of Thomas Scheffey, were invaluable.

I do want to cite some specific sources that do not appear in the book itself. The primary source on the history of poor children in sixteenth-century London is drawn from *Children in English Society* by Ivy Pinchbeck and Margaret Hewitt. The history of the evolution of the orphanage in the United States comes from the work of historian Michael Sherraden. The number of public institutions in the early twentieth century comes from *In the Shadow of the Poor House* by Michael B. Katz. Material on the history and present state of Lexington, Mississippi, is drawn from articles in the *Los Angeles Times.* The material on the impact of inflation on funding for child welfare is drawn from the *Washington Monthly.* The chapter on the Center for Family Life is drawn from an article I wrote in *New York* magazine.

What follows is a listing of additional source material, first books and then scholarly and legal articles.

BOOKS

Addams, Jane. *Twenty Years at Hull-House.* New York: Signet, 1961.

Areen, Judith. *Family Law: Cases and Materials.* Westbury, N.Y.: Foundation Press, 1992.

Aries, Philippe. *Centuries of Childhood: A Social History of Family Life.* New York: Vintage, 1962.

Auletta, Ken. *The Underclass.* New York: Vintage, 1983.

Barthel, Joan. *For Children's Sake: The Promise of Family Preservation.* New York: Edna McConnell Clark Foundation, 1992.

Bartholet, Elizabeth. *Family Bonds: Adoption and the Politics of Parenting.* New York: Houghton Mifflin, 1993.

Beier, A.L. *Masterless Men: The Vagrancy Problem in England, 1560–1640.* London: Methuen, 1985.

Bender, Thomas. *Toward an Urban Vision: Ideas and Institutions in Nineteenth-Century America.* Baltimore: Johns Hopkins University Press, 1975.

Benzola, Edward J., with Neva Beach. *Temporary Child: A Foster Care Survivor's Story.* Fremont, Calif.: Real People Publishing, 1993.

Boswell, John. *The Kindness of Strangers.* New York: Pantheon Books, 1988.

Boyer, Paul. *Urban Masses and Moral Order in America, 1820–1920.* Cambridge: Harvard University Press, 1978.

Brace, Charles Loring. *The Dangerous Classes of New York and Twenty Years Among Them.* New York: Wynkoop & Hallenbeck, 1872.

Sources

Coles, Robert. *Anna Freud: The Dream of Psychoanalysis*. Reading, Mass.: Addison Wesley, 1992.

Courter, Gay. *I Speak for This Child: True Stories of a Child Advocate*. New York: Crown, 1995.

Cray, Robert E. *Paupers and Poor Relief: In New York City and Its Environs, 1700–1830*. Philadelphia: Temple University Press, 1988.

Desetta, Al, ed. *The Heart Knows Something Different: Teenage Voices from the Foster Care System*. New York: Persea, 1996.

Ellwood, David T. *Poor Support: Poverty in the American Family*. New York: Basic Books, 1988.

Fanschel, David, and Eugene B. Shinn. *Children in Foster Care: A Longitudinal Investigation*. New York: Columbia University Press, 1978.

Foucault, Michel. *Madness and Civilization*. New York: Random House, 1965.

Fry, Annette R. *The Children's Migration*. New York: Children's Aid Society, 1974.

Gillis, John R. *A World of Their Own Making: Myth, Ritual, and the Quest for Family Values*. Cambridge: Harvard University Press, 1997.

Goldstein, Joseph, Anna Freud, and Albert J. Solnit. *Beyond the Best Interests of the Child*. New York: The Free Press, 1973.

———. *Before the Best Interests of the Child*. New York: The Free Press, 1979.

———. *In the Best Interests of the Child*. New York: The Free Press, 1986.

Grubb, W. Norton, and Marvin Lazenson. *Broken Promises: How Americans Fail Their Children*. New York: Basic Books, 1982.

Hawes, Joseph. *The Children's Rights Movement: A History of Advocacy and Protection*. Boston: Twayne Publishers, 1991.

Herman, Stephen P. *Parent vs. Parent*. New York: Pantheon, 1990.

Hewlett, Sylvia Ann. *Child Neglect in Rich Nations*. New York: Unicef, 1993.

Holloway, Susan D., Bruce Fuller, Marylee F. Rambaud, and Costanza Eggers-Pierola. *Through My Own Eyes: Single Mothers and the Cultures of Poverty*. Cambridge: Harvard, 1997.

Janchill, Sister Mary Paul. *Guidelines to Decision Making in Child Welfare*. New York: Human Resources Workshop, 1981.

Karen, Robert. *Becoming Attached: Unfolding the Mystery of the Infant-Mother Bond and Its Impact on Later Life*. New York: Warner, 1994.

Katz, Michael B. *In the Shadow of the Poor House: A Social History of Welfare in America*. New York: Basic Books, 1986.

Kelso, Robert. *The History of Public Poor Relief in Massachusetts, 1620 to 1920*.

Ladd-Taylor, Molly. *Mother-Work: Women, Child Welfare, and the State, 1890–1930*. Urbana: University of Illinois Press. 1994.

Lemann, Nicholas. *The Promised Land: The Great Black Migration and How It Changed America*. New York: Knopf, 1991.

Lindsay, Duncan. *The Welfare of Children*. Oxford: Oxford University Press, 1994.

Mason, Mary Ann. *From Father's Property to Children's Rights: The History of Child Custody in the United States*. New York: Columbia University Press, 1994.

Mnookin, Robert H. and D. Kelly Weisberg. *Child, Family, and State: Problems and Materials on Children and the Law*. Boston: Little Brown, 1989.

Murphy, Patrick T. *Wasted: The Plight of America's Unwanted Children*. Chicago: Ivan R. Dee, 1997.

Myers, John E., ed. *The Backlash: Child Protection under Fire*. Thousand Oaks, Calif.: Sage, 1994.

Pinchbeck, Ivy, and Margaret Hewitt. *Children in English Society*. London: Routledge & Kegan Paul, 1969.

Polier, Justine Wise. *Everyone's Children, Nobody's Child: A Judge Looks at Underprivileged Children in the United States*. New York: Scribner's, 1941.

Rothman, David J. *The Discovery of the Asylum: Social Order and Disorder in the New Republic*. Boston: Little Brown, 1971.

Slack, Paul. *Poverty and Policy in Tudor and Stuart England*. London: Longman, 1988.

Solnit, Albert J., Barbara F. Nordhaus, and Ruth Lord. *When Home Is No Haven: Child Placement Issues*. New Haven: Yale University Press, 1992.

Trattner, Walter I. *From Poor Law to Welfare State: A History of Social Welfare in America*. New York: Free Press, 1994.

Vardin, Patricia A., and Ilene N. Brody, eds. *Children's Rights: Contemporary Perspectives*. New York: Teachers College Press, 1979.

Wheeler, Leslie. *The Orphan Trains. American History Illustrated*. Harrisburg, Penn.: 1983.

Williams, Perny. *The Tudor Regime*. Oxford: Oxford University Press, 1979.

Wilson, William Julius. *The Truly Disadvantaged: The Inner City, the Underclass, and Public Policy*. Chicago: University of Chicago Press, 1987.

Zelizer, Viviana A. *Pricing the Priceless Child: The Changing Social Value of Children*. New York: Basic Books, 1985.

PERIODICALS

Adams, Paul. "Marketing Social Change: The Case of Family Preservation." *Children and Youth Services Review* (1994).

Anderson, Paul G. "Professionalism in Child Protection." *Social Service Review* (June 1989).

Barbell, Kathy, et al. "Child Abuse and Neglect: A Look at the States." *Child Welfare League of America* (1995).

Bartlett, Katherine T. "Rethinking Parenthood as an Exclusive Status: The Need for Legal Alternatives When the Premise of the Nuclear Family Has Failed." *Virginia Law Review* (June 1984).

Bartolet, Elizabeth. "Beyond Biology: The Politics of Adoption and Reproduction." *Duke Journal of Gender Law and Policy* (Spring 1995).

Besharov, Douglas J. "Looking Beyond 30, 60, and 90 Days." *Children and Youth Services Review* (1994).

Besharov, Douglas J., with Karen N. Gardiner. "Tough Love, Safety Net Keys to Welfare Reform." *Forum for Applied Research and Public Policy* (Winter 1997).

Bowlby, John. "Maternal Care and Mental Health." World Health Organization (1952).

Brenneman, Frederica S. "Striking a Balance Between Family Privacy and Child Protection: The View from Connecticut." NCJFCJ Fall College (1983).

Clement, Priscilla F. "Families and Foster Care in 19th-Century Philadelphia." *Social Service Review* (June 1983).

Collins, Ann, and Lawrence J. Aber. "Children and Welfare Reform: How Welfare Reform Can Help or Hurt Children." *National Center for Children in Poverty* (1997).

Davis, Peggy C. "Contested Images of Family Values: The Role of the State." *Harvard Law Review* (April 1994).

———. "Law as Microaggression." *Yale Law Journal* (June 1989).

———. "Neglected Stories and the Lawfulness of Roe v. Wade." *Harvard Civil Rights Civil Liberties Law Review* (Summer 1993).

———. " 'There Is a Book Out . . .': An Analysis of Judicial Absorption of Legislative Facts." *Harvard Law Review* (May 1987).

———. "Use and Abuse of the Power to Sever Family Bonds." *New York University Review of Law and Social Change* (1983–1984).

Department of Children and Family Services, State of Illinois, *Executive Statistical Summary,* 1994.

———, *Executive Summary: Five-Year Trend Report, Fiscal Years 1990–1994.*

Dore, Martha Morrison. "Family Preservation and Poor Families: When 'Homebuilding' Is Not Enough." *Journal of Contemporary Family Services* (1993).

Eagle, Rita S. "Airplanes Crash, Spaceships Stay in Orbit: The Separation of Experience of a Child 'In Care.' " *Journal of Psychotherapy Practice and Research* (Fall 1993).

English, Diana J., and Peter J. Pecora. "Risk Assessment as a Practice Method in Child Protective Services." *Child Welfare League of America* (1994).

Fineman, Martha L. "The Politics of Custody and the Transformation of American Custody Decision Making." *University of California Davis Law Review* (Spring 1989).

Flynn, Frank. "Early Days of Chicago Juvenile Court." *Social Service Review* (March 1954).

Fraser, Mark W., Kristine E. Nelson, and Jeanne C. Rivard. "Effectiveness of Family Preservation Services." *Social Work Research* (September 1997).

Garrison, Marcia. "Why Terminate Parental Rights?" *Stanford Law Review* (February 1983).

————. "Child Welfare Decisionmaking: In Search of the Least Drastic Alternative." *Georgetown Law Journal* (1987).

George, Robert M., Fred H. Wulczyn, and Allen W. Harden. "Foster Care Dynamics, 1983–1993: An Update from the Multistate Foster Care Data Archive." *The Chapin Hall Center for Children* (1995).

————. "Foster Care Dynamics, 1983–1992." Chicago. *The Chapin Hall Center for Children* (1994).

Greenberg, Mark, Steve Savner, and Rebecca Swartz. "Limits on Limits: State and Federal Policies on Welfare Time Limits." *Center for Law and Social Policy* (1996).

Guggenheim, Martin. "The Right to Be Represented but Not Heard: Reflections on Legal Representation of Children." *New York University Law Review* (April 1984).

————. "The Effects of Recent Trends to Accelerate the Termination of Parental Rights of Children in Foster Care: An Empirical Analysis of Two States." 1994

Hanna, Agnes K. "Dependent Children under Care of Children's Agencies: A Review of Census Findings." *Children's Bureau* (1933).

Hess, Peg McCartt. "Reflecting in and on Practice: A Role for Practitioners in Knowledge Building."

Hess, Peg McCartt, with Brenda G. McGowan, and Michael Botsko. "Preserving and Supporting Families over Time: The Center for Family Life's 'Preventive Services Program' Model." *Columbia University School of Social Work* (1998).

Hess, Peg McCartt, with Gail Folaron. "Ambivalences: A Challenge to Permanency for Children." *Child Welfare League of America* (1991).

Hess, Peg McCartt. "Placement Considerations for Children of Mixed African-American and Caucasian Parentage." *Child Welfare* (1992).

Korn, Kirsten. "The Struggle for the Child: Preserving the Family in Adoption Disputes between Biological Parents and Third Parties." *North Carolina Law Review* (June 1994).

Lerner, Steve. "The Geography of Foster Care: Keeping Children in the Neighborhood." *Foundation for Child Development* (February 1990).

Lindsay, Duncan. "Family Preservation and Child Protection." *Children and Youth Services Review* (1994).

McGowan, Brenda G. "Family-based Services and Public Policy: Context and Implications."

McGowan, Brenda G., with Alfred J. Kahn and Sheila B. Kamerman. "Social Services for Children, Youth, and Families: The New York City Study." *Columbia University School of Social Work* (1990).

McKenzie, Richard B. "Orphanages: The Real Story." *The Public Interest* (Spring 1996).

Nagle, Ami, Chuck Shubart, and Regina McGraw. "Chicago Kids Count: Community by Community Profiles of Child Well-Being." *Voices for Illinois Children* (1994).

Sources

Nelson, Kristine E. "Child Placing in the Nineteenth Century." *Social Service Review* (March 1985).

Pardeck, John T. "The Forgotten Child: A Study of the Stability and Continuity of Foster Care." *University Press of America* (1982).

Rodham, Hillary. "Children under the Law." *Harvard Educational Review* (November 1973).

Ross, Jane L. *Child Welfare: Complex Needs Strain Capacity to Provide Services.* Washington. Government Accounting Office Report, 1995.

Rossi, Peter H., John R. Scheurman, and Stephen Budde. "Understanding Child Placement Decisions and Those Who Make Them." *Chapin Hall Center for Children* (1994).

Wolpert, Julian. "What Charity Can and Cannot Do." *Twentieth Century Fund Press.* 1996.

Zainaldin, Jamil. "The Emergence of Modern American Family Law: Child Custody, Adoption, and the Courts, 1796–1851." *University of Louisville Law Review* (1979).

Index

A (foster-care teenager), 246
Abandonment
  of Baby Girl B, 12, 13, 14, 49–50,
    75, 80–81, 179, 201, 207, 220,
    284, 300
  Canadian case about, 216
  definition of, 49
  and history of family, 30–31
  and intentions of mother, 12–13, 14
  in New York State, 181, 299–300
  questions concerning, 16
  and role of state, 13, 31
  in Russia, 222
  and termination of rights, 49
  and time issues, 49
Abortion, 15, 121, 125, 145, 238
Adams, Paul, 134
Addams, Jane, 148–54
Administration for Children's Services
    (New York City), 255–56
Adoption
  and Center for Family Life, 261
  Connecticut's reconsideration of
    laws about, 176–77
  and finality, 208–9, 210
  finalizing of, 177, 202–4
  in Illinois, 282, 288, 292

of Melton children, 281, 282
  See also Adoptive parents
Adoption Assistance Act (1980), 33,
    36, 50, 132, 133
Adoptive parents
  impact of Baby Girl B case on, 170
  legal standing of, 300
  probation for, 65
  refusal to surrender child by, 216
  rights of, 170
  screenings/inspections of, 4–6, 8
  subsidizing of, 231
  and time issues, 300
  See also LaFlamme, Cynthia and
    Jerry
Aid for Families with Dependent Chil-
    dren (AFDC), 155, 293
Aid to Dependent Children (ADC),
    155
Ainsworth, Mary, 60
Ainsworth Strange Situation Test,
    60–62, 71–72
Almshouses, 100
American Bar Association, Center on
    Children and the Law of, 50
American Civil Liberties Union
    (ACLU), 131–32, 135

Amish case, 21
Anaya-Allen, Angelica
  and abuse of Gina, 199
  clients of, 33–34, 68
  and Connecticut's reconsideration of
    adoption and termination laws,
    176, 177
  death threats against, 172
  Gina names child after, 174
  as Gina's lawyer, 35, 224
  and Gina's living arrangements, 77,
    78
  and "infinite patience" concept, 242
  and LaFlammes' visitation rights,
    183–84, 185–86, 190, 192–93
  professional background of, 33–34
  and publicity about Baby Girl B, 78,
    169–70
  and removal of baby from
    LaFlammes, 44, 77, 78
  and stay of Downey's decision, 182
  and termination of rights issue, 32–33,
    35–36, 67, 201, 208–10, 218
  and worthiness issue, 220
Anderson, Arthur, 143–44
Angelica. *See* Baby Girl B
Anne (psychotic mother), 254–55,
    256–59, 264, 268, 286
Apprenticeships, 28–29
Aries, Philippe, 26, 28
Art Institute of Chicago, 148, 149
Asylums, 100, 112, 113
Attachment, 60–61, 74. *See also*
    Ainsworth strange situation test;
    Parent-child relationship
Attorney general, Connecticut
  amending of Pellegrino case by,
    49–50, 218–19
  and appeal of Downey's decision,
    172, 173–74, 175, 177
  and final decision in Baby Girl B
    case, 218–19
  and LaFlammes' visitation rights, 183
  and public debate about Baby Girl
    B, 171, 172
  rebuke of, 219

  and refusal to appeal Downey's deci-
    sion, 49–50, 218, 219
  and stay in Downey's ruling, 174
  See also Blumenthal, Richard
Attorneys
  for children, 186–90
  court-appointed, 104, 187–88
  fees for, 187–88
  See also specific person

B (teenage mother), 238–39
Baby Girl B
  Baby Girl B
  abandonment of, 12, 13, 14, 49–50,
    75, 80–81, 179, 201, 207, 220,
    284, 300
  appeal in case of, 173–74, 201–4,
    205–10
  appearance of, 224
  attorneys for, 183–84, 186–87
  best interests of, 16, 59, 66, 169,
    173, 175, 178, 183–84, 194, 200,
    205–7, 210, 215–16, 220–21
  birth of, 3, 219–20
  Connecticut Department of Chil-
    dren and Youth Services responsi-
    ble for, 176
  and Connecticut's reconsideration of
    laws about adoption and termina-
    tion, 176–77
  father of, 284
  final decision for, 218–23
  foster parents of, 7–9
  Gill's views about, 213–15
  impact of case of, 170
  LaFlammes' surrender of, 76–82,
    171, 175, 179, 183, 184–85, 186,
    193, 194
  and myth of family, 299
  naming of, 6–7, 174
  and parent-child relationship, 16,
    224–25, 284
  placement of, 6–7, 65
  and psychological parents, 185–86
  and psychologists/psychiatrists, 47,
    61–62, 190, 199–200

public debate about, 16, 177–78
publicity about, 15–16, 76–80,
169–70, 171, 172–73, 174,
178–79, 186
and "rescue fantasy," 67–68, 283
and role of state, 4, 15, 81, 190–94,
221
and time issues, 24, 36, 66–67,
300
See also Connecticut Department of
Children and Youth Services;
Downey, John; LaFlamme, Cynthia and Jerry; Pellegrino, Gina
Baby Jessica, 22, 23, 24, 220
Baby Lenore, 201, 202, 208, 209
Baby Richard, 22–23, 24, 59, 213–14,
215, 220
Baby Robert, 70–75
Bakulsky, Paul, 49–46, 173
Berdon, Robert, 206, 207, 208, 209
The Bertice Berry Show, Melton sisters
on, 94–95, 97, 106
Best interests of child
and Baby Girl B, 16, 59, 66, 169,
173, 175, 178, 183–84, 194, 200,
205–7, 210, 215–16, 220–21
and Baby Richard, 214
basis for deciding, 136
in Canada, 216
and centrality of mother, 298
and children's resilence, 60
and Connecticut's reconsideration of
adoption and termination laws,
176
experts' views about, 59–61
and finality, 205–7, 210
Gill's views about, 211–16
Guggenheim's views about, 179–82
and Indiana case, 270
and material benefits, 214
and Melton children, 232
and poor, 155
and role of state, 154
and termination of rights, 53–54, 56,
206
and time issues, 66

Biological parents
and basic parent-child relationship,
180
child's bond with, 60–62, 180,
192–93
and foster parents, 20–22
and hierarchy of claims to children,
16, 21, 22, 65, 181–82
and "infinite patience" concept,
202–4
saving children from, 112–18
See also Fathers; Mothers; *specific
person*
Birth parents. *See* Biological parents
Blackmun, Harry, 51–52
Block, Gerald, 104, 107
Bloss, William, 19, 56, 57, 171, 207–8
Blumenthal, Richard
and appeal of termination rights,
79–80, 173, 177, 201, 205–7, 210
and Connecticut's reconsideration of
adoption and termination laws,
185
and stay of Downey's decision, 182
Borden, David, 203–4, 206, 207,
208–9, 218, 219
Boswell, John, 30–31
Bowlby, John, 52–53, 54, 60, 61
Brace, Charles Loring, 112–16,
148–49, 150, 155, 240, 291
Brennan, William, 20–21, 22, 218
Brenneman, Fredrica, 40, 41–42, 62,
203, 204
Brooklyn, New York. *See* Center for
Family Life
Burke, Anne, 127–28, 148

C (foster-care teenager), 246–47, 248
Calica, Richard, 121–22, 240–45,
249–50, 253, 279, 287
Callahan, Robert, 208
Canada, best interests of child in, 216
Case workers. *See* Social workers
Catholic Charities, 88
Catholic church, 26–27, 28, 31, 112,
116

Causes, 237–39, 275, 290

Center for Family Life
and Anne's case, 254–55, 256–59
budget for, 293
as community-centered, 250, 259,
291, 292
and foster parents, 259, 260–61
functions/programs of, 251–54
as model for others, 266, 294
open adoptions at, 261
parents' role at, 252–54, 258,
259–60, 268, 286
and removal of children, 261–64
role of state compared with work of,
253, 262
social workers at, 251, 252, 254,
255, 259–60, 261–64, 267
and unsalvageable families, 267

Chicago, Illinois. *See* Melton sisters

Child abuse
and children's feelings about mothers, 247
and emancipation of children, 63
federal reporting about, 132
in Illinois, 291
legislation about, 63
in Melton/Turner case, 88, 92, 104,
119, 278, 286
and mothers on drugs, 95
and rights of children, 212
and termination of rights, 49

Child labor, 101, 154

Child neglect
Clinton administration concern
about, 89
federal reporting about, 132
in Melton case, 88, 89, 92, 103, 119
and termination of rights, 49

Child welfare agencies
assumptions of, 288–89
boards of, 155–56
as community-based programs,
289–92
county, 155–56, 268–71
criticisms of, 128–39
daily activities of, 289–90

inspections by, 81
options available to, 288–89
private, 155, 288
publicity about, 129
See also Child welfare system; Social
workers; *specific agency*

Child welfare system
costs/funding of, 132–33, 231, 255,
276, 288, 293–96
criticisms of, 234–35
dilemmas facing, 158, 268
doubts and concerns of workers in,
189
federal role in, 132–34
goals in, 295
ignorance about, 214
as intrusive, 139, 234–35
limits of, 234–35
and Melton sisters, 88
as noble cause, 135
and obstacles to poor, 180
overstepping bounds by, 69–70
philosophy for, 137–39
as reactive, 136–37
reform of, 130–31, 155, 232,
255–56, 266–67, 288–89, 293–96
rise of, 98–102
successes in, 266
See also Child welfare agencies; Family preservation; Social workers;
State, role of; *specific agency*

Children
acting up by, 272–74
answers for failed, 289–92
attorneys for, 186–90
as caretakers of mothers, 121–22
centrality of mothers in lives of,
232–33, 244–48, 265, 271,
272–74, 279–81, 283, 284,
297–98
as chattel, 28–29, 62–63, 154, 171
death of, 92, 93, 255, 288
depression of, 248, 257, 269, 270
divorcing of parents by, 212
emancipation of, 63
emotional needs of, 279

feelings about separation from
mothers of, 232–33, 244–48, 265,
271, 272–74, 283
future of failed, 275, 280, 288
hierarchy of claims to, 16, 21, 22,
65, 181–82
as innocents, 29, 114, 154, 230
and myth of family, 299
as "nobody's child," 118
of poor, 98–102, 150–54
prevailing attitudes about, 214–15
as "priceless," 297
resiliency of, 60, 244
return to parents of, 231
rights of, 63, 104, 211–13, 216–17,
271
"sacralization" of, 154
saving of, 112–18
school attendance of, 270–71
self-blame of, 286
"special needs," 278, 288, 294
unborn, 203–4
violent/troubled, 268–71, 294
See also Abandonment; Best interests
of child; Melton children; *specific
child*
Children's Aid Society, 113, 115–18
Christian, Claudine, Melton children
with, 119, 120, 164–65, 232–33,
244, 276, 277, 279, 280, 281, 286,
288, 293
Cities
child welfare as problem of, 291
poor in, 101
as source of problems, 92, 115
Clinton, William J./Clinton Administration, 89, 134, 155, 288
Cohen, Donald, 59–60, 65, 66, 73, 74,
75, 220, 244
Columbia University, National Center
for Children in Poverty at, 294
Columbus-Maryville, 272–74
Community
and assistance to troubled families,
250
standards of, 249

Community-based program
benefits/importance of, 268, 289–92
Center for Family Life as, 250, 259,
291, 292
child welfare agencies as, 289–92
and families as unsalvageable, 266–67
Confidentiality
and child welfare agencies' work,
129, 270
of legal proceedings, 15–16, 37, 62
Connecticut Appellate Court, 182,
203–4
Connecticut Civil Liberties Union, 201
Connecticut Department of Children
and Youth Services
and abandonment of Baby Girl B,
13, 31
and appeal of Downey's decision,
173–74
Baby Girl B in care of, 4, 19, 176, 182
choosing sides by, 67–68
Gina's initial contacts with, 14–15,
17
and Gina's transportation, 198
and Gina's visitation rights, 44
impact of Baby Girl B case on, 170
and LaFlammes' visitation rights, 183
placement of Baby Girl B by, 6–7
and removal of child from Gina,
173–74
and "rescue fantasy," 67–68
screenings/inspections of LaFlammes
by, 4–6, 8
supervision of Gina and child by,
199
and termination of rights, 32, 41, 300
and time issues, 66–67
and Valerie D case, 203
See also Baby Girl B; LeMay, Patricia; Senatore, Rose Alma
Connecticut, State of
and costs of Baby Girl B care, 170
reconsideration of adoption and termination laws in, 16, 176–77,
202, 204
See also specific agency

Connecticut Supreme Court, 201–4, 205–10, 218–21, 242

Constitution, U.S., 213, 215

"Continuity of care," 53

Cook County Public Guardian, 91, 104, 134. *See also* Murphy, Patrick

Cook County. *See* Cook County Public Guardian; Melton sisters

Cortigiano, Betty Lou and Louis, 7–9, 65, 66

Costs/funding
  of child welfare system, 132–33, 231, 255, 276, 288, 293–96
  for foster care, 133, 155, 293–94, 295–96

Council for Equal Rights in Adoption, 178

County child welfare agencies, 155–56, 268–71

Courts
  responsibilities of, 179
  as ultimate control of fate of child, 32
  See also specific court

Cult of Mary, 27

Cult of motherhood, 154

Daley, Richard M., 89

Dandridge, Lance, 188–90

The Dangerous Classes (Brace), 113–15

Davis, Peggy, 53, 54

Depression
  of children, 248, 257, 269, 270
  of mothers/parents, 123–24, 138, 166, 236

DeShaney, Joshua, 212

Dewey, John, 152

Divorce
  of child from parents, 212
  and history of family, 29
  and screening of adoptive parents, 4–5

"Doe, Jean," 203–4

Dohrn, Bernardine, 157–58, 240

Domph, Ellen, 277

Downey, John
  appeal to decision of, 79–80, 172, 173, 175, 201–4, 205–10
  and best interests of child, 220
  as Chinese prisoner, 38–40, 195
  and Connecticut's reconsideration of adoption and termination laws, 202
  death threats against, 172
  decisions of, 66, 70, 75, 76, 79–80, 169, 174, 182, 300
  and final decision in Baby Girl B case, 218–23
  gag order imposed by, 176
  and Gina's late filing, 36, 42
  and Gina's visitation rights, 32, 43
  Guggenheim's views about decision of, 182
  idealism of, 283–84
  and LaFlammes' powerlessness and uncertainty, 43
  and LaFlammes' visitation hearing, 184–87, 190–95, 197
  and parent-child relationship, 171, 284
  personal and professional background of, 37–40
  and psychological/psychiatric reports, 44, 62, 195–96
  public debate about ruling of, 178
  reconsideration of his termination decision by, 173, 174, 175
  reconsideration of termination rights by, 19, 32, 36, 37–42, 49, 66, 70, 219
  refuses to talk about case, 76, 79
  Ruhe's views about decision of, 169
  and Solnit's testimony, 185, 190–94
  state refuses to appeal decision of, 49, 218
  stays in ruling of, 174, 176, 182
  termination of Gina's rights by, 7, 17, 23, 183–84, 201–4, 300
  and transportation for Gina, 198

Drugs
  and family preservation projects, 104

and Melton sisters, 89, 95, 106, 114, 122, 125, 126, 145, 157, 159, 229, 230, 243, 285, 287, 292, 293
mothers on, 70, 72, 89, 95, 114, 122, 126, 158, 159, 203–4, 229, 230, 236–37, 243, 260–61, 284, 285, 287
and termination of mother's rights, 33
Dudley, Richard, 54

Edgar, James, 127
Edna McConnell Clark Foundation, 134
Education, Addams' views about, 152
Emergency shelters, 88–89, 91, 238, 244
Endangerment, 33, 51, 56, 75
England, poor in, 98–102, 150, 250, 291
Experts
and best interest of child, 59–61
overstepping boundaries by, 187
See also Psychologists/psychiatrists; *specific person*

Family First, 133–34
Family preservation, 103–5, 133–35, 213, 237, 267, 279, 285, 288, 296
Family/families
and Baby Robert's case, 74–75
cult of, 30
definition of, 21, 25–26
as essential economic and social unit, 29
history of, 25–31
legal decisions about, 20–22
myth of, 80, 298–99
state's relationship to, 63–64, 267, 298–99
as unsalvageable, 267–68
what constitutes, 16, 21, 23
Father/fathers
and Anne's case, 254, 257, 264
in Baby Girl B case, 284
of Baby Richard, 59, 214
children as belonging to, 29
of foster-care children, 246–47, 248
grandparents versus, 65
and history of family, 28
impact on children of, 126
in Indiana case, 271
and material benefits, 65
of Melton children, 88, 91, 95, 109, 121, 126, 145, 281
of Melton sisters, 143–44
missing, 155
and public assistance, 230
rights/power of, 22–23, 28
and role of state, 297
termination of rights of, 261
Fay, Marion, 36, 37, 174, 183–84, 186, 187, 190, 193, 203
Federal government
funding by, 293–95
role of, 132–34, 230
and welfare reform, 232
Finality
and adoption, 208–9, 210
and appeal of Downey's decision, 205–10
and best interests of child, 205–7, 210
and bonding, 206
of termination of rights, 201–4, 205–7, 208–10
See also Permanence
Florida
adoption laws in, 202
child welfare in, 212
Foster care
and best interests of child, 100, 101, 104, 112, 148, 155–56, 240, 271, 292
Brace's views about, 155
costs/funding for, 133, 155, 293–94, 295–96
and "doing" transportation, 109, 118
and emergence of child welfare system, 101
and feelings of children about mothers, 245–48

Foster care (*cont'd*)
  goal of, 22
  in Illinois, 291–92
  inadequacy of, 155
  in Indiana case, 270
  legal decisions about, 20–22
  "legal orphans" in, 51
  legislation concerning, 33
  Melton children in, 91, 109, 110, 159,
    164–65, 229–30, 231, 232–33,
    234, 276, 277, 278, 281, 287
  as option for child welfare agencies,
    271, 288
  and saving children from parents,
    115–18
  and time issues, 55, 300
  See also Foster parents; "Foster-care
    drift"
Foster Care Youth United, 245–48, 279,
  287
Foster parents
  ambivalence and fatigue of, 73, 74–75
  attachment/bonding with, 158, 259
  of Baby Girl B, 7–9
  and Baby Robert's case, 70–75
  and biological parents, 20–22
  and Center for Family Life, 259,
    260–61
  fees for, 231
  LaFlammes as, 195
  and parent-child relationship,
    299–300
  as psychological parents, 52–53
  and resolution of cases, 158
  rights of, 20–22
  and termination of rights, 55, 261
  and time issues, 55, 300
  See also Foster care
"Foster-care drift," 33, 93–94, 132,
  255, 275, 281
Foucault, Michel, 98
Foundling hospitals, 31
Freud, Anna, 52–53, 59, 60, 64, 65, 69,
  181, 187, 216
Freud, Sigmund, 156
Friedman, Sonya, 169, 170

G (foster-care teenager), 246, 247, 248
Gage, Michael, 70–75
Gallanis, Kathryn, 91, 103, 104, 106,
  107, 278
Garrison, Marcia, 53–54
Gill, Charles, 211–17, 220, 221
Gillis, John R., 27, 28, 30
Gina. *See* Pellegrino, Gina
Ginrich, Newt, 236, 240, 242
Goldberg, Sidney, 137–39
Goldstein, Joseph, 53, 59, 64, 69, 181,
  187, 216
Graham, Janet, 116, 117–18
Grandparents
  and custody of children, 65, 71–74,
    140
  as source of parenting skills, 142
  See also Melton, Josephine
Gray, Edward, 116
Gregory K (termination of rights case),
  63, 212
Guggenheim, Martin, 50–51, 179–82,
  202, 221, 287
Guiliani, Rudolph, 255

Haley, Alex, 64
Hall, E. Stanley, 152, 154
Hardin, Mark, 50
Hauser, Jennifer, 58, 174–75, 176,
  198–99
Heiple, James, 59, 214
"Hereditary pauperism," 113–14, 240
Herzlich, Ken, 87–88, 89, 179, 232
Hess, Peg, 266
Holy Family, 28
HomeBuilders, 133, 134
HomeRebuilders, 295–96
Horton, Wesley, 219, 220
House of Representatives, U.S., 230
Houses of refuge, 101
Hull-House, 105, 148, 149–54

Illinois Department of Children and
  Family Services
  caseload of, 92–93, 130
  children taken to, 272–73

creation of, 132
criticisms/public anger of, 92,
    93–94, 105, 127–28
funding for, 132, 133
hiring and training in, 130–31
lawsuits against, 131–32
and Melton sisters, 88, 92, 93–94,
    127–28, 130, 277, 281–82
minority workers in, 128
monitor of, 131–32
referrals by, 240
reform of, 133–34
responsibilities of, 136
and return of children to parents, 231
vision for, 136–37
See also McDonald, Jess
Illinois Masonic Medical Center,
    Maryville Parenting-Teen Center
    of, 237–39, 272–76
Illinois, State of
adoption in, 282, 288, 292
child abuse in, 291
child care costs in, 276
child welfare reform in, 291–92
foster care in, 291–92
termination of rights in, 288
See also specific agency
Illinois Supreme Court, 213–14
In re Gault, 63
Indiana, violent children case in,
    268–71, 286
"Infinite patience," for parental failure,
    201–4, 242
Institutions
and role of state, 98–102
space in, 288
See also type of institution
Interest development, 138–39
Iowa, custody cases in, 65
Izquierdo, Elisa, 255, 288

Jane (Anne's daughter), 254–55,
    256–57, 258, 259, 264, 265
Johnson, Gordon, 105
Judges
powers of, 33

and process versus "results," 40–42
and psychological parents, 60
and resolution of cases, 159
responsibilities of, 63
types of, 40–42
See also specific judge
Juvenile court, 148, 159
Juvenile Protective Association
    (Chicago), 121–22. *See also* Cal-
    ica, Richard

Kate (termination case), 55, 56
Kawamoto, Lynne
and alternatives of state, 288–89
decision of, 119, 157
feelings about Melton sisters of, 104,
    119, 283, 285–86
idealism of, 283–84, 287
and Melton sisters regaining custody
    of children, 125, 157, 285–86
and Meltons' hopes of regaining cus-
    tody, 120
Newsweek story about, 278–81, 285
and trial of Melton sisters, 106–7
Kelso, Robert, 29
Kennedy, Duncan, 40
Keystone Avenue. *See* Melton sisters
Kindergarten, 152
"Kindly intentions," 64, 69
King v. Low, 216
Krawiecki, Edward, 176
Kristina (termination case), 55, 56

Labrie, Richard, 237
LaFlamme, Cynthia and Jerry
and appeal to Downey's decision,
    205–10
and attachment/bonding with baby,
    61–62, 193, 221
attorneys for, 19, 170, 171
Baby Girl B placed with, 6–7, 65
Baby Girl B's early months with,
    8–10
birth mother's initial contact with,
    19–20
and Cindy's diary, 46–48

LaFlamme, Cynthia and Jerry (*cont'd*)
and Cindy's legal disposition, 175
commitment of, 75
and Connecticut's reconsideration of
laws about adoption and termination, 176, 177
consider having Gina live with
them, 56
contract of, 196–97
and Downey's imprisonment, 39
emotional distancing from baby of,
47–48
as family, 300
final decision for, 218–23
finalizing of adoption by, 10, 17, 19
as "foster parents," 195
and Gina's return, 9–10, 17, 18–19
and Gina's visitations, 43–48, 57–59,
174, 175
impact of case on, 35
initial knowledge about Gina of, 7
legal standing of, 17, 19, 20, 23, 173,
194, 195, 207–8, 218, 219
and myth of family, 299
and naming of baby, 6–7
and parent-child relationship, 284
post-decision life of, 221–23
powerlessness and uncertainty of,
43–48, 81, 200
psychiatric interviews/recommenda-
tions concerning, 43, 44, 47, 59,
61–62, 185, 195–96
and publicity, 76–77, 78–79,
169–70, 171, 174, 177–78, 220
re-placement of child with, 173–74,
176, 182
and reconsideration of termination
rights, 20, 36, 219
and "rescue fantasy," 67–68
in Russia, 221–22
screening/inspections of, 4–6, 8
state's assurances to, 81, 181, 221
surrender of Baby Girl B by, 76–82,
171, 175, 179, 183, 184–85, 186,
193, 194
and time issues, 24, 66–67, 300

views about Gina of, 56, 169–70,
192, 196–97
visitations to baby by, 7–9, 170,
183–87, 190–97, 199, 210
worthiness of, 284
LaFlamme, Gerard Konstantine, 222
LaFlamme, Megan Marie. *See* Baby
Girl B
Laslett, Peter, 27
Legal Aid Society of New York,
188–90
Legal assistance, 15, 35. *See also* Attorneys
"Legal orphans," 51, 287
Legal proceedings
confidentiality of, 15–16, 37, 62
See also specific proceeding
Legal system
and "critical legal issues" school of
thought, 40
responsibilities of, 179
See also Courts
LeMay, Patricia
Gina's contacts with, 14–15, 17,
35–36, 206, 209
places Baby Girl B with LaFlammes,
7, 8–9, 65
and reconsideration of termination
rights, 35–36, 37
rescue fantasy of, 67, 72
and return of Baby Girl B's mother,
9–10, 17, 18–19, 218
and time issue, 66–67
Levine, Daniel, 152
Lexington, Mississippi, Melton sisters
from, 143
Lord, Gretchen, 255, 256–60, 261,
262, 263, 264, 265, 267, 276

McDonald, Jess, 92, 128, 130–31, 132,
133, 135–37, 139, 158, 240, 291
Maddux, William, 135, 148
Malcolm X, 64, 69
Martin, Sara, 183, 184, 186, 190,
193–94, 203, 210
Mary, cult of, 27

Mary Ellen (child abuse case), 63
Maryville Parenting-Teen Center (Illinois Masonic Medical Center), 237–39, 272–76
Mason, Mary Ann, 29
Material benefits, 64–65, 214
Megan Marie. *See* Baby Girl B
Melton, Cassandra
  appearance and personality of, 96, 166
  background of, 95
  and drugs, 145
  and family reunion, 109
  hopes for regaining custody of children by, 122–23, 157
  in jail, 157
  living arrangements of, 87, 96, 229
  as mother, 229, 234, 281, 301
  mother's relationship with, 141
  removal of children of, 88
  and sisters' pregnancies, 121
  termination of rights of, 277
  trial of, 106–8
  visits with children of, 106
  See also Melton children; Melton sisters
Melton, Cassandra Henderson, 107–8, 119–21, 122–26, 141, 144, 147, 160–63, 235–36, 237
Melton children
  adoption of, 281, 282
  and best interests of child, 232
  cost to state for, 231
  and depression of mothers, 124
  in emergency shelter, 88–89, 91, 244
  fathers of, 88, 91, 95, 109, 121, 126, 145, 281
  feelings about separation from mothers of, 232–33, 244–45, 279–81, 283
  in foster care, 91, 109, 110, 159, 164–65, 229–30, 231, 232–33, 234, 276, 277, 278, 281, 287
  future of, 278–79, 280, 284, 286–87, 288
  Gill's views about, 215

and grandmother, 110, 140
hopes for regaining custody of, 93–94, 119–21, 122–23, 125–26, 140, 157–58, 160–63, 164–66, 229–30, 243, 285–86
impact of removal on, 233, 267
as instruments of punishment, 285
mothers' centrality in lives of, 232–33, 244–45, 279–81, 283, 285–87
mothers' commitment to, 242–43
mothers' treatment of, 96–97
mothers' visits with, 119, 120, 126, 140, 159, 160, 165, 229–30, 243, 285
and myth of family, 299
observation of, 110
pictures of, 106
relatives care for, 119–21, 159, 282, 286
remanded to custody of state, 157
removal of, 82, 86–88, 179, 232, 239–40, 243, 245, 249, 250, 286
reunion of, 109–11
rights of, 104
and role of state, 93–94
self-blame of, 286
splitting up of, 164, 229–30
surrender of, 277–82, 301
total number of, 281
and worthiness, 104
See also Melton sisters; *specific person*
Melton, Crystal, 108, 124–25, 126
Melton, Denise
  appearance and personality of, 96, 292
  on *Bertice Berry Show*, 94–95, 97
  and drugs, 95, 106, 159, 229, 230, 243, 292, 293
  and family reunion, 109
  hopes for regaining custody of children by, 122–23, 159–63, 230, 243, 244, 293
  living arrangements of, 87, 89, 96–97, 127, 229
  as mother, 96–97, 160

Melton, Denise (*cont'd*)
mother's relationship with, 141
motivation of, 292
and removal of children, 87, 89
surrender of children by, 277
trial of, 106–8, 119
visits to children of, 159, 160
See also Melton children; Melton sisters

Melton, Diane
on *Bertice Berry Show*, 94–95
birth of, 143
and drugs, 95, 122, 157, 230, 243
and family reunion, 109, 110
father of, 143
in jail, 106
living arrangements of, 229
as lost soul, 122
as mother, 97, 281, 293
motivation of, 292
and regaining custody of children, 230, 243
removal of children of, 87, 89
termination of rights of, 157, 277
trial of, 106–8
See also Melton children; Melton sisters

Melton, Johnny, 88

Melton, Josephine
appearance and personality of, 96, 140–47
background of, 142–44
on *Bertice Berry Show*, 94–95
and care of Melton children, 110, 146
daughters' relationship with, 89–90, 121, 125, 141–42, 145–47, 229, 243, 274, 301
and drugs, 145
and family reunion, 109
and father of sisters, 143–44
and hopes for regaining custody of children, 140, 160–63
mother of, 142–43
relatives of, 89–90, 144, 282
teaches parenting to daughters, 142–43

See also Melton children; Melton sisters

Melton, Maxine
appearance and personality of, 96, 145, 165–66
assistance for, 249
and child neglect charges, 103
children's feelings about separation from, 279–81
and drugs, 89, 145
father of, 143, 144
Henderson Melton's comments about, 107, 122–23
hopes for regaining custody of children by, 119–21, 122–23, 125, 159, 160–63, 164–66, 243
in jail, 95, 103, 106, 109, 119
living arrangements of, 86–89, 127, 146–47, 229, 240–41
as mother, 147, 286
mother's relationship with, 121, 141, 147
motivation of, 292
parenting skills of, 292–93
on public assistance, 96
and removal of children, 86–88, 97
termination of rights of, 277, 279–81
testimony at trial about, 107
visits with children of, 165, 243
See also Melton children; Melton sisters

Melton, May Fay
appearance and personality of, 96, 144–45, 163, 166, 292
assistance for, 249
background of, 95
and drugs, 106, 125, 126, 229, 230, 243, 292, 293
as ex-convict, 162
and family reunion, 109
Henderson Melton's views about, 147, 237
hopes for regaining custody of children by, 122–23, 125–26, 159, 160–63, 230, 243, 244, 293

living arrangements of, 87, 88, 96,
127, 146–47, 229
as mother, 147, 241–42, 293
mother's relationship with, 125,
141, 142, 145–47
motivation of, 292
preganancy of, 145
on public assistance, 96
public defender for, 104
and removal of children, 87, 88
self-confidence of, 235
surrender of children by, 277
trial of, 106–8
visits with children by, 126
See also Melton children; Melton sisters
Melton sisters
as adversaries to state, 286
on *The Bertice Berry Show*, 94–95,
97, 106
blame for losing children by, 94
Calica's views about, 240–43
centrality in children's lives of,
232–33, 244–45, 279–81, 283,
285–87
and child abuse/child neglect, 88,
89, 92, 103, 104, 119
children's feelings about separation
from, 232–33, 244–45, 279–81,
283
commitment to children of, 242–43
and community standards, 249
dependency on each other of, 90
depression of, 123–24
desire for return of children of,
93–94
as "dirty house" case, 95, 104, 105,
285
and drugs, 89, 95, 106, 114, 122,
125, 126, 145, 157, 159, 229, 230,
243, 285, 287, 292, 293
and family preservation projects,
134–35
father of, 143–44
Henderson Melton's life compared
with, 122–24

hopes for regaining custody of children by, 93–94, 119–21, 122–23,
125–26, 140, 157–58, 160–63,
164–66, 230, 232–33, 242–43,
285–86
and Illinois Department of Children
and Family Services, 88, 92,
93–94, 127–28, 130, 277, 281–82
initial removal of children of, 86–88,
94, 97
Kawamoto's feelings about, 104,
119, 278–79, 283, 285–86
lack of understanding about removal
of children by, 97
living arrangements of, 85–90,
91–92, 96–97, 107, 141, 146–47,
301
mother's relationship with, 89–90,
121, 125, 141–42, 145–47, 229,
243, 274, 301
motivation of, 236–37, 292
and myth of family, 299
number of children by, 281
and parent-child relationship, 284
and psychologists, 110
on public assistance, 91, 94, 96, 107,
143, 161, 230
public attitudes about, 104–6, 114
publicity about, 89, 94–95, 106,
157–58, 162, 232, 267, 277–81,
287
punishment of, 232, 285
relatives of, 89–90, 159, 282
reunion of, 109–11
and role of state, 82, 93–94, 97,
103–4, 221, 278–79, 283
Sisters Mary Paul's and Geraldine's
views about, 292–93
and social workers, 89–90, 109–11,
120, 127, 140, 142, 233,
267–68
teaching parenting/successful living
to, 249, 267–68, 274, 285
termination/surrender of rights of,
277–82, 287, 301
trial of, 103, 104, 106–8, 109, 119

Melton sisters (*cont'd*)
  and Wallace death, 92, 93, 128
  worthiness of, 104, 285
  See also Melton children; *specific person*
Meskill, Thomas, 39
Michigan, termination of rights in, 50–51
Milford Mental Health Center, 197, 210
Mindell, Robert, 158
Mnookin, Robert, 22
Moore, Jaime, 143
Morris, William, 150
Mothers
  as adversaries, 286
  blame on, 119
  and Center for Family Life goals, 252–54, 259–60
  centrality in lives of children of, 29–30, 232–33, 244–48, 265, 271, 272–74, 279–81, 283, 284, 297–98
  children as caretakers of, 121–22
  children's feelings about separation from, 232–33, 244–48, 265, 271, 272–74, 279–81, 283
  and cult of motherhood, 154
  depression of, 123–24, 166, 236
  discouragement of, 158
  on drugs, 70, 72, 89, 95, 114, 122, 126, 158, 159, 203–4, 229, 230, 236–37, 243, 260–61, 284, 285, 287
  as emotionally stunted, 239
  enhanced stature of, 29–30, 297
  and history of family, 27, 29–30
  intentions in abandonment of, 12–13, 14
  motivation of, 231–32
  passive acceptance of unwanted events by, 121–22
  "proper," 28–29
  punishing of, 232
  "romantic" view of, 29
  in school, 237
  teenage, 121, 125, 145, 232, 237–39, 245–48
  what it takes to be good, 120–21
  worthiness of, 104, 154–55, 180, 204, 220, 284, 285, 297, 298–99
Moynihan, Daniel Patrick, 230
Mrs. A (foster parent), 260–61, 267
Mrs. J (Baby Robert's case), 71–74
Murphy, Patrick, 104–5, 114, 134, 232, 234–35, 237, 239, 267, 287, 288, 289
"Mutuality," 184

National Center for Children in Poverty (Columbia University), 294
National People's Uhuru Movement, 94
National Task Force for Children's Constitutional Rights, 211–12
New York Child Welfare Administration, 70–74
New York City
  child deaths in, 288
  foster-care teenagers in, 245–48
  funding for child welfare in, 293
  welfare reform in, 255–56, 266–67
  See also Center for Family Life
New York State
  abandonment in, 181, 299–300
  Baby Lenore case in, 202
  child abuse in, 63
  child welfare reform in, 293, 295–96
  foster parents in, 20–22, 299–300
  termination of rights in, 50–51, 52, 181
Newsweek, Kawamoto story in, 278–81, 285
Nicole (teenage parent), 272–74, 275, 276
Norcott, Flemming, 203–4, 208, 209
Nordhaus, Barbara, 66–67, 69, 72, 79, 219, 222, 283
Northwestern University Law School, Children and Family Justice Center at, 157–58

Orphan trains, 115–18, 148, 240, 292
Orphanages, 100, 101, 104, 112, 148,
 155–56, 240, 271, 292

P (teenage mother), 238
Painter v. Bannister, 65
Parens patriae, state as, 63–64
Parent-child relationship
 and Baby Girl B, 16, 224–25, 284
 biological relationship as primary to,
  171–72, 180
 and community-based agencies, 290
 failure to sustain, 218–19
 and foster parents, 299–300
 irreparable break in, 16
 and Melton sisters, 284
 and myth of family, 299
 psychological bond in, 61–62,
  171–72
 and removal of children, 240–43
 state as mediator in, 15, 216–17
 state-parent relationship as, 249–50
 and worthiness, 284
 See also Adoptive parents; Attachment; Best interests of child; Biological parents; Foster parents;
  Psychological parents; Termination
  of rights
Parenting
 basic, 137
 classes for, 5, 55, 103, 138, 157, 165,
  199, 237, 269, 285
 learning about, 142–43, 147, 170,
  249–50, 262, 267–68, 292
Parents
 and Center for Family Life goals,
  252–54, 258, 259–60, 268, 286
 children who divorce, 212
 commitment of, 253–54
 and community-based programs,
  289–90
 depression of, 123–24, 138
 emotionally-stunted, 239, 290
 excuses of, 290
 hurdles for, 242
 punishment of, 297

responsibility of, 121–22
saving children from, 112–18
second chance for, 16–17
social workers as stand-in, 259–60
staff as stand-in, 273, 275
teenage, 272–74, 279
 See also Biological parents; Family;
  Fathers; Mothers; Parent-child
  relationship; Psychological parents
Pearlman, Susan, 173–74, 203
Peer pressures, 124–25, 274
Pellegrino, Angelica. *See* Baby Girl B
Pellegrino, Gina
 abandonment of child by, 12, 13, 14,
  49–50, 75, 80–81, 179, 207, 220,
  284, 300
 abuse of, 199
 appeal of termination rights of,
  173–74, 201–4, 205–10
 attorney for, 15, 19
 beliefs/intentions of, 12–13, 14
 and birth of Baby Girl B, 3, 12–13,
  219–20
 boyfriends of, 13, 44, 198, 199, 200
 death threats against, 172
 defense of, 179–81, 201–2
 determination of, 17, 68, 75, 220
 and dressing for court, 33–34
 final decision for, 218–23
 Gill's views about, 215–16
 hospital records concerning, 1, 3–4,
  12–13, 16
 impact of case on, 35
 LaFlammes' initial contact with,
  19–20
 LaFlammes' views about, 56,
  169–70, 192, 196–97
 and LaFlammes' visitations, 170,
  196–97, 199, 210
 living arrangements of, 44, 56, 58,
  62, 64, 77, 78, 172, 174, 176,
  198–99
 move to take child from, 173–74
 and parent-child relationship,
  218–19, 224–25, 284

Pellegrino, Gina (*cont'd*)
    parenting skills of, 170, 172, 199,
        224, 299
    parents' relationship with, 11–12,
        13–14, 17, 43–44, 56, 58, 64, 78,
        80–81, 172–73, 174
    psychological/psychiatric reports
        about, 47, 59, 61–62, 185,
        195–96, 199
    on public assistance, 169–70
    publicity about, 172–73, 177–78
    reconsideration of termination rights
        of, 19, 20, 32–42, 62, 218–19
    removal of child from, 182,
        183–84
    and "rescue fantasy," 67–68
    returns to claim child, 9–10, 17
    and social workers, 12–13, 35–36,
        198–99, 206, 209, 220
    Solnit's testimony concerning,
        190–94
    state's search for, 206
    surrender of child to, 76–82
    termination of rights of, 4, 7, 13–15,
        17, 23, 183–84, 300
    and time issues, 66–67
    visits with baby of, 32, 43–48,
        57–59, 175, 220
    worthiness of, 284
Pellegrino, Mr. and Mrs.
    defense of Gina by, 172–73
    Gina's relationship with, 11–12,
        13–14, 17, 43–44, 56, 58, 64, 78,
        80–81, 174
    and Gina's visits with baby, 43–44,
        45, 58
    and reconsideration of termination,
        35–36
    and surrender of baby, 78
"Permanency," 16, 54, 56, 72, 158,
    177, 300. *See also* Finality
Peters, Ellen, 205, 207, 208, 209, 218,
    219–20
Philip, James "Pate," 128
Police, Chicago. *See* Melton children:
    removal of

Poor
    and best interests of child, 155
    as categories, 148–49
    and causes of poverty, 156
    child welfare system as intrusive to,
        180, 234–35
    children of, 150–54
    community as responsible for, 250
    in England, 98–102, 150, 250, 291
    history of, 98–102, 250
    images of, 98–102
    motivation of, 292
    and role of state, 130, 152–56
    saving children of, 112–18
    worthiness of, 154, 180
    See also Addams, Jane
Pregnancy
    lack of knowledge about, 121
    and need for someone to love, 274
Prestley, Linda Pearce, 173–74, 175,
    190
Psychological parents
    accepted orthodoxy of, 54
    and Baby Girl B, 185–86
    and Baby Robert's case, 71–72, 74
    experts views about, 52–53, 59–61
    foster parents as, 52–53
    and judges, 60
    legal decisions about, 22
    priority of rights of, 16, 22
    and termination of rights as merciful
        act, 52–53
Psychologists/psychiatrists
    and Baby Girl B, 47, 61–62, 190,
        199–200
    and Baby Robert's case, 71–72,
        73–74
    and Melton sisters, 110
    See also specific person
Public assistance
    cutting/ending of, 230, 232
    and fathers, 230
    Gina Pellegrino on, 169–70
    Melton sisters on, 91, 94, 96, 107,
        143, 161, 230
    and worthiness, 154–55

Public debate, about Baby Girl B, 16,
    177–78
Publicity
    about Baby Girl B, 15–16, 76–80,
        169–70, 171, 172–73, 174,
        178–79, 186
    about child welfare agencies, 129
    about deaths of children, 288
    about Melton sisters, 89, 94–95,
        106, 157–58, 162, 232, 267,
        277–81, 287
    and social workers, 77

Q (foster-care teenager), 246, 248
Queens County Family Count (New
    York), 70–75, 188–89

R (teenage mother), 238–39
Reagan Administration, 134
Rehnquist, William, 51
Religion, 112, 116, 123, 124. *See also*
    Catholic church
Removal of children. *See specific case or
    agency*
"Rescue fantasy," 67–68, 72, 283
Rhode Island, termination of rights in,
    55, 56
Richmond, Mary, 156
Rothman, David, 101
Rousseau, Jean-Jacques, 31
Ruhe, Barbara, 169, 170–72, 175, 177,
    183, 188, 190, 191, 194–95, 224
Ruskin, John, 150
Rutter, Michael, 54

Santosky v. Kramer, 221
School
    apprenticeships in, 28–29
    and history of family, 28–29
    mother's failure to send children to,
        270–71
    mothers in, 237
Schooling, and worthiness of mothers,
    154
Scoppetta, Nicholas, 255
Segal, Valerie, 260, 261

Senate, U.S., 230
Senatore, Rose Alma, 173, 177, 184,
    185
Settlement house movement, 149–54,
    156
Siblings, separation of, 89, 91, 116,
    147, 164, 229–30, 238, 271
Sister Geraldine, 250–55, 258, 259,
    262–63, 264, 275, 286, 291, 292,
    293
Sister Mary Paul, 250–59, 263–64,
    266, 268, 275, 279, 286, 291, 292,
    293
Smyth, John, 244, 272, 274, 275, 276
Social engineering, 182
Social workers
    arbitrariness of, 34
    and Baby Girl B case, 4–6, 8, 12–13,
        43, 44–45, 57, 58, 76, 77, 175,
        182, 200, 206, 220
    in Baby Robert's case, 72–73
    biases of, 175, 180
    burn out of, 130, 131
    caseload of, 92, 130
    casework approach for, 156
    at Center for Family Life, 251, 252,
        254, 255, 259–60, 261–64, 267
    Center for Family Life workers com-
        pared with government, 262
    clients' relationship with, 267
    criticisms of, 127–28
    discretionary power of, 51
    dismissal of, 127–28
    and family preservation projects,
        133–34
    images of, 262
    kindly intentions of, 69
    and Melton sisters, 89–90, 109–11,
        120, 127, 140, 142, 233, 267–68
    overstepping bounds by, 69–70
    and permanency, 158
    professionalization of, 156
    psychiatric, 156
    and publicity, 77
    quality of, 130–31
    "rescue fantasy" of, 67–68, 283

Social workers (*cont'd*)
and resolution of cases, 158–59
role of, 267–68
salary of, 263
screening/inspections by, 4–6, 8, 81
as stand-in parents, 259–60
and stay of Downey's decision, 182
training of, 131
turnover rate of, 263
See also Child welfare system; *specific person or agency*
Solnit, Albert
and best interests of child, 53, 59, 60, 64, 66, 69, 74, 181, 187, 200, 216
and LaFlammes' visitation hearings, 184–87, 190–94, 195
Solomon, Robert, 186–87, 188
Sonya Live (CNN), 169
Spector, Robert, 239, 290
Stanley v. Illinois, 214
Starr, Ellen, 150
State
arbitrariness of, 33
dilemmas faced by, 295, 298
failure of, 296–99
limitations on accomplishments of, 296–97
number of children removed by, 287
options available to, 271, 276
See also State, role of; *specific agency*
State, role of
and abandonment, 13, 31
ambiguous relationship of family and, 63–64, 267, 298–99
and assistance with failing parents, 249–50
in Baby Girl B case, 4, 15, 81, 190–94, 221
and best interests of child, 154
and caseload, 92–93
Center for Family Life compared with, 253, 262
and endangerment, 75
and hurdles for parents, 242
and "infinite patience," 201–4

as intrusive, 82, 248
"kindly intentions" of, 64, 69
as mediator between parent and child, 15, 216–17
and Melton sisters, 82, 93–94, 97, 103–4, 221, 278–79, 283
and mothers as adversaries, 286
as *parens patriae,* 63–64
and parent-child relationship, 15
as parent-child relationship, 249–50
and poor, 98–102, 130, 152–56
questions about, 241, 278–79
and relationship with mothers, 297–98
and termination of rights, 51–52, 54, 55, 205–10
and unborn children, 203–4
State's attorney, Illinois, 281
Steward, Potter, 22
Strange Situation Test. *See* Ainsworth Strange Situation Test
Sunset Park (Brooklyn, New York). *See* Center for Family Life
Supreme Court, U.S., 51–52, 202, 212, 214, 218, 221
Symth, John, 88–89, 91

Teenagers
foster-care, 245–48, 268, 287
as parents, 272–74, 279
"Tender years doctrine," 29
Termination of rights
and appeal in Baby Girl B's case, 201–4, 205–10
in Baby Robert's case, 71–74
and best interests of child, 53–54, 56, 206
children asking for, 63
Connecticut's reconsideration of laws about, 176–77
and "continuity of care," 53
definition of grounds for, 202–3
and endangerment, 33, 51, 56
examples of, 54–55
and family preservation projects, 135
of fathers, 22–23, 261

finality of, 205–7, 208–10
and foster parents, 55, 261
and Gregory K case, 63
Guggenheim's studies of, 50–51
and hierarchy of rights, 271
history of, 50–51
idealization of, 50
in Illinois, 288
in Indiana case, 270
and "infinite patience" of state,
    201–4
lack of knowledge about, 13–14
and "legal orphans," 51
legislation concerning, 33
as merciful act, 52–53
in New York State, 181
as open-ended, 170
and "permanency," 54, 56
"pre-adoptive" parents appearance at
    hearings about, 20
problems inherent in, 53–54
and psychological reports, 62–63
as relief, 261
and role of state, 54, 55
Solnit's views about, 185
standards for decisions about, 51–52
Supreme Court decisions about,
    51–52
and time issues, 36, 55, 66–67, 172
See also Melton sisters; *specific person*
Time issues
and adoptive parents, 300
and Baby Girl B case, 24, 36, 66–67,
    300
and best interests of child, 66
and child's time with foster parents,
    55
and definition of abandonment, 49
and foster parents, 55, 300
and termination of rights, 36, 55,
    66–67, 172
Toynbee Hall (London, England), 150
Trattner, Walter, 153

Tulisano, Richard, 176, 177, 188
Turner, Denise, 87, 88, 103, 106–8,
    109, 127, 278, 279, 281, 286, 292,
    293
Turner, Gregory, 88, 145

United Nations, 213
University of Chicago, Chapin Hall
    Center for Children at, 133–34

Valerie D case, 203–4
Visitations
    by Gina Pellegrino, 32, 43–48,
        57–59, 175, 220
    by LaFlammes, 7–9, 170, 183–87,
        190–97, 199, 210
    contract for, 196–97
    with Melton children, 119, 120,
        126, 140, 159, 160, 165, 229–30,
        243, 285
    to Melton children, 119, 120, 126,
        140, 159, 160, 165, 229–30, 243,
        285

Wallace, Amanda, 92, 93, 242
Wallace, Joseph, 92, 93, 128, 130, 179,
    277
White House Conference on Depen-
    dent Children (1909), 154
Wilson, Edmund, 153
Wisconsin, DeShaney case in, 212
Wood, Kimba, 299–300
Workhouses, 101
Worthiness, 104, 154–55, 180, 204,
    220, 284, 285, 297, 298–99
Wulczyn, Fred, 293–96

Y (foster-care teenager), 246, 247–48
Yale Child Study Center, 59, 61–62,
    184, 185, 219
Youth Communication, 245

Zelizer, Viviana, 154, 297

About the Author

MICHAEL SHAPIRO is the author of *Japan: In the Land of the Broken-hearted; The Shadow in the Sun: A Korean Year of Love and Sorrow;* and *Who Will Teach for America?* His work has also appeared in such publications as *The New Yorker, Esquire, Sports Illustrated, The Wall Street Journal,* and *The New York Times Magazine.* He is an assistant professor at the Columbia University Graduate School of Journalism and lives in New York with his wife, Susan Chira, and their two children.